PT735
PLO

The Radical Subject

Britische und Irische Studien
zur deutschen Sprache und Literatur

Etudes parues en Grande-Bretagne et en Irlande
concernant la philologie et la littérature allemandes

British and Irish Studies
in German Language and Literature

herausgegeben von H.S. Reiss
und W.E. Yates

Band 13

PETER LANG
Bern · Berlin · Frankfurt /M. · New York · Paris · Wien

Andrew Plowman

The Radical Subject

Social Change and the Self in
Recent German Autobiography

PETER LANG

Bern · Berlin · Frankfurt /M. · New York · Paris · Wien

Die Deutsche Bibliothek – CIP-Einheitsaufnahme

Plowman, Andrew:
The radical subject : social change and the self in recent German
autobiography / Andrew Plowman. – Bern ; Berlin ; Frankfurt/M. ;
New York ; Paris ; Wien : Lang, 1998
(British and Irish studies in German language and literature ; Bd. 13)
ISBN 3-906760-52-9

ISSN 0171-6662
ISBN 3-906760-52-9
US-ISBN 0-8204-3449-3

© Peter Lang AG, European Academic Publishers, Berne 1998

Printed in Germany

Acknowledgements

This study would never have been written without the award of a Major Postgraduate Studentship from the British Academy. I am grateful to Jesus College, Cambridge, for the generous bursaries which helped to fund research visits to the Federal Republic of Germany. I wish to thank also family and friends for their support during the completion of this project, in particular my mother, and my brother and sister-in-law, David and Emma. I owe a more practical debt to colleagues in the German Department at the University of Liverpool for their assistance in the preparation of this manuscript. Helpful comments on this study were provided at different stages by Dr Peter Hutchinson, Dr Martin Kane and Professor Hans Reiss. My greatest debt of thanks, however, is to Dr Michael Minden, whose calm and patient guidance has seen this project through from its conception to its conclusion.

Table of Contents

Abbreviations

Primary Texts

First references to the primary texts by Vesper, Brinkmann, Struck, Buhmann and Stefan are given in footnote form and in full at an appropriate point in the study. Thereafter, the following abbreviations are used when citing from texts:

DR	*Die Reise*
E	*Die Erkundungen für die Präzisierung des Gefühls für einen Aufstand*
K	*Klassenliebe*
G	*Ich habe mir eine Geschichte geschrieben*
H	*Häutungen*

Secondary Literature

The following common and accepted abbreviations have been used for the titles of academic journals:

MLN	*Modern Language Notes*
NLH	*New Literary History*

CHAPTER 1

Beyond New Subjectivity: Situating the Self in Recent German Autobiography

I   New Subjectivity and Autobiography

Criticism has repeatedly characterised the 1970s in the Federal Republic of Germany as a decade of autobiographical writing. Already in 1976, Hugo Dittberner identified a 'Tendenz zum Autobiographischen' as a significant literary trend of the time.[1] And Michael Rutschky's *Erfahrungshunger. Ein Essay über die siebziger Jahre* (1980) observed a parallel and widespread 'Lesen von Texten als Autobiographie'.[2] Himself the author of an autobiographical text, Dittberner's evaluation possibly contained a personal component;[3] and Rutschky proved his own point by reading all manner of texts as autobiographical utterances. Again in 1983, however, Sandra Frieden's *Autobiography: Self into Form. German-Language Autobiographical Writings of the 1970s* fixed 'a burgeoning of autobiographical writings' as the 'literary phenomenon of the decade'.[4] The claim that autobiography constitutes the dominant literary mode of the 1970s has of course been contested and ignored. Nonetheless, it persists into the present: as recently as 1994, Barbara Kosta's *Recasting Autobiography: Women's Counterfictions in Contemporary German Literature and Film* has presented 'an unprecedented surge in autobiographical expression' as the keynote of the decade.[5]

It is not our aim to trade assertions or counter-assertions about the competing literary trends of the decade. Faced with the evidence, it would be futile to dispute the existence of a robust interest in autobiography, whether it represented the decade's major tendency or just one of many. Our starting point here is rather the relationship between two discrete literary-critical discourses about the self in recent West German literature: first, a debate that has crystallised around the concept of 'New Subjectivity'; second, the criticism and theory of autobiography as a genre. Both nourish the perception of the

---

1   Hugo Dittberner, 'Die autobiographische Tendenz', *Literarische Hefte*, 52 (1976), 69-71 (p. 70).

2   Michael Rutschky, *Erfahrungshunger. Ein Essay über die siebziger Jahre* (Cologne, 1980), p. 245.

3   Hugo Dittberner, *Das Internat. Papiere vom Kaffeetisch* (Darmstadt and Neuwied, 1974).

4   Sandra Frieden, *Autobiography: Self into Form. German-Language Autobiographical Writings of the 1970s* (Frankfurt am Main, Bern and New York, 1983), p. 42.

5   Barbara Kosta, *Recasting Autobiography: Women's Counterfictions in Contemporary German Literature and Film* (Ithaca and London, 1994), p. 1.

1970s as an autobiographical decade. Yet there exists an unreflected discontinuity between them, and between the interpretative frameworks they provide.

An autobiographical impulse is manifestly at work in the texts forming the basis of this study: Bernward Vesper's *Die Reise. Romanessay* (published posthumously in 1977), Rolf Dieter Brinkmann's *Erkundungen für die Präzisierung des Gefühls für einen Aufstand: Reise Zeit Magazin. (Tagebuch)* (published posthumously in 1987), Karin Struck's *Klassenliebe. Roman* (1973), Verena Stefan's *Häutungen. Autobiografische Aufzeichnungen Gedichte Träume Analysen* (1975) and Inga Buhmann's *Ich habe mir eine Geschichte geschrieben* (1977). These texts lay a dual claim to our attention. Written by individuals involved in the social and cultural upheavals in the Federal Republic of Germany during the 1960s and 1970s, they are important social and historical documents. They engage with a preoccupation with subjectivity that marks the West German student movement of the 1960s, the pop subculture at its fringes, and the New Women's Movement of the 1970s. However, they also belong to the genre of autobiography. They command our interest for the way they situate themselves in relation to autobiographical discourse and challenge our critical assumptions about the genre – even (as in Vesper's 'Romanessay' or Struck's 'Roman') where they seem to refuse the generic label.

Literature, in Adorno's famous dictum, is both social fact and aesthetic artefact.[6] Accordingly, our chosen texts merit analysis both as social documents and autobiographical texts. Yet the dominant literary-critical discourses about the self in the West German literature of the 1970s – the debates surrounding New Subjectivity and the autobiography of the period – fail to provide a workable model for their analysis as such. The debate surrounding New Subjectivity does not eschew all aesthetic questions; and some definitions of autobiography, conversely, are predicated on an interpenetration of psychological and social structures. However, it is not the category of autobiography, but of New Subjectivity, that has supplied the focus for the investigation of the broader social and cultural issue of subjectivity in West German literature after 1968. Ralf Schnell's description in 1986 of New Subjectivity as a 'Schlagwort, das [...] den inneren Zusammenhang einer sich verändernden Perspektive auf politisch-gesellschaftliche Verhältnisse benennt' illustrates this social orientation.[7]

6   Theodor W. Adorno, *Ästhetische Theorie*, ed. by Gretel Adorno and Rolf Tiedemann (Frankfurt am Main, 1970), pp. 374-75.

7   Ralf Schnell, *Die Literatur der Bundesrepublik. Autoren, Geschichte, Literaturbetrieb* (Stuttgart, 1986), pp. 256-57.

The birth of 'Neue Subjektivität' has been dated as the publication in 1973 of Peter Schneider's *Lenz* and Karin Struck's *Klassenliebe*.[8] Used synonymously with 'Neue Innerlichkeit' and 'Neue Sensibilität', the term has been so loosely applied – above all to prose – that its value has been questioned. Besides *Lenz* and *Klassenliebe*, the work of Peter Handke, Botho Strauß and Nicholas Born, and a spate of 'Vater-Bücher' late in the 1970s are typically associated with it.[9] Critical debate about the topic has from the outset been bound up with the perception of a reactionary shift in the political climate of the Federal Republic: the *Tendenzwende*. (This term signals a retrenchment of the spirit of democratic fundamentalism as the radical hopes awakened by the student movement dissipated in the face of recession and a sinister growth of the powers of the state between the *Radikalenerlaß* of 1972 and the 'deutscher Herbst' of 1977.)[10]

In the 1970s, critical debate was mostly locked in a battle of claim and counter-claim regarding the political status of the trend. Some critics saw New Subjectivity's preoccupation with the self as a retreat from the political radicalism of the student movement; others claimed that it was inherently political.[11] Since the 1980s, scholars have offered a more subtle analysis of the relationship of literature, subjectivity and politics in the wake of 1968. Many have observed that the concern with the self considered the defining trait of New Subjectivity had itself been central to the anti-authoritarian student movement of the 1960s. In '"Neue Subjektivität"' (1989), Moray McGowan notes that the term 'Neue Sensibilität' (a synonym of 'Neue Subjektivität') derived from the thought of Herbert Marcuse, whose conception of a mobilisation of phantasy and desire 'subversive of the false needs generated by capitalism' had influenced the movement.[12] According to McGowan, elements within New Subjectivity, such as Schneider's *Lenz* and the feminist literature of the 1970s, mark an extension of the student movement's analysis of the relationship between self and society. Central to recent debates has been the claim that the trend is linked to a paradigm shift within political discourse. David Roberts's 'Tendenzwenden. Die sechziger und siebziger Jahre in literaturhistorischer Perspektive' (1982) remains the most forceful statement

---

8   Anz, Thomas, 'Neue Subjektivität', in *Moderne Literatur in Grundbegriffen*, ed. by Dieter Borchmeyer and Viktor Zmegac (Frankfurt am Main, 1987), pp. 283-86 (p. 283).

9   Moray McGowan, '"Neue Subjektivität"', in *After the 'Death of Literature': West German Writing of the 1970s*, ed. by Keith Bullivant (Oxford, New York and Munich, 1989), pp. 53-68 (p. 54).

10   Rob Burns and Wilfried van der Will, *Protest and Democracy in West Germany: Extra-Parliamentary Opposition and the Democratic Agenda* (Basingstoke and London, 1988), p. 62.

11   Karin Ruoff Kramer, *The Politics of Discourse: Third Thoughts on "New Subjectivity"* (Bern, Frankfurt am Main, New York and Paris, 1993), pp. 29-32.

12   McGowan, p. 56.

of this claim. The 1960s, Roberts argues, marked the end of the post-war period in the Federal Republic, its political agenda set by reconstruction and integration into the West; and they ushered in a new agenda defined by the problems of the post-industrial society (such as the rise of a mass intelligentsia and a loss of confidence in economic growth). This new agenda, Roberts argues, contributed to a transformation of political discourse in which a traditional class-based politics yielded to a pluralistic politics grounded in personal experience and exemplified by the women's and alternative movements of the 1970s. New Subjectivity, he suggests, forms part of a process in which, parallel to the new social movements of the 1970s, the relationship between self and society was redefined in the face of a pervasive sense of 'Entfremdung in der modernen Industriegesellschaft'.[13]

The critical debates about New Subjectivity are useful for us here because they suggest that the problem of the self in the West German literature of the 1970s is linked to fundamental shifts in political discourse. McGowan's brief comments on Marcuse's influence on the student movement notwithstanding, however, there is a striking lacuna even in recent assessments of New Subjectivity as the working out of the relationships between literature, politics and subjectivity in the wake of 1968: the discourses of the student and feminist movements themselves. These discourses are, by contrast, crucial to our own readings of Vesper's *Die Reise*, Brinkmann's *Erkundungen*, Struck's *Klassenliebe* (a text viewed as an inaugural moment of New Subjectivity), Stefan's *Häutungen* and Buhmann's *Ich habe mir eine Geschichte geschrieben*. The New Subjectivity debate moves largely on the level of tendential shifts; there is clearly room for a more resolutely contextual approach to individual texts.

Its fulcrum the student movement, the character of the critical debate about New Subjectivity is social. Though 'Autobiographische Bekenntnisliteratur' features prominently amongst the forms ascribed to the trend,[14] the debate scarcely addresses the problematic of autobiographical writing. A substantial body of criticism about recent German autobiography, from Germany and beyond, has appeared since the 1970s. Yet discussions have tended to confront the question of autobiography rather than the social and political issues surrounding New Subjectivity.[15] There results, moreover, a

---

13 David Roberts, 'Tendenzwenden. Die sechziger und siebziger Jahre in literaturhistorischer Perspektive', *Deutsche Vierteljahresschrift für Literaturwissenschaft und Geistesgeschichte*, 56 (1982), 290-313 (pp. 297).

14 Stephan Reinhardt, '"Nach innen führt der geheimnisvolle Weg, aber er führt auch wieder heraus." Unvollständige Anmerkungen zum neuen Irrationalismus in der Literatur', in *Nach dem Protest. Literatur im Umbruch*, ed. by W. Martin Lüdke (Frankfurt am Main, 1979), pp. 158-84 (p. 160).

15 Exemplary in this regard is Barbara Saunders, *Contemporary German Autobiography: Literary Approaches to the Problem of Identity* (London, 1986).

14

striking imbalance when New Subjectivity and the criticism of autobiography meet, an awkward discursive rupture in which the categories are elided with or subsumed under one another; or else the critical encounter altogether fails to bring them into a dialogue.

A case in point is Sandra Frieden's *Self into Form* of 1983, which explicitly proposes an examination of the German autobiography of the 1970s sensitive both to the historical context of its emergence and to generic questions about autobiography. Frieden's study opens with an account of the historical context with which it is concerned, and continues by arguing the case for a speech act theory of autobiography. The treatment of context is on its own terms unsatisfactory, producing generalisations about changes in the 'the social and intellectual mood' that fall behind more informative work on New Subjectivity; above all, though, it is Frieden's account of individual texts that fails to bring '"New Subjectivity" and the autobiographical impulse' into a dialogue.[16] Though the social and political context established by Frieden is the Federal Republic, she closes with readings of Ingeborg Bachmann's *Malina* (1971), Elisabeth Plessen's *Mitteilung an den Adel* (1976), Christa Wolf's *Kindheitsmuster* (1976) and Peter Handke's *Das Gewicht der Welt* (1977). In short, Frieden fails to explore the intersections between autobiographical practices and their ideological context precisely where this would be most illuminating: in the interpretation of individual texts.

By contrast, this study offers an approach to autobiographical texts of the 1970s that overcomes both the aesthetic limitations of the debates about New Subjectivity and the social and historical blind spots of many accounts of the autobiography of the period – an approach, in short, able to situate texts both in relation to the historical context of their composition and to autobiographical discourse. For here, the texts by Vesper, Brinkmann, Struck, Buhmann and Stefan are placed squarely in the discursive contexts of the student and the feminist movements; and they are set also in relation to a range of recent critical and theoretical discourses about autobiography. In approaching individual texts, we will ask, put simply: what is the relationship in them between the discourses of the student and women's movements and the autobiographical act?

A treatment of this question has as yet occurred only in partial isolation from the wider New Subjectivity debate. Critics have readily accepted the cultural challenge of feminism and women's writing as part of the social, political and cultural complex of New Subjectivity. Yet critical treatments of the women's autobiography of the 1970s have tended to claw questions of gender back from this context and instead relate them to broader historical continuities in women's writing. (An extreme statement of this position, Kosta's *Recasting Autobiography* of 1994 argues that 'placing into the

16   Frieden, p. 47 and 44.

category of New Subjectivity women's texts that perform self-explorations into female identity and subjectivity in the 1970s is a gross misrepresentation'.)[17] A continuity of women's writing needs no justification as a context for the study of women's autobiography. However, it belongs also, as we place it here, in the context of a concern with subjectivity more historically specific to the 1960s and 1970s.

This first chapter of the study outlines the historical context in which the chosen texts are placed, and introduces the concepts taken from the theory of autobiography that are brought to bear on them. Chapter 2 then examines how Vesper's *Die Reise* uses the Freudo-Marxist theories of Wilhelm Reich and Herbert Marcuse influential within the student movement to construct a revolutionary case history designed to prepare its author for political action. But this aim is rendered problematic, it argues, by Vesper's fraught engagement with the problem of autobiography. Chapter 3 places Brinkmann's *Erkundungen* in the context of debates about the mass media during the 1960s. We examine how Brinkmann's autobiography, suspended between the cultural pessimism of the Frankfurt School and the more utopian perspectives of Marshall McLuhan, mobilises the metaphors provided by the media to dismantle traditional notions of autobiographical subjectivity. Chapter 4, on Struck's *Klassenliebe*, Buhmann's *Ich habe mir eine Geschichte geschrieben* and Stefan's *Häutungen*, confronts the poststructuralist approaches that have dominated the criticism of women's autobiography during the 1980s. It argues for a more differentiated historical understanding of the discursive function of autobiographical texts within the New Women's Movement. Where the diary form of *Klassenliebe* cannot transcend the private sphere, this chapter argues that precisely the forms of feminist autobiography under attack from poststructuralist feminism can be grasped as symbolic fictions which formulate, like *Ich habe mir ein Geschichte geschrieben*, the entry of women into the historical process and act, like *Häutungen*, as a form of political discourse that disseminates and consolidates feminist positions. Let us proceed now with an examination of the discourses of the student and feminist movements that represent the context for our discussion of individual texts.

II   The Revolution of the Bourgeois Subject

Central connections between our texts and the ideological context of the student and feminist movements of the 1960s and 1970s present themselves naturally. *Die Reise*'s fragmented subject matter is in part the whole sweep of the student movement from its origins to its decline. The text paints a vivid picture of the ideological conformity of the Federal Republic during the 1950s

17   Kosta, p. 40.

and early 1960s from which the movement arose. It has been associated also with the rise of urban terrorism as the movement declined, Vesper's fiancée – Gudrun Ensslin – being a founder member of the *Rote Armee Fraktion* (RAF), the activities of which disproportionately shaped the political culture of the Federal Republic during the 1970s. The fragmentary notes of a controversial figure within the pop culture feeding into the (sub)cultural currents of the anti-authoritarian student movement, Brinkmann's *Erkundungen* record their author's disillusionment with a perceived turn in the course of the movement around 1968 towards an orthodox class politics that weakened its anti-authoritarian currents and drove a wedge between its political and life-style elements. To a point, Brinkmann's text resembles the retreat into the self described by some accounts of New Subjectivity. *Klassenliebe* appears poised between the decline of the student movement and the rise of the New Women's Movement as a political entity. More vividly than *Die Reise, Ich habe mir eine Geschichte geschrieben* charts the development of the student movement, from meetings of *Subversive Aktion* in the mid-1960s to the emergence of the politics of gender as the movement ebbed. (A situationist group whose members included Dieter Kunzelmann and Rudi Dutschke, *Subversive Aktion* crucially shaped the discourses of anti-authoritarianism upon joining the *Sozialistischer Deutscher Studentenbund*, or SDS, the nucleus of the student movement, in 1965.) *Häutungen*, finally, is bound up with the emergence of the New Women's Movement. Stefan was a member of *Brot und Rosen*, amongst the first groups within the women's movement in the Federal Republic to strive for ideological and organisational autonomy from the male-dominated left, and her autobiography became itself a central document of West German feminism upon its publication in the Frauenoffensive press.

Beyond such apparent connections to the contexts of their composition, however, our texts also illuminate a more complex shift in political discourse within the student and feminist movements. We must open out that shift here, identifying the issues to which the texts relate.

David Roberts has related the concept of New Subjectivity to the emergence of a pluralistic politics of personal experience that began with the student movement. Yet without engaging its discourses, he suggests that the student movement viewed itself in terms of an outmoded Marxist model of class struggle. By contrast, our texts illuminate the movement's 'Janus face' better. They force us to balance more satisfactorily the view that it could not understand itself in terms of a development that was after all yet to occur with the perception that its anti-authoritarian currents contributed already to a more active revision of political discourse than Roberts admits – a view supported by various studies of the political culture of the left in the Federal

Republic since 1968.[18] For what is at stake in both the anti-authoritarianism of the student movement and the feminism of the New Women's Movement is: first, a conception of politics as a process centred on the needs of the human subject; second, a reassessment of radical social critique and the opportunities for opposition in the light of changing historical circumstances or the emergence of gendered perspectives; and third, the development of forms of practice balancing participants' needs against broader processes of political enlightenment and change. Let us consider these points briefly.

'Anti-authoritarianism' is perhaps the most elusive term connected to the student movement. It seems to extend from a critique of authority (be it a theoretical critique of the '"autoritäre[...] Staat[...]"' or a practical experimentation with 'nicht-autoritäre Lebensformen')[19] to a broader cultural sensibility not always cognate with its political manifestations. A favoured self-designation of student theorists like Bernd Rabehl and Rudi Dutschke, however, it certainly embraced a powerful impetus within the student movement towards, as Dutschke put it in 1965, the 'Ausarbeitung einer neuen Revolutionstheorie, die den qualitativen neuen Erscheinungen der sozioökonomischen Wirklichkeit gerecht werden muss'.[20] Like the international New Left's endeavour in the 1950s and 1960s to elaborate a humanist Marxism distinct from the scientific orthodoxies of Soviet Marxism and the reformism of social democracy, anti-authoritarianism represented a fragmentary but distinctive 'Theorieansatz'.[21] From *Subversive Aktion* to the student movement's orthodox turn, it espoused a subjective Marxism that refused to limit the theoretical and practical problem of human alienation and emancipation to the productive sphere. This subjective emphasis derived from sources that included Lukács and the critical theory of the Frankfurt School generally. But in particular the attempted synthesis of Marxism and psychoanalysis in the work of the psychoanalyst Wilhelm Reich and the critical theorist Herbert Marcuse amongst others furnished anti-authoritarianism with a powerful anthropological basis.[22] Further, anti-authoritarianism sought to

---

18   For example, Burns and van der Will; Andrei S. Markovits and Philip S. Gorski, *The German Left: Red, Green and Beyond* (Cambridge, 1993); and Gerd Langguth, *Protestbewegung. Entwicklung – Niedergang – Renaissance. Die Neue Linke seit 1968* (Cologne, 1983).

19   Langguth, p. 37; Tilman Fichter and Siegward Lönnendonker, *Kleine Geschichte des SDS. Der Sozialistische Deutsche Studentenbund von 1946 bis zur Selbstauflösung* (Berlin, 1977), p. 103.

20   Frank Böckelmann and Herbert Nagel, eds., *Subversive Aktion. Der Sinn der Aktion ist ihr Scheitern* (Frankfurt am Main, 1976), p. 307.

21   Bernd Rabehl, *Am Ende der Utopie. Die politische Geschichte der Freien Universität Berlin* (Berlin, 1988), p. 250.

22   See Jörg Bopp, 'Geliebt und doch gehaßt. Über den Umgang der Studentenbewegung mit Theorie', *Kursbuch*, 78 (1984), 121-42 (pp. 124-25).

revise Marxist social critique in the light of shifting historical constellations and new forms of social control, in the process questioning central assumptions about the crisis-prone nature of capitalism and the historical role of the working class. Finally, it comprised also a highly practical momentum, developing practices that reflected both its subjective emphasis and its social critique. Using limited acts of civil disobedience to provoke a disproportionate reaction, for example, the strategy of 'begrenzte Regelverletzung' popular within the SDS after the mid-1960s sought both to 'create contexts of political enlightenment' and afford participants an immediate sense of self-actualisation.[23]

At the same time, anti-authoritarianism's commitment to social transformation as the revolutionary reorganisation of the relations of production bound it to Marxist traditions. Often divided into 'liberal', 'socialist' or 'Marxist', and 'radical' currents, the feminism of the second wave women's movements hardly represented a unified ideology. Yet with the ascendancy of radical feminism, the shift in political discourse is more complete. The New Women's Movement did not so much ground its politics within an anthropological framework as formulate a gendered critique of the *anthro*pological bias of existing political ideologies, elaborating instead a gendered perspective. Gender, not class, formed the basis of its social critique, which radically politicised the private sphere. The movement's early actions during the (unsuccessful) campaign between 1971 and 1975 to abolish §218 – the law governing the legal availability of abortion in the Federal Republic – bore the imprint of the symbolic provocation favoured by the student movement, with its characteristic balancing of wider political objectives against participants' needs.[24] During the latter part of the 1970s this balance shifted: relinquishing longer-term perspectives of social change, the New Women's Movement built a counterculture – an expanding network of feminist publishing houses, bookshops and self-help centres – that combined the radical feminist demand for autonomy from the male-dominated left with a stress on personal change in the here and now. An important feature of the shift in political discourse in the women's movement was also a shift in the very medium in which the political was articulated: from theoretical to more personalised, autobiographical forms of discourse.

A comprehensive analysis of these shifts in political discourse lies beyond our scope. It would arguably have to consider also the transformation of the critical impulses of the student movement in the alternative movement, the citizens' initiatives and the ecology movement. Crucial here is how our texts relate to the discursive contexts of the student and women's movements, how

---

23   Burns and van der Will, p. 109.
24   Ute Frevert, *Frauen-Geschichte. Zwischen bürgerlicher Verbesserung und neuer Weiblichkeit* (Frankfurt am Main, 1986), pp. 279-81.

19

they engage with the shifts outlined above. For example, Vesper's *Die Reise* illuminates both the anthropological dimension of anti-authoritarianism – especially its reception of Reich and Marcuse – and a crisis of revolutionary subjectivity within it. Brinkmann's *Erkundungen*, by contrast, situate themselves in relation to anti-authoritarianism in a more complex way, taking up contradictory discourses about the mass media and their impact on the individual. Suspended between the dystopian perspectives of Marcuse and anti-authoritarianism on the one hand and the more utopian ones of Marshall McLuhan on the other, the text throws into relief the awkward relationship between political and cultural currents within the upheavals of the 1960s. The autobiographies of Struck, Buhmann and Stefan, finally, illuminate the emergence of a feminist politics in ways better documented. Whilst Struck's *Klassenliebe* ultimately declares an allegiance to neither the left nor feminism, Buhmann's *Ich habe mir eine Geschichte geschrieben* and Stefan's *Häutungen* articulate, against the background of the ascendancy of radical feminism, a clearer turn towards the politics of gender. Moreover, these latter two texts also tell us something about the function of autobiographical discourse within the New Women's Movement. Let us examine these points.

The work of Reich and Marcuse is central to Vesper's *Die Reise* – as it was to anti-authoritarianism itself. For the purposes of critique, Reich's most explicitly Marxist work – including *Die Massenpsychologie des Faschismus* (1933) – furnished anti-authoritarianism with an armoury of psychoanalytic terms circumscribing the isolation and misery of the individuals produced by the nuclear family under capitalism; and Marcuse's *Eros and Civilization: A Philosophical Enquiry into Freud* (1955) provided a conceptual language that exposed the deformation of human needs under a cruel 'performance principle' ('the prevailing historical form of the *reality principle*').[25] Moreover, in *Eros and Civilization*'s libidinised concept of the 'free play of human faculties' and *An Essay on Liberation*'s (1969) notion of a 'New Sensibility' expressing 'the vital need for the abolition of injustice and misery', Marcuse offered a powerful and aesthetic and erotic vision of human emancipation.[26] The work of Reich and Marcuse furnished weapons of critique, a resource for opposition and a vision of emancipation: a revolutionary anthropology, in short, at the heart of anti-authoritarianism – from *Subversive Aktion*'s vision in 1964 of life 'unterm Prinzip der Lust' to Dutschke's critique of the prevailing 'bürgerliche Charakterstruktur' and his

---

25   Herbert Marcuse, *Eros and Civilization: A Philosophical Enquiry into Freud* (Boston, 1955), p. 35. Published in German as *Triebstruktur und Gesellschaft. Ein philosophischer Beitrag zu Sigmund Freud* (Frankfurt am Main, 1965).

26   Marcuse, *Eros and Civilization*, p. 156; Herbert Marcuse, *An Essay on Liberation* (Boston, 1969), pp. 23-24. German: *Versuch über die Befreiung* (Frankfurt am Main, 1969).

appeal to 'vitalen Bedürfnisse [...] nach Frieden, Gerechtigkeit und Emanzipation' in *Rebellion der Studenten oder Die neue Opposition* (1968).[27]

A comparable reception of their work occurs in *Die Reise*. Here, Reich's synthesis of Marx and Freud grounds an account of Vesper's relationship with his oppressive father – the one-time blood and soil poet Will Vesper – that issues into a wider critique of repressive mechanisms of socialisation within capitalist societies. In addition, Marcuse's vision of an aesthetic and erotic human emancipation underpins Vesper's account of an LSD trip that provides him with a glimpse of a sensuous and non-repressive alternative experience of self. But the theoretical discourses of Reich and Marcuse do not just perform critical or anticipatory functions in Vesper's autobiography, they are fundamental to the very narrative construction of the text. They underpin a narrative of subjective radicalisation designed to prepare its author to engage in transformative political action. Although class politics are not foregrounded in the text, *Die Reise* thus responds to a perceived crisis of revolutionary subjectivity within the theoretical discourses of anti-authoritarianism.

Critical theory had contemplated an indefinite stabilisation of capitalism and questioned the historical role of the working class since the catastrophe of fascism. However, in particular Marcuse's *One-Dimensional Man: Studies in the Ideology of Advanced Industrial Society* (1964) offered anti-authoritarianism a social analysis that appeared to fit the stabilising processes at work in the Federal Republic. These included a progressive harmonisation of the major political parties in the *Bundestag* and a defusing of the antagonism between capital and labour that was underwritten by the affluence of the West German economic miracle. In advanced capitalism, Marcuse suggested, new 'forms of social control' (the mass media, the advertising and entertainment industries) could 'contain and manipulate' the forces able to negate the status quo; this ultimately meant 'a weakening of the negative position of the working class' such that it no longer embodied 'the living contradiction to the established society'.[28]

This perceived loss of working-class radicalism arguably came to dominate anti-authoritarianism. For clearly, the apparent passivity of the working class threw open the question of revolutionary subjectivity. *One-Dimensional Man* raised the spectre of a society without opposition. Yet like Marcuse, the theorists of anti-authoritarianism refused to relinquish a Marxist dialectic of productive forces. On the contrary, they insisted – to cite Dutschke's famous

---

27   Böckelmann and Nagel, p.132; Uwe Bergmann, Rudi Dutschke, Wolfgang Lefèvre and Bernd Rabehl, *Rebellion der Studenten oder Die neue Opposition* (Reinbek, 1968), pp. 75 and 86.

28   Herbert Marcuse, *One-Dimensional Man: Studies in the Ideology of Advanced Industrial Society* (Boston, 1964), pp. 9, 23 and 31. German: *Der eindimensionale Mensch. Studien zur Ideologie der fortgeschrittenen Industriegesellschaft* (Berlin and Neuwied, 1967).

altercation with Jürgen Habermas at the SDS's June 1967 'Bedingungen und Organisation des Widerstandes' conference:

> Die Entwicklungen der Produktivkräfte haben einen Prozeßpunkt erreicht, wo die Abschaffung von Hunger, Krieg und Herrschaft materiell möglich geworden ist. Alles hängt vom bewußten Willen des Menschen ab.[29]

If this was so, was there a revolutionary subject able to set the dialectic between the actual and the possible into motion? With the escalation of the student movement and the forces arrayed against it after 1967, this question became urgent. Marcuse put his scant hope for change in marginal groups, 'Außenseiter innerhalb des Bestehenden'; 'die Opposition der Intellektuellen, besonders der Studenten', he argued, lacked revolutionary force.[30] For the theorists of anti-authoritarianism, however, the 'Suche nach dem revolutionären Subjekt'[31] entailed an inflation of their role as intellectuals. The American New Left sociologist C. Wright Mills had argued in the early 1960s that intellectuals should assume the historical role vacated by the working class. Anti-authoritarianism never expressed this view so unequivocally, but it travelled far down the road of a 'Substitutionalismus' in which intellectuals and students sought to take the place of the working class.[32]

Some theorists, like Reimut Reiche in 'Verteidigung der "neuen Sensibilität"' (1968), looked to students' 'intellektuell, ökonomisch und psychisch privilegierte Lage' in the university to assign them a radical edge.[33] Hans-Jürgen Krahl's 'Thesen zum allgemeinen Verhältnis von wissenschaftlicher Intelligenz und proletarischem Klassenbewusstsein' (1969), by contrast, explored whether the subsumption of technical knowledge under the productive process could endow the radical intelligentsia with 'industrieproletarisches Klassenbewusstsein'.[34]

With greater resonance, Dutschke's writings after 1967 – notably 'Das Sich-Verweigern erfordert Guerilla Mentalität' (a paper co-authored with Krahl in 1967) and his contribution to *Rebellion der Studenten* in 1968 –

29 Rudi Dutschke, untitled, in *Bedingungen und Organisation des Widerstands. Der Kongreß in Hannover. Protokolle Flugblätter Resolutionen*, ed. by Bernward Vesper, *Voltaire Flugschrift*, 12 (1967), 78-82 (p. 78).

30 Herbert Marcuse, *Das Ende der Utopie. Vorträge und Diskussionen in Berlin 1967* (Frankfurt am Main, 1980), p. 45, 21 and 25.

31 Bopp, p. 128.

32 Hans Manfred Bock, *Geschichte des 'Linken Radikalismus' in Deutschland. Ein Versuch* (Frankfurt am Main, 1976), pp. 225-28.

33 Reimut Reiche, 'Verteidigung der "neuen Sensibilität"', in *Die Linke antwortet Jürgen Habermas*, ed. by Wolfgang Abendroth and others (Frankfurt am Main, 1968), pp. 90-103 (p. 91).

34 Hans-Jürgen Krahl, *Konstitution und Klassenkampf. Schriften und Reden 1966-1970* (Frankfurt am Main, 1971), pp. 330-47 (p. 334). Compare Bock, pp. 228-29.

explored the revolutionary potential of Third World guerrilla strategies. Arguing that the revolutionary impasse within advanced capitalism was offset by a global dialectic of exploiters and exploited, Dutschke suggested that the reception of Che Guevara's 'focus' theory – 'daß [die Revolutionäre...] über die bewaffnete Avantgarde des Volkes die objektiven Bedingungen für die Revolution durch subjektive Tätigkeit schaffen können'[35] – could bring the struggle for emancipation from the margins of capitalism to its centre. An urban 'Guerilla-Tätigkeit', he (and Krahl) suggested, would trigger 'einen Bewußtseinsprozeß für agierende Minderheiten innerhalb der passiven und leidenden Massen, denen durch sichtbare irreguläre Aktionen die abstrakte Gewalt des Systems zur sinnlichen Gewißheit werden kann'.[36] The step from here to the theory and practice of the RAF is manifest.

Another intriguing response to the anti-authoritarian crisis of revolutionary subjectivity came from the *Kommune 2* in Berlin. Its *Versuch der Revolutionierung des bürgerlichen Individuums. Kollektives Leben mit politischer Arbeit verbinden!* (1969) gave familiar arguments about a loss of working-class radicalism a practical slant, asking:

> Wie können bürgerliche Individuen ihre bürgerliche Herkunft und ihre davon geprägte psychische Struktur soweit überwinden, daß sie zu einer kontinuierlichen Praxis befähigt werden?[37]

Reich's work offered a solution. If capitalism was, as he suggested, supported by 'an infantile Bedürfnisse und irrationale Autoritäten fixierte Individuen' formed within the bourgeois family, then the dissolution of individuals' rigid character structures could enable them, 'beizutragen zur radikalen Veränderung aller unterdrückenden Gesellschaftsverhältnisse'.[38] The projected 'Revolutionierung des bürgerlichen Individuums', however, failed as the commune lost itself in microstructural processes of change. The text details the challenges of establishing an anti-authoritarian life style, from running the household to organising a Christmas celebration, but the result was a near total retreat from political activity. Like *Kommune 2*'s collective protocol, Vesper's autobiography deploys the work of Reich – and Marcuse – toward the goal of subjective radicalisation. But could Vesper's *Die Reise* prove more successful? Arguably, *Kommune 2* foundered on the limitations of anti-authoritarianism itself. For anti-authoritarianism extended the Marxist concept of alienation

---

35   Bergmann, Dutschke, Lefèvre and Rabehl, p. 69.

36   'Das Sich-Verweigern erfordert Guerilla-Mentalität' is reprinted in Rudi Dutschke, *Geschichte ist machbar. Texte über das herrschende Falsche und die Radikalität des Friedens*, ed. by Jürgen Miermeister (Berlin, 1980), pp. 89-95 (p. 94).

37   Kommune 2, *Versuch der Revolutionierung des bürgerlichen Individuums: Kollektives Leben mit politischer Arbeit verbinden!* (Berlin, 1969), p. 11.

38   Kommune 2, pp. 70 and 297.

beyond the productive sphere and sought to privilege the agency of students and intellectuals, whilst hinging social transformation on a rearrangement of the relations of production from which these students and intellectuals, whatever their changing role, were debarred.

Brinkmann's *Erkundungen* do not share the anti-authoritarian preoccupation with the fate of the working class. However, they engage with a partly related problematic: the impact of the mass media on the individual. Engaging with a range of discourses about the mass media that enjoyed popular currency in the late 1960s, they bring into focus the difficult relationship between the political elements of the revolt and the cultural currents that initially at least formed part of its wider milieu. In *Die Reise*, Vesper's fascination with the Beat literature of William Burroughs and Jack Kerouac, with the pop and drugs culture that also belong to the discursive networks of 1968 feeds into the text's narrative of radicalisation. Brinkmann's text, however, points to a more radical discursive disjunction, appearing suspended between contradictory discourses on the mass media. It appeals to a dystopian Marcusean and anti-authoritarian discourse that accords the mass media a pivotal position in controlling individual consciousness in the interest of perpetuating the cycles of consumption through which late capitalism reproduces itself. Yet the text takes up also the more utopian and, for the pop culture of the 1960s, influential perspectives of Marshall McLuhan, whose *Understanding Media: The Extensions of Man* (like *One-Dimensional Man* of 1964) celebrated the media as the instruments of a 'technological extension of consciousness'.[39]

For Marcuse and anti-authoritarianism, the mass media represented powerful means of social control. Marcuse's views on their impact on the working class have been discussed above; for the individual, they entailed, *One-Dimensional Man* argued, a closing down of 'the critical power of Reason' and a 'repressive desublimation' of instinctual energy whereby 'the Pleasure Principle is [...] deprived of the claims which are irreconcilable with the established society'.[40]

A dystopian Marcusean vision of the liquidation of the subject in the face of new means of social control that included the mass media played a substantial part in the discourses and practices of anti-authoritarianism. Anti-authoritarianism concurred with Marcuse that, as *Subversive Aktion* put it in the mid-1960s, the 'immer sublimeren Auffangsmechanismen der hochindustrialisierten, neokapitalistischen Gesellschaft' enabled an increasingly effective, and even pleasurable 'Vergewaltigung des Menschen'.[41] The critique

---

39   Marshall McLuhan, *Understanding Media: The Extensions of Man* (New York, 1964), p. 57. German: *Die magischen Kanäle* (Düsseldorf and Vienna, 1968).
40   Marcuse, *One-Dimensional Man*, pp. 11, 56 and 75.
41   Böckelmann and Nagel, pp. 305 and 271.

of new forms of social control – for *Subversive   Aktion*
'Bewusstseinsmanipulation' and 'Konsumzwang'[42] – found both theoretical
and practical expression throughout the course of the student movement. The
actions of *Subversive Aktion*'s Munich cell under Dieter Kunzelmann were
levelled before 1965 against the institutions of the culture industry. These
included, for instance, the disruption of advertising conferences with leaflets
proclaiming 'Hört auf mit der totalen Manipulation des Menschen!'[43] The
critique of a consumerism fostered by the organs of the mass media as the
repressive creation and satisfaction of false needs continued during the student
movement's initial period of unrest in West Berlin between 1965 and mid-
1967. It surfaced, for example, in a notorious pamphlet – 'Warum brennst Du,
Konsument?' – distributed by Berlin's infamous *Kommune I* following the
bombing of a Brussels department store in 1967.[44] The pamphlet's intent was
satirical, aping the language of advertising and the Springer press. Yet its basic
critique of the mechanisms of manipulation binding individuals into the status
quo had already found more violent expression in April 1967 when Gudrun
Ensslin (now separated from Vesper) and Andreas Baader fire-bombed a
Frankfurt department store in one of the founding acts of the RAF. As the
revolt escalated, the critique of 'manipulation' again found expression,
increasingly centred on the perceived passivity of the working class, in the
student movement's full-blown campaign against the Springer press following
the attempted assassination of Dutschke by a young labourer in April 1968.
For the students of the SDS, the perceived influence of the Springer press's
attacks on Dutschke and the SDS over Josef Bachmann, a reader, vividly
dramatised the culture industry's power over a pacified working class. As
Michael Schneider put it in one of Bernward Vesper's *Voltaire Flugschrift*
pamphlets (1968): 'In der Bundesrepublik ist es u.a. die Springer Presse,
genauer: die Boulevard-Zeitungen BILD und BZ, die die lohnabhängigen
Massen [...] bei der Stange hält'.[45]

Inasfar as they theorised the role of the mass media, the left's discourses
on manipulation increasingly converged on the (Springer) press and its impact
on the working class. By contrast, Brinkmann's *Erkundungen* consistently
focus on the corrosive impact of the mass media more widely (including
television and radio) on the individual human consciousness. Following
Marcuse, they present a dystopian vision of the liquidation of the human
subject – the obliteration of critical faculties and a mobilisation of instinctual

42   Böckelmann and Nagel, p. 133.
43   Böckelmann and Nagel, p. 147.
44   Jürgen Miermeister and Jochen Staadt, eds., *Provokationen. Die Studenten- und
      Jugendrevolte in ihren Flugblättern 1965-1971* (Darmstadt and Neuwied, 1980), p. 27.
45   Michael Schneider, untitled, in *DER SPIEGEL oder Die Nachricht als Ware. Nachwort
      von Bernward Vesper*, ed. by Bernward Vesper, *Voltaire Flugschrift*, 18 (1968), 5-18
      (p. 6).

energy in support of the status quo – in the face of mass media. The images and voices of the mass media allow no possibility of escape beyond their reach or of retreat into inner resources of the self. On the contrary, the *Erkundungen* raise the spectre that the media prove capable of transforming the psychological structure of the individual so effectively that established forms of socialisation, in the family for instance, are rendered obsolete. In this, the *Erkundungen* appear to illustrate a thesis advanced in Marcuse's 'The Obsolescence of the Freudian Concept of Man', originally a lecture of 1963. According to Marcuse, the mass media make possible the social construction of individuals incapable of autonomous thought and action: 'society's direct management of the nascent ego', he argued, transformed the 'mental structure, the ego shrink[ing] to such an extent that it seems no longer capable of sustaining itself, as a self, in distinction from id and superego'.[46]

To set Brinkmann in the context of a Marcusean concept of 'New Sensibility' would hardly be novel. Translator and champion of an iconoclastic American pop literature in collections of poetry and essays like *Silverscreen. Neue amerikanische Lyrik* (1969) and *ACID. Neue amerikanische Szene* (1969), and a leading exponent of a German pop literature, Brinkmann's work certainly took up Marcuse's call for 'a revolution in perception'.[47] (In *ACID*, indeed, Brinkmann and his co-editor Ralf-Rainer Rygulla openly declared their allegiance to the 'neuen Sensibilität' – albeit to a depoliticised version of the concept.)[48] It is Brinkmann's alignment with a Marcusean critique of the mass media that might appear more surprising. For where the mass media are concerned, Brinkmann's work of the late 1960s evidences a more positive appraisal of the implications of the media that derives from his reception of American Beat and pop discourses and of the theories of McLuhan. The Beat and pop literature taken up in the Federal Republic by Brinkmann, Bazon Brock, Peter Chotjewitz and Wolf Wondratschek amongst others embodied a powerful anti-elitism that belonged to a culture of anti-authoritarianism in a literal sense. Yet its iconoclastic force derived precisely in part from its proximity to the media. For the advocates and practitioners of pop, the icons and symbols of popular culture, the popular myths circulated within and by the mass media, represented a potent weapon against the rhetoric of poetic authority. Following the influential American critic Leslie Fiedler's endeavour

---

46   See 'The Obsolescence of the Freudian Concept of Man', reprinted in Herbert Marcuse, *Five Lectures: Psychoanalysis, Politics and Utopia* (Boston, 1970), pp. 44-61 (p.47). A German version of 'The Obsolescence of Psychoanalysis', the lecture's original title, was published as 'Das Veralten der Psychoanalyse' in Herbert Marcuse, *Kultur und Gesellschaft*, 2 vols (Frankfurt am Main, 1965), II, 85-106.

47   Marcuse, *An Essay on Liberation*, p. 37.

48   Rolf Dieter Brinkmann and Ralf-Rainer Rygulla, eds., *ACID. Neue amerikanische Szene* (Berlin and Schlechtenwegen, 1969), pp. 417-18 (p. 418).

to 'Close the Gap' between 'Pop Art' and the bastions of 'High Art',[49] Brinkmann's introduction to *Silverscreen* argued that the deployment of 'Filme, Reklame, eine Dose Bier, Salat, Billy the Kid, Pot, Pepsi' militated against the 'herrische Geste des Besserwissens, des Belehrens sowie die gußeiserne Autorität "Dichter"' central to received literary forms.[50] Pop's enthusiasm for the myths of popular culture garnered mistrust on the left. However, by the time he wrote the *Erkundungen* in the early 1970s, Brinkmann had retreated to the Marcusean position outlined above. Significantly, though, this position remains counterbalanced in the *Erkundungen* by the enduring influence of McLuhan.

McLuhan's groundbreaking *Understanding Media* argued that the technical media represented 'an extension or self-amputation of our physical bodies' which for the human cognitive apparatus generated new sensory and aesthetic possibilities.[51] They appropriated, he suggested, the functions of human senses and organs – such as the phonograph the voice (some of McLuhan's examples now appear old-fashioned) – and in so doing transformed both those senses and, by shifting the ratios among them, the whole process of perception. The media, McLuhan asserted, could extend the 'central nervous system itself', effecting a 'technological simulation of consciousness'; for human consciousness the reward was the dissolution of a 'lineal structuring of rational life by phonetic literacy' itself bound up with the outmoded hegemony over all media of the printed word.[52] Moreover, *Understanding Media* also explored the impact of the mass media on modes of literary production, examining how a given medium could generate new forms of literary discourse – as the 'typewriter [...] an entirely new attitude to the written and printed word [which...] altered the forms of the language and of literature'.[53]

McLuhan's work found an enthusiastic reception in the pop scene of the Federal Republic. Rejecting the 'für den europäischen Bereich anerzogene anti-technische Affekt', Brinkmann's conclusion to *ACID*, for example, both saw in 'den Gebrauch von Technik' the key to an 'Erweiterung des menschlichen Bewußtseins' and advocated a literature 'die [...] Erfahrungen aus dem Umgang mit technischen Geräten integriert hat'; 'die Verwendung technischer Apparate' could, Brinkmann argued, both contribute to the 'Steigerung des Einzelnen' and generate a literature of 'Vermischungen' – 'Bilder, mit Wörtern durchsetzt, Sätze, neu arrangiert zu Bildern und Bild-

49 See 'Cross the Border — Close the Gap', an essay of 1970, in Leslie A. Fiedler, *The Collected Essays of Leslie Fiedler*, 2 vols (New York, 1971), II, 461-85 (pp. 480-81).
50 Rolf Dieter Brinkmann, 'Notizen 1969 zu amerikanischen Gedichten und zu dieser Anthologie', in *Silverscreen. Neue amerikanische Lyrik*, ed. by Rolf Dieter Brinkmann (Cologne, 1969), pp. 7-32 (pp. 16 and 9).
51 McLuhan, p. 46.
52 McLuhan, pp. 3 and 85.
53 McLuhan, p. 260.

(Vorstellungs-)zusammenhängen' that attained, in its break with established literary discourses, 'ein Stückchen befreite Realität'.[54] Admittedly, the practice of pop both in the United States and more so in the Federal Republic often fell short of the programme of cognitive and aesthetic transformation through the channels of the technical media: precisely the contrived banality of its preoccupation with advertising and popular icons militated against such a project (the literature of the European avant-garde had arguably proved more successful in this respect). But between the mid-1960s and the start of the 1970s, the pop literature that flourished in the Federal Republic did witness interesting explorations of McLuhan's themes. These ranged from Jürgen Becker's *Felder* (1964), its central image a 'Radiokopf' through which human consciousness tuned in 'to the multifarious messages of experience in the present and, through the effects of association, from the past',[55] through the work of Brinkmann to the collections representing the peak of pop's popularity in the Federal Republic: Vagelis Tsakiridis's *Super Garde. Prosa der Beat- und Pop-Generation* (1969), which included a contribution by Brinkmann ('Flickermaschine'); the *März Texte 1* (1969) combining the contributions of American writers like J. G. Ballard, Ted Berrigan and Burroughs with those of German writers such as Bazon Brock, Peter Chotjewitz, and Brinkmann again; and Renate Matthaei's *Trivialmythen* (1970), which included a photographical essay by Brinkmann. Pop's appeal in the Federal Republic soon evaporated in the climate of retrenchment that followed the disintegration of the student movement. Yet a McLuhanite interest in the transformative, even liberating impact of the technical media on human subjectivity and patterns of discourse remained a crucial element within Brinkmann's work until his death in 1975. To be sure, the *Erkundungen* contain a powerful vision of the liquidation of the human subject that owes more to Marcuse and the New Left than to McLuhan. Nonetheless, this is offset by an exploration of the possibilities and limits of the transformation of the human subject through its assimilation to the channels, codes and frequencies of the media that is crucially shaped by the perspectives of the latter.

In contrast with the autobiographies of Vesper and Brinkmann, the discursive context to which Struck's *Klassenliebe*, Buhmann's *Ich habe mir eine Geschichte geschrieben* and Stefan's *Häutungen* relate is better documented by literary scholars. It is the emergence of feminism, particularly in its radical variety, as movement and discourse during the 1970s; and the

---

54   Rolf Dieter Brinkmann, 'Der Film in Worten', in *ACID. Neue amerikanische Szene*, ed. by Rolf Dieter Brinkmann and Ralf-Rainer Rygulla (Berlin and Schlechtenwegen, 1969), pp. 381-99 (pp. 381-82 and 384).

55   R. Hinton Thomas and Keith Bullivant, *Literature in Upheaval: West German Writers and the Challenge of the 1960s* (Manchester, 1974), pp. 5-6 (p. 6).

related rise of the autobiographical as a mode of political discourse within the New Women's Movement. Within the politics of the left in the Federal Republic, feminism was born at the SDS's September 1968 conference, when Helke Sander, of the *Aktionsrat zur Befreiung der Frau*, spoke to condemn the sexual division of labour within the SDS. It emerged speaking the language of anti-authoritarianism, whose rhetoric of human needs and commitment to the world-wide struggles of marginal groups rendered it a potent theoretical language with which to grasp, as Sander's speech put it, 'das spezifische Ausbeutungsverhältnis, unter dem die Frauen stehen'.[56] For Karin Schrader-Klebert, also of the *Aktionsrat*, in 'Die kulturelle Revolution der Frau' (1969) it was no coincidence that:

> wo der Kampf unterdrückter entmenschter Völker gegen imperialistische und kolonialistische Gewalt, der Kampf entmündigter und politisch entrechteter Gruppen innerhalb der monopolkapitalistischen Länder selbst geschichtsmächtig geworden ist, auch die Frauen ihre prinzipielle Entmenschung zu erkennen beginnen.[57]

Significantly, though, the early feminism of Sander and Schrader-Klebert attacked the gender-blindness of anti-authoritarianism from within a shared framework of assumptions. Sander insisted, 'daß eine Emanzipation nur gesamtgesellschaftlich möglich ist'; and for both women that emancipation required the 'Umwandlung der Produktionsverhältnisse und damit der Machtverhältnisse'.[58]

Informed by Kate Millett's *Sexual Politics* (1969), Germaine Greer's *The Female Eunuch* (1970) and Shulamith Firestone's *The Dialectic of Sex: The Case for Feminist Revolution* (1970) among others,[59] the ascendant radical feminist currents within the movement took the earlier critique beyond the parameters of a radical project shared with the left. For contributors to the *Frauenjahrbuch '75*, the left was structurally blind to '*den* Teil der

---

56 Helke Sander, 'Rede des "Aktionsrates zur Befreiung der Frauen"', in *Autonome Frauen. Schlüsseltexte der Neuen Frauenbewegung seit 1968*, ed. by Ann Anders (Frankfurt am Main, 1988), pp. 39-47 (p. 40).

57 Karin Schrader-Klebert, 'Die kulturelle Revolution der Frau', *Kursbuch*, 17 (1969), 1-46 (p. 1).

58 Sander, pp. 42-43; see also Schrader-Klebert, p. 5.

59 These texts were published in German as: Kate Millett, *Sexus und Herrschaft. Die Tyrannei des Mannes in unserer Gesellschaft* (Munich, 1974); Germaine Greer, *Der weibliche Eunuch. Aufruf zur Befreiung der Frau* (Frankfurt am Main, 1974); Shulamith Firestone, *Frauenbefreiung und sexuelle Revolution* (Frankfurt am Main, 1975).

gesellschaftlichen Wirklichkeit, auf Grund dessen wir überhaupt in einer Frauengruppe waren: die Frauenunterdrückung'.[60]

During the 1970s, Marxist feminism could draw on classic analyses of the 'woman question' – like Friedrich Engels's *Der Ursprung der Familie, des Privateigentums und des Staates* (1884) or August Bebel's *Die Frau und der Sozialismus* (1879). Radical feminism, however, was forced to develop an alternative account of female oppression and emancipation. Underwritten by the §218 campaign, a gender-specific issue politicising the reproductive sphere in a most immediate sense, that account crystallised around the discourses about vaginal orgasm in circulation in the second wave women's movements. For Alice Schwarzer's *Der 'kleine Unterschied' und seine großen Folgen. Frauen über sich – Beginn einer Befreiung* (1975), among the first indigenous statements of radical feminism in the Federal Republic:

> Nur der Mythos vom vaginalen Orgasmus (und damit von der Bedeutung der Penetration) sichert den Männern das Sexmonopol über Frauen. Und nur das Sexmonopol sichert auch Männern das private Monopol, das das Fundament des öffentlichen Monopols der Männergesellschaft über Frauen ist.[61]

This radically psychological and sexual account of women's oppression unmistakably bears the influence of anti-authoritarianism's psychosexual rhetoric. However, it seeks not so much to compensate the left's blind spots as furnish radical politics with a new grounding in which social critique is formulated along the fault lines of gender. For Schwarzer, the socialist concept of capitalism is accordingly displaced by a broader 'Männerherrschaft' lasting 'Jahrtausende': '[das] Patriarchat'.[62]

The feminist critique of the left and the emergence of radical feminist positions are central to the autobiographies of Struck, Buhmann and Stefan. *Klassenliebe* plays leftist and feminist positions off against one another without declaring allegiance to either. By contrast, *Ich habe mir eine Geschichte geschrieben* and *Häutungen* articulate more clearly a gendered critique of the left. In *Ich habe mir eine Geschichte geschrieben* that critique comes from outside the positions of the left; in *Häutungen* it is unambiguously a radical feminist one. These two latter texts also exemplify a shift in the very medium of political discourse – a shift towards autobiographical forms of writing – that merits clarification.

---

60 'Vom SDS zum Frauenzentrum', no author, in *Frauenjahrbuch '75*, ed. by Frankfurter Frauen (Frankfurt am Main, 1975), pp. 9-48 (p. 22).

61 Alice Schwarzer, *Der 'kleine Unterschied' und seine großen Folgen. Frauen über sich – Beginn einer Befreiung* (Frankfurt am Main, 1975), p. 204. Compare Burns and van der Will, pp. 142-43.

62 Schwarzer, *Der 'kleine Unterschied'*, pp. 185-86.

That a theorist like Schwarzer found the theoretical formulation of a positive account of female emancipation difficult is hardly surprising given the monolithic character she ascribed to patriarchy. *Der 'kleine Unterschied'* nonetheless offered its readers the outlines of a more positive account. An example of the 'Protokolliteratur' that flourished in the wake of the student movement, the text combined a conventional theoretical analysis of the mechanisms of women's oppression with individual 'Protokolle' based on Schwarzer's interviews with various women, which both inform and illustrate that analysis. A vision of female emancipation is not provided by Schwarzer's theoretical commentary, but rather, tentatively upheld within some of the 'Protokolle' – like 'Anne H.' or 'Annegret O.' – which document the small triumphs of a personal struggle against oppression.[63] Put briefly, these 'Protokolle' combined political insights with personal experience in a powerful new discourse which could offer positive examples of the struggle for emancipation too.

Schwarzer's text testifies eloquently to a shift toward experience-based discourses within the New Women's Movement. Conventional theoretical discourses remained a crucial tool in the politicisation of the reproductive sphere in debates on abortion and domestic labour. During the 1970s, however, a confluence of factors contributed to a valorisation of autobiographical discourse as a medium suited to negotiating the dichotomies of private and public, the personal and political, the singular and universal. The ascendancy of radical feminism within the movement located women's oppression in the reproductive sphere and placed a high premium on women's experience (as was evidenced by the flowering of 'Selbsterfahrungsgruppen' designed to encourage women, not always successfully, to abstract from their personal experience to the general patterns underlying it).[64] This created a climate in which 'Protokolliteratur' could flourish. Most famously associated with Erika Runge's *Bottroper Protokolle* (1968), 'Protokolliteratur' – the attempt to let disenfranchised voices speak through a medium of a committed editor – predated the women's movement. Under partisan feminist editors, however, it became a favoured form of political expression which, like the 'Selbsterfahrungsgruppen' ideally, moved from women's individual experience to the general features of their oppression. (Feminist examples of 'Protokolliteratur' included: Erika Runge's *Frauen. Versuche zur Emanzipation*, 1969; Alice Schwarzer's *Frauenarbeit – Frauenbefreiung*, 1973, and *Der 'kleine' Unterschied*, 1975; and Freia Hoffmann's *Ledige Mütter*, 1976.) Further, the valorisation of the autobiographical occurred within the framework of the movement's expanding literary counterculture. A

---

63   Schwarzer, *Der 'kleine Unterschied'*, pp. 62-72 and 138-51.
64   Herrad Schenk, *Die feministische Herausforderung. 150 Jahre Frauenbewegung in Deutschland* (Munich, 1980), pp. 88-94.

growing network of feminist publishing houses and journals – such as the Frauenoffensive press in which *Häutungen* was published, and its journal (both founded in 1974) – generated an enormous pressure for texts to be published. Finally, the shift towards autobiographical discourses was nourished also by a sub-literary culture which predated the publication of *Häutungen* in 1975, and thereafter issued into the network of feminist journals and of 'Treffen schreibender Frauen'.[65] This culture fostered processes of writing above all connected with the need for 'Selbsterfahrung'. As one woman put it in her account of an 'Autobiographie AG' ('Arbeitsgruppe') at a 1978 'Treffen schreibender Frauen': 'Nicht literarischer Ruhm ist unser Ziel, sondern besseres Selbstverständnis durch und mit und in Sprache'.[66]

The step from the feminist 'Protokolle' to more fully developed forms of autobiographical writing was small. That autobiographical discourse represented a form of political communication appears a commonplace among studies of West German feminist writing published since the 1980s. In *Inszenierungen des Weiblichen. Die literarische Darstellung weiblicher Subjektivität in der westdeutschen Frauenliteratur der siebziger und achtziger Jahre* (1992), for example, Renate Becker contemplates a 'dialektisches Verhältnis von Frauenbewegung und Frauentexten'.[67] Or in *Frauenliteratur und weibliche Identität. Theoretische Ansätze zu einer weiblichen Ästhetik und zur Entwicklung der neuen deutschen Frauenliteratur* (1986), Karin Richter-Schröder considers whether the autobiographical literature of the 1970s might have provided an important medium for the construction of a female subjectivity, as classical autobiography did for bourgeois subjectivity according to Habermas's *Strukturwandel der Öffentlichkeit* (1962).[68] However, these studies, informed by a poststructuralist feminist aesthetic, exhibit a preference for a playful and disruptive textuality that obscures the political value of the movement's autobiographical culture, with its often unsophisticated conception of the relationships between female subjectivity and literary form. Our reading of *Ich habe mir eine Geschichte geschrieben* and *Häutungen* will by contrast grasp with greater sensitivity to the historical context of the West German New Women's Movement how the autobiographical drew its force as a medium of political discourse. This issue

---

65 Sigrid Weigel, *Die Stimme der Medusa. Schreibweisen in der Gegenwartsliteratur von Frauen* (Dülmen-Hiddingsel, 1987), p. 48.

66 Anke Schneemann, 'Autobiographie AG', *Schreiben 1. Frauenliteraturzeitung*, 3/4 June 1978, pp. 42-43 (p. 43).

67 Renate Becker, *Inszenierungen des Weiblichen. Die literarische Darstellung weiblicher Subjektivität in der westdeutschen Frauenliteratur der siebziger und achtziger Jahre* (Frankfurt am Main, Bern, New York and Paris, 1992), p. 57.

68 Karin Richter-Schröder, *Frauenliteratur und weibliche Identität. Theoretische Ansätze zu einer weiblichen Ästhetik und zur Entwicklung der neuen deutschen Frauenliteratur* (Frankfurt am Main, 1986), pp. 123-28.

is more fully discussed in the following section on the history and theory of autobiography.

III   Theories of Autobiography

Setting our texts in relation to the student and the women's movements – already here we touch upon the topic of autobiography – helps us to grasp them as social fact. Yet the question of autobiographical writing in them is not peripheral to more pressing social and political issues. Vesper's fraught engagement with the autobiographical act sets *Die Reise* apart from other narratives about the student movement and its aftermath, like Uwe Timm's *Heißer Sommer* (1974) or Roland Lang's *Ein Hai in der Suppe* (1975). An exploration of the implications of the mass media for human subjectivity and, crucially, for autobiographical discourse, Brinkmann's *Erkundungen* represent a remarkable contribution to the genre of autobiography. And, as suggested above, texts like *Ich habe mir eine Geschichte geschrieben* and *Häutungen* illustrate the significance of autobiographical discourse for the articulation of a feminist politics and of a gendered subjectivity within the New Women's Movement. The theoretical problem of autobiography is central to our texts; our task here is to relate them to it.

For all the critical attention devoted in recent years to the subject of autobiography, the contours of the genre have not emerged with entire clarity. On the contrary, as William Spengemann's *The Forms of Autobiography: Episodes in the History of a Literary Genre* (1980) notes, 'the more the genre gets written about, the less agreement there seems to be on what it properly includes'.[69] (Indeed, to add to a proliferation of theoretical approaches, autobiographical theory currently seems to be turning on itself, generating theories about the theory, as if this were easier to pin down than autobiography itself.) Nonetheless, Spengemann's claim that the 'only arguable definition of autobiography would be a full account of all the ways in which the word has been used' is surely disingenuous.[70] Autobiographical criticism has consistently focused on specific concerns. The 'nature and expression of subjectivity; the generic specificity of autobiography; the truth-status and referentiality of autobiography in relation to the fact-fiction dichotomy and the status of fictional entities' are not just concerns of recent theory, as Laura Marcus's *Auto/biographical discourses: criticism, theory, practice* (1994)

---

69   William Spengemann, *The Forms of Autobiography: Episodes in the History of a Literary Genre* (New Haven and London, 1980), p. xi.
70   Spengemann, p. 185.

implies,[71] but have been fundamental to autobiographical criticism from its inception. Moreover, the handling of these concerns in the critical literature reveals a number of distinct theoretical and methodological approaches to the genre. These include a tendency to view autobiography in terms of the historical evolution of an impulse to bring coherence, form and meaning to human experience; an interest in the relation between autobiography and psychoanalysis; and an interest in the linguistic structure of the autobiographical text that has given rise to speech act and deconstructive theories of autobiography. Feeding methodological questions into political ones, feminist criticism has taken on existing assumptions about the genre too. Rather than adhere rigidly to one critical approach, this study will employ a range of theories in order to illuminate different aspects of the autobiographical act in our texts. A brief discussion of autobiographical theory can help us understand how.

A dominant approach to the study of autobiography can be traced to a concept of human life as a meaningful totality – the notion of a 'Zusammenhang des Lebens' – elaborated by the nineteenth-century German philosopher Wilhelm Dilthey.[72] Following Dilthey, Georg Misch's massive *Geschichte der Autobiographie* (published between 1907 and 1969) and Roy Pascal's *Design and Truth in Autobiography* (1960), for example, have interpreted autobiography as a hermeneutic in which the autobiographer brings form and cohesion to his life experience, relating its parts to its whole meaning, and his self to the world. According to Misch, the autobiographer 'uncovers' through the autobiographical act a totality of part and whole in his life which pre-exists that act.[73] For Pascal, by contrast, autobiography represents a more active shaping of the past, but the resulting totality, an 'interpenetration and collusion of inner and outer life, of the person and society', remains similar.[74] At any rate, the concept of autobiography as totality associated with Misch and Pascal has provided the basis for recurrent critical assumptions about the genre: that the autobiographical text has a representative significance for its era; and that it provides a psychological truth which transcends questions of historical verifiability. Misch in particular has given shape to a conception of the history of autobiography that has cast a long shadow over subsequent scholars.

71   Laura Marcus, *Auto/biographical discourses: theory, criticism, practice* (Manchester and New York, 1994), p. 179.
72   Michael Sheringham, *French Autobiography: Devices and Desires. Rousseau to Perec* (Oxford, 1993), p. 2.
73   Georg Misch, *Geschichte der Autobiographie*, 4 vols (Frankfurt am Main, 1949-69), I (Pt. 1), 9-10.
74   Roy Pascal, *Design and Truth in Autobiography* (London, 1960), p. 185. See Sheringham, p. 4.

At first sight, Misch's conception of the genre appears very broad. His study presents autobiography as nothing short of a transhistorical category extending from Egyptian tomb inscriptions to Goethe's *Dichtung und Wahrheit* (1811-33) – 'eine Geschichte des menschlichen Selbstbewußtseins', no less.[75] However, if this understanding of autobiography as a transhistorical category of human expression appears too broad to be useful, Misch's view of the literary value accruing to the genre is actually very narrow. His critical ideal of the genre as a totality of part and whole, self and world allows but few texts truly able to embody that ideal. For all his historical sweep, Misch centres his understanding of the genre, in short, on the classical autobiography of the nineteenth century, installing Goethe's *Dichtung und Wahrheit* – the poetic incarnation of the 'typisch Menschlichen'[76] – as its apogee.

The privileged position Misch assigns classical autobiography, particularly *Dichtung und Wahrheit*, has shaped criticism, especially of German autobiography, enduringly. The value system fixing *Dichtung und Wahrheit* as the consummation of the genre is displayed, for instance, in Pascal's assertion that since Goethe 'little enrichment in the conception of [autobiography's] central purpose and scope' has occurred.[77] It also provides the backdrop against which critics of German autobiography sceptical of Misch's undertaking have been constrained to elaborate alternative accounts. Bernd Neumann's *Identität und Rollenzwang. Zur Theorie der Autobiographie* (1970) charges Misch with perpetuating a blind 'Goetheverehrung' irreconcilable with a truly historical understanding of autobiography.[78] For his part, Neumann draws on a tradition of critical social psychology from Freud to the Frankfurt School in order to frame the evolution of autobiography within a materialist conception of history and reveal the autobiographer as 'das Objekt sozialer und psychischer Zwänge'. Classical autobiography, he argues, evidences a high degree of autonomy on the part of the autobiographer – he terms this 'Identität' – in response to the demand of mercantile capitalism for a free economic subject. With progressive capital concentration and the advent of new means of socialisation which foster conformity, that free economic subject becomes obsolete and the 'Identität' of classical autobiography is displaced by a mechanical 'Rollenzwang'. Autobiography, with its emphasis on its writer's 'psychische Ergehen', dissolves into memoir, which focuses on 'das Ergehen eines Individuums als Träger einer sozialen Rolle'. (This account of the passage of autobiography

75   Misch, I (Pt. 1), 6 and 11.
76   Misch IV (Pt. 2), 944.
77   Pascal, p. 55. Compare Marcus pp. 164-65.
78   Bernd Neumann, *Identität und Rollenzwang. Zur Theorie der Autobiographie* (Frankfurt am Main, 1970), p. 3. See pp. 1-25 for further references to Neumann's study in the discussion above.

into memoir surely reproduces, albeit in the language of historical materialism, central assumptions of the Goethe cult that Neumann rejects.)

Perhaps it is hardly surprising that a diversification of critical methodologies has occurred largely beyond the criticism of German autobiography. Since the start of the 1970s, critics have turned to psychoanalytic, linguistic, speech act and deconstructive theories to provide fresh critical vocabularies for autobiography. Psychoanalysis and autobiography 'paradigmatically involve the reconstruction of a life in narrative and the shaping of events into a meaningful framework'.[79] Psychoanalytic approaches like Bruce Mazlish's 'Autobiography and Psycho-analysis: Between Truth and Self-Deception' (1970) have thus explored the relationships between autobiography, psychoanalytic theories of subjectivity and the analytic process. Anticipating the advent of speech act and deconstructive theories of the genre, by contrast, Louis Renza's 'The Veto of the Imagination: A Theory of Autobiography' (1977) and Jean Starobinski's 'The Style of Autobiography' (1971) explore the role of language in the construction of autobiographical subjectivity. For Renza, the autobiographical act is split between the autobiographer's private intention to bring his past into the 'purview of his present narrative project' and the public structures of language, which 'displaces this past whenever he speaks of it to others'.[80] According to Starobinski, however, language anything but frustrates the accurate 'transcription of past events'; rather, it feeds into a notion of 'style' as a 'system of revealing indices' that represents the most radically 'individualizing' feature of autobiography.[81] For Starobinski, autobiographical truth thus resides above all in the revelatory force of language.

Communication models offer another account of the problem of truth in autobiography. In the speech act theory of J. L. Austin and John Searle, the meaning of a linguistic utterance is evaluated according to conventions shared by sender and receiver as members of a speech community. Analogously, Elisabeth Bruss's *Autobiographical Acts: The Changing Situation of a Literary Genre* (1976) conceives the autobiographical text as a message transmitted from author to reader within a common framework of expectations. The genre designation 'autobiography', she argues, binds author and reader into a system of 'rules': that author, narrator and protagonist, for example, be

79   Marcus, p. 214.
80   Louis A. Renza, 'The Veto of the Imagination: A Theory of Autobiography', *NLH*, 9 (1977), 1-26 (pp. 3 and 7).
81   Jean Starobinski, 'The Style of Autobiography', in *Literary Style: A Symposium*, ed. by Seymour Chatman (London and New York, 1971), pp. 285-96 (pp. 286-87).

identical, and that reported events 'are asserted to have been, to be, or to have potential for being the case'.[82]

On this view, autobiographical truth lies in a pragmatic acceptance of certain utterances as truthful.[83] However, precisely Bruss's sensitivity toward the literary issues raised by autobiography shows up the theory's limitations. She acknowledges that the rules of the autobiographical act 'occasionally are broken'; vital for 'the illocutionary force of the text is that the author purport to have met these requirements'. Yet to claim that an 'autobiographer can be convicted of "insincerity" or worse if he is caught in a premeditated distortion' is to evade the implications of texts which situate themselves ambiguously in relation to the 'rules' governing the autobiographical act.

Deconstructive critics have for their part attacked the speech act theorists account of autobiographical truth as the product of a phonocentrism that privileges speech as a metaphor of authenticity over the lifeless emanations of writing. In 'Autobiography as De-facement' (1979), Paul de Man famously exposed the authenticity of autobiographical discourse as rhetorically produced. He put it like this:

> We assume that life *produces* the autobiography [...], but can we not suggest, with equal justice, that the autobiographical project may itself produce and determine the life and that whatever the writer *does* is in fact governed by the technical demands of self-portraiture and thus determined in all its aspects, by the resources of his medium?[84]

Because they turn 'the author as subject, as one who authorizes, gives authority to, is responsible for a text' into a fiction, one might expect, as Michael Sprinker argues in 'Fictions of the Self: The End of Autobiography' (1980), that poststructuralist theories have rendered the concept of autobiography meaningless.[85] As long as writers and critics continue to write or write about 'autobiography', though, it seems premature to dispense with the category. Indeed, the notion of the self as fiction has, on the contrary, been taken up by critics keen to recuperate the challenge of deconstruction for a new understanding of the genre. John Paul Eakin's *Fictions of the Self: Studies in the Art of Self-Invention* (1985), for example, endeavours to preserve the integrity of the autobiographical act by feeding poststructuralist theories into a

---

82   Elisabeth Bruss, *Autobiographical Acts: The Changing Situation of a Literary Genre* (Baltimore and London, 1976), pp. 10-11 (p. 11). See pp. 11-16 for other references to Bruss in the discussion above.
83   Frieden, p. 30.
84   Paul de Man, 'Autobiography as De-facement', *MLN*, 94 (1979), 919-30 (pp. 920-21).
85   Michael Sprinker, 'Fictions of the Self: The End of Autobiography', in *Autobiography: Essays Theoretical and Critical*, ed. by James Olney (Princeton, 1980), pp. 321-42 (p. 322).

concept of 'self-invention' designed to avoid the pitfalls of a deconstructive approach that simply views the self as an effect of rhetoric. Arguing that 'the fiction-making process [is] a central constituent of the truth of any life as it is lived', Eakin claims that 'self and language are mutually implicated in a single, interdependent system of symbolic behaviour'.[86]

Autobiographical discourse, we suggested, played a substantial role in the evolution of a feminist politics within the New Women's Movement. Conversely, a criticism taking feminist politics as a point of departure has recently recast critical assumptions about the genre. The broad scope of feminist approaches to autobiography combines historical scholarship with impulses from psychoanalysis and poststructuralism. But here too there are central concerns. Linking the construction of gender to the institution of genre, feminist approaches offer a critique of the historical and critical mechanisms through which the genre of autobiography and the theories based upon it have been constructed so as to exclude women's texts. They seek also to reconstruct histories and theories of autobiography from a perspective that acknowledges forms of self-expression historically available to women.

Feminist critique has focused on the conflation of masculinity and universality underpinning established conceptions of autobiography. For feminist critics, this conflation has barred autobiography to women or disqualified their writings as inconsequential. Its focus German autobiography, Marianne Vogt's *Autobiographik bürgerlicher Frauen. Zur Geschichte weiblicher Selbstbewußtwerdung* (1981) argues that a 'Gattungspoetik' developing from the eighteenth century onwards through the models provided by the '"Selbstbiographien berühmter Männer"' excluded women from the evolving genre; confined within bourgeois society to the domestic sphere, women were deprived of the 'Teilnahme am öffentlichen Diskurs' that was the prerequisite of a claim to public significance fundamental to autobiography.[87] To this account of women's exclusion, Kay Goodman adds, in *Dis/Closures: Women's Autobiography in Germany between 1790 and 1914* (1986) and in 'Elisabeth to Meta: Epistolary Autobiography and the Postulation of the Self' (1988), a critique of the normative character of autobiographical theory. Above all, she takes Misch to task for helping to found an ideal of the genre as a 'universal synthesis of historical, professional, intellectual, and personal struggles' that fits *Dichtung und Wahrheit*, but overlooks women's strategies of self-representation.[88]

---

86   John Paul Eakin, *Fictions in Autobiography: Studies in the Art of Self-Invention* (Princeton, 1985), pp. 5 and 192.

87   Marianne Vogt, *Autobiographik bürgerlicher Frauen. Zur Geschichte weiblicher Selbstbewußtwerdung* (Würzburg, 1981), pp. 15 and 25.

88   Kay Goodman, *Dis/Closures: Women's Autobiography in Germany between 1790 and 1914* (New York, Bern and Frankfurt am Main, 1986), p. iv.

In feminist approaches, however, critique above all provides the springboard for a reconstruction of the history and theory of autobiography from a gendered perspective. Vogt's study, for instance, locates early in the nineteenth century the inception of a tradition of women's autobiographical writing running askew to received critical histories. Women's expanding range of social experience, she argues, facilitated their access to autobiographical discourse. Yet where men's autobiographies inscribed the codes of bourgeois subjectivity, women's autobiographical writings were split between a desire for 'Selbstbestimmung' and the dominant cultural constructions of femininity.[89] According to Goodman, women explored modes of self-expression 'based on other constructions of experience' and often developed hybrid forms outside received generic definitions, like Isabella von Wallenrodt's 'epistolary' autobiography *Das Leben der Frau von Wallenrodt in Briefen an einen Freund* (1797).[90]

Poststructuralist thought has been a powerful influence in recent feminist approaches to autobiography too. Its 'destabilisation of monolithic notions of self and author' has, as Kosta's *Recasting Autobiography* of 1994 acknowledges, proved crucial in opening the genre to the heterogeneous voices of women.[91] Unwilling to relinquish the self to a process of rhetorical figuration, however, even feminist critics sympathetic to poststructuralism have insisted on texts' connection to individual lives and upheld, in Goodman's words, the 'concreteness of women's (and men's) existence' against 'the radical deconstruction of the subject'.[92] Others have voiced open disquiet about the alliance of feminism and poststructuralism, particularly in the influential poststructuralist feminisms of Hélène Cixous, Luce Irigaray and Julia Kristeva. Evelyne Keitel's 'Frauen, Texte, Theorie. Aspekte eines problematischen Verhältnisses' (1983), for instance, problematises a 'mangelnde Korrelierbarkeit' between the often simple autobiographical narratives written within the New Women's Movement and the poststructuralist feminist theories increasingly the focus for feminist debates about literature.[93] More assertively, Rita Felski's *Beyond Feminist Aesthetics: Feminist Literature and Social Change* (1989) claims that poststructuralist feminism's tendency to equate the 'feminine' with a deconstruction of fixed identities cannot grasp the autobiographical narrative that is the mainstay of feminist writing. Felski advocates a recontextualisation of feminist autobiography that engages

---

89 Marianne Vogt, *Autobiographik bürgerlicher Frauen*, p. 48.
90 Katherine R. Goodman, 'Elisabeth to Meta: Epistolary Autobiography and the Postulation of the Self', in *Life/Lines: Theorizing Women's Autobiography*, ed. by Bella Brodzki and Celeste Schenk (Ithaca and London, 1988), pp. 306-19 (pp. 311 and 318).
91 Kosta, p. 3.
92 Goodman, 'From Elisabeth to Meta', p. 309.
93 Evelyne Keitel, 'Frauen, Texte, Theorie. Aspekte eines problematischen Verhältnisses', *Das Argument*, 25 (1983), 830-41 (p. 830).

'sympathetically with the issue of identity formation as a defining feature of recent feminist literature and an important stage in the development of an oppositional politics'.[94]

Studies of recent German autobiography have adopted diverse positions towards the theoretical problem of autobiography. At one extreme, Barbara Saunders's *Contemporary German Autobiography: Literary Approaches to the Problem of Identity* (1985) fails to clarify its critical stance toward texts by Canetti, Bernhard, Frisch, Koeppen and Christa Wolf. At the other, Frieden's 1983 *Autobiography: Self into Form* rigidly applies speech act theory. Steering by contrast a path of theoretical pluralism, this study offers a richly theorised approach to autobiography, but no global or comprehensive theory. This stance follows from a new departure in autobiographical criticism, in which the problem itself of theorising autobiography is foregrounded.

Of recent studies, Laura Marcus's *Auto/biographical discourses* of 1994, which elevates the theory itself into the object of critical scrutiny, takes this self-conscious concern with theorising autobiography the furthest. For Marcus, autobiographical theory represents in its own right a medium for exploring epistemological questions about the relationship between truth and fiction, literary questions about the process of canon formation and political questions about the formation of cultural and gendered identities. Yet in its self-consciousness theory has not lost sight of autobiography itself. Drawing on Marcus's work (as dissertation) Michael Sheringham's *French Autobiography: Devices and Desires. Rousseau to Perec* (1993) on the contrary advances an inclusive notion of autobiography as 'act and narrative process' that folds such epistemological, literary and political questions back into the autobiographical act.[95] Far from 'the apotheosis of the sovereign ego', autobiography is for Sheringham 'an anxious genre' in which each text performs 'a negotiation with different forms of otherness': 'other texts, other ideas, other people'. Thus autobiographers never simply write the self, they always already 'write [it] in the margins of major conceptual systems, existing narratives, or paradigms of selfhood at large in philosophy and psychology'. Autobiography, in short, itself already is a kind of autobiographical theory engaging the epistemological, literary and political questions that Marcus ascribes to the theory proper. For us here, Sheringham's work upholds the ideal of a theoretical approach to autobiography. Yet it eschews prescriptive assumptions about the genre in favour of a more subtle notion of 'negotiation' that allows us to range between theoretical approaches to illuminate the varying ways in which our texts engage with autobiographical discourse. Just

---

94   Rita Felski, *Beyond Feminist Aesthetics: Feminist Literature and Social Change* (London, 1989), pp. 44.

95   Sheringham, p. 2. See pp. vii-ix for further references to Sheringham in the discussion above.

as they relate diversely to the ideological context of their production, so each text constructs the autobiographical act differently.

Die Reise, we suggested, is constructed as a radical 'case history' grounded in the work of Reich and Marcuse. But Vesper's engagement with the autobiographical act renders the project a more fraught affair. Put briefly, the text appears split between opposing conceptions of the autobiographical act. In the fashion described by Renza's 'The Veto of the Imagination', Vesper's endeavour to yield up his past to a present intention (a process of personal radicalisation) is frustrated as it dissipates in the language used to seize it. The autobiographical act thus holds Vesper in thrall to an unmasterable past. Yet Vesper intuits also, more in line with Starobinski's 'The Style of Autobiography', that the language which frustrates him might function as an instrument of reconciliation between past and present, a medium in which the autobiographer invents himself according to his present needs. This is not to say that *Die Reise* misrecognises the character of the autobiographical act. Rather, it dramatises a fundamental theoretical problem: namely, whether autobiographical discourse represents a means of self-knowledge or self-invention.

The *Erkundungen*, we argued, are suspended between contradictory constructions of the relationship between the mass media and human subjectivity: a Marcusean vision of the liquidation of the subject in the face of the mass media, and a McLuhanite emphasis on the transformation of human experience through them. Accordingly, the *Erkundungen* also grasp as contradictory the implications of the media for the autobiographical act. Like Neumann's *Identität und Rollenzwang*, they suggest that if the mass media as direct means of socialisation render obsolete the autonomous individual, so too they assail an interplay of self and world, of past and present that is central to autobiography as a genre. Brinkmann's text documents his failure to write an 'autobiographical novel' as he struggles to protect a realm of interiority against the mass media. Yet the *Erkundungen* also grasp in the media the key to a fundamental transformation of the autobiographical act. Manfred Schneider's *Die erkaltete Herzensschrift. Der autobiographische Text im 20. Jahrhundert* (1986), a work *sui generis* in autobiographical theory, has drawn on McLuhan and others to argue that the autobiographical act occurs within the framework of the writing and recording technologies available in a given social and cultural formation. A culture of the written word, he suggests, produced classical autobiography, its author both representative and unique (a 'character' after all was both a standardised symbol and a system of personal traits). Yet the ascendancy of other media – 'die öffentlichen und privaten Bild-, Fernseh-, Film- und Tonarchive' – in recording information about the self undermines the 'Paradigma der Erinnerung' based on written and printed discourse and furnishes autobiography with 'Metaphern' for fresh constructions of experience, memory and selfhood.[96] In the *Erkundungen*, the metaphors provided by the technical media – here the camera, the tape recorder and the typewriter (or computer) – turn the autobiographical act into a form of information processing that erases the interiority of the subject, but in so doing provides the basis for a radical concept of self-invention.

The critical context for our discussion of the texts by Struck, Stefan and Buhmann is the disparity noted by Keitel's 'Frauen, Texte, Theorie' between the autobiographical practices of the women's movement and the elaboration of theoretical discourses about women's writing. Where the moment of autobiographical writing within the New Women's Movement is concerned, the academic institutionalisation of poststructuralist feminist discourses during the 1980s has surely heightened this mismatch of text and theory. Karin Richter-Schröder's *Frauenliteratur und weibliche Identität* of 1986 and Renate Becker's *Inszenierungen des Weiblichen* of 1992 acknowledge a specific historical relationship between autobiographical discourse and the New Women's Movement. However, the poststructuralist feminist aesthetic informing their work dissipates the specific historicity of the texts concerned. The fixing of 'der im literarischen Experiment spielerisch vollzogenen Verweigerung der Sinnstiftung'[97] as the ideal of a subversive feminine textuality entails the rejection of the teleological narratives of texts like Stefan's *Häutungen* or Buhmann's *Ich habe mir eine Geschichte geschrieben* in favour of more self-conscious writing. Key texts are thus charged with an aesthetic naivety that robs them of their transformative impetus.

In *Beyond Feminist Aesthetics*, Rita Felski has by contrast argued that there exists no automatic link between specific signifying practices, whether perceived as subversive or feminine, and the wider aims and practices of an oppositional movement like feminism. The political meanings of women's writing, she writes, cannot be theorised 'in an a priori fashion': they can be addressed only through examining the discursive status and function of texts 'within historically specific contexts'.[98] To uphold an ideal of subversive textuality runs various risks in respect of texts like *Ich habe mir eine Geschichte geschrieben* or *Häutungen*. It devalues the way in which they adopt, open up and adapt existing cultural traditions like autobiography; and it confuses the legitimate but specialised reading practices of (feminist) academics with the broader needs of feminism as a movement.

Our discussion of *Klassenliebe*, *Ich habe mir eine Geschichte geschrieben* and *Häutungen* in the final chapter of the study takes up precisely these questions about the appropriation of existing genres and the needs of

---

96   Manfred Schneider, *Die erkaltete Herzensschrift. Der autobiographische Text im 20. Jahrhundert* (Munich, 1986), pp. 28 and 42.
97   Richter-Schröder, p. 157.
98   Felski, p. 48.

oppositional communities. Following a brief introductory section, the chapter's second part examines the relationship between history, life history and form in the texts by Struck and Buhmann. In contrast to the diary form of Struck's *Klassenliebe*, which remains locked into the private sphere, the synthetic and teleological autobiographical narrative of Buhmann's *Ich habe mir eine Geschichte geschrieben*, it argues, provides a medium in which female subjectivity and historical discourse are brought into a dialogue through the collective agency of the New Women's Movement. The third part of the chapter focuses on Stefan's *Häutungen* and explores the relation between autobiography and political discourse. Taking on critiques of the text's essentialism in the light of recent debates about the 'identity politics' of oppositional movements, it argues that *Häutungen* provided the New Women's Movement with a symbolic fiction in which a concept of autobiographical self-invention, more happily than in the more complex texts by Vesper and Brinkmann, is linked to an oppositional politics.

CHAPTER 2

Bernward Vesper's Revolutionary Autobiography: *Die Reise*

I   German Autumn: The Reception of *Die Reise*

Before his suicide in 1971, Bernward Vesper made radical claims for the autobiography he was writing. A letter to his publishers, März, dated 11 September 1969 (and reprinted as part of an appendix to *Die Reise*), suggests that he believed the text without precedent in German literature:[1] 'Wir haben in Deutschland keine Tradition. D. h. jenseits von Realismus, Bekenntnisliteratur und "fiction" – nichts' (*DR*, 607). This letter outlines Vesper's ambition to combine radical subject matter with radical form in his autobiography through the 'Verschmelzung' of three narrative levels: the 'Bericht [einer] realen Reise' recently undertaken from Dubrovnik to Tübingen, its climax a drugs trip in Munich; an 'Einfacher Bericht' charting Vesper's political development, from the '"subtilen Faschismus"' of his childhood to his later 'politische, literarische Tätigkeit'; and finally a level of '"momentane Wahrnehmung"' pertaining to the present of writing (*DR*, 606-07). Another letter to März, undated, reflects the high hopes which Vesper, founder and editor of the influential *Voltaire Flugschrift* pamphlets during the student movement, had for the political impact of his autobiography on its future readership. Vesper clearly thought his autobiography a key document of anti-authoritarianism in the Federal Republic, able to clarify its positions at home and represent them to the New Left abroad (*DR*, 616-17). Ending in '"neuer Tätigkeit – neuer Sensibilität"' (*DR*, 606), the text, he believed, would sweep its readers along with it, impelling them '*mitzumachen*'; 'bei den wenigen Leuten,' he added, 'die das Ms. bisher sahen, wurde dieser Effekt sichtbar' (*DR*, 616).

The autobiography, which Vesper variously considered naming 'Trip', 'Die Reise' and 'Logbuch' (*DR*, 603, 606, 618), was never completed. In 1971, after rampaging under the influence of drugs, Vesper was committed to psychiatric institutions first in Munich and then near Hamburg where, on 15 May 1971, he committed suicide. Financial problems after 1973 left März unable to publish Vesper's unfinished manuscript, thus it was only in 1977 after Jörg Schröder, März's director, had gone into partnership with

---

1   Bernward Vesper, *Die Reise. Romanessay. Ausgabe letzter Hand*, ed. by Jörg Schröder and Klaus Behnken (Reinbek, 1983), pp. 605-08. References to this edition are given in the main body of the text using the abbreviation *DR*.

Zweitausendeins, a Frankfurt-based mail-order distributor, that a first edition of *Die Reise. Romanessay* – Schröder's chosen title – appeared.[2] Containing in an appendix Vesper's correspondence with März, *Die Reise* proved a popular success, selling 40,000 copies in a year.

In 1979, Schröder published a new edition of the text, subtitled the *Ausgabe letzter Hand*.[3] Based on a further manuscript that came to light in 1978, the *Ausgabe letzter Hand* contained significant additions to the 1977 edition, including passages written days before Vesper's suicide. (These additions were also published separately in 1979 in a supplementary volume for readers owning the 1977 edition.)[4] A first paperback edition appeared in 1981,[5] but it is the most widely available form of the *Ausgabe letzter Hand*, published by Rowohlt in 1983, that is used here. Identical to the editions of 1979 and 1981, it includes Vesper's correspondence with März (*DR*, 601-24) and a second appendix comprising his working notes to the text (*DR*, 625-703). It also lists the items left by Vesper at the psychiatric clinic in Hamburg-Eppendorf upon his suicide (*DR*, 704-08).

Nothing less than a cult book, *Die Reise* has enjoyed enduring popularity on the German left. Those on the left quick to recognise the text's significance included the Marxist dramatist and novelist Peter Weiss, who hailed it in his *Notizbücher* of 1981 as the 'intellektuelle Höhepunkt der Bewegung des Jahrs 68'.[6] Given Vesper's role as founder and editor of the *Voltaire Flugschrift* pamphlets, it is hardly surprising that *Die Reise* should constitute a powerful intellectual record of some of the West German student movement's central political preoccupations. The text's fragmented narrative encapsulates a number of short essays on subjects as diverse as the relationship between capitalism and fascism; the justification for revolutionary violence; the black liberation movements of the United States; and even the political implications of hallucinogenic drugs like LSD.

However, *Die Reise* is fascinating not simply for its overtly political and essayistic passages, but also for its central autobiographical narrative. Refracting a whole segment of German history through the prismatic view of an individual perspective, it tells the story of Vesper's infancy during the final years of the Third Reich; and of his repressive upbringing at the hands of his father, the one-time blood and soil poet Will Vesper, during what he perceived as the stifling ideological conformity of the Federal Republic under Adenauer

2   Bernward Vesper, *Die Reise. Romanessay*, ed. by Jörg Schröder (Jossa, 1977).
3   Bernward Vesper, *Die Reise. Romanessay. Ausgabe letzter Hand*, ed. by Jörg Schröder and Klaus Behnken (Jossa, 1979).
4   Bernward Vesper, *Ergänzungen zu: Die Reise. Romanessay. Aus der Ausgabe letzter Hand*, ed. by Jörg Schröder and Klaus Behnken (Jossa, 1979).
5   Bernward Vesper, *Die Reise. Romanessay. Ausgabe letzter Hand*, ed. by Jörg Schröder and Klaus Behnken (Berlin and Schlechtenwegen, 1981).
6   Peter Weiss, *Notizbücher 1971-1980*, 2 vols (Frankfurt am Main, 1981), II, 672.

in the 1950s. It also tells a personal story of radical hopes awakened and frustrated during the political upheavals of the 1960s. Clearly, *Die Reise* is of more than just intellectual interest, as Weiss suggests. It merits analysis both as a historical document and as an autobiographical text.

However, *Die Reise* has not always received the critical attention that it deserves. The reason for this lies in the shift in the political climate of the Federal Republic that occurred during the delay between Vesper's suicide in 1971 and the publication of his autobiography in July 1977. For *Die Reise* finally appeared just as a spiral of Red Army Faction terrorism and state reaction was reaching its climax in the so-called 'deutscher Herbst' of 1977. This was when the employers' leader, Hanns-Martin Schleyer, was abducted by the RAF and a Lufthansa jet was hijacked by Palestinian and German terrorists demanding the release from the notorious Stammheim prison of Andreas Baader and Gudrun Ensslin amongst others, the latter Vesper's fiancée (until she left him in 1967) and the mother of his son, Felix. With the failure of the hijacking, Baader and Ensslin committed suicide and Schleyer was killed.

When it appeared, Vesper's ambition that his autobiography should illuminate positions on the left posthumously fulfilled itself. Yet if Vesper had hoped that his autobiography might illuminate the radical euphoria of 1968, in the fraught climate of the 'deutscher Herbst' reviewers turned to the text for clarifications of another sort.

Many reviews in the press treated Vesper's autobiography simply as representative of the collective history of what Peter Mosler in the *Frankfurter Allgemeine Zeitung* (11 October 1977) described as the 'Generation der Studentenrevolte'.[7] Yet under the shadow of Vesper's suicide, the exemplary status that critics accorded *Die Reise* related above all to the perceived failures of the student movement. In the *Frankfurter Rundschau* (29 October 1977), for example, Uwe Schweikert asserted that in Vesper's 'individuellem Scheitern [...] spiegelt sich das kollektive Scheitern jener Generation wider, die Mitte der sechziger Jahre aufbrach, die versteinerte Gesellschaft der westlichen Industriestaaten zu verändern'.[8] Viewing it as the record of an individual and collective failure, these reviews placed *Die Reise* in the wider context of the erosion of left-wing hopes in the Federal Republic during the 1970s, the *Tendenzwende*.

Against the backdrop of the 'deutscher Herbst', other early reviews set the text more directly in relation to the rise of urban terrorism in the Federal Republic. An important factor shaping the critical reception of Vesper's

---

7   Peter Mosler, 'Bericht über eine verlorene Generation oder Reise ohne Ankunft. Bernward Vespers Roman', *Frankfurter Allgemeine Zeitung*, 11 October 1977, ('Literatur') p. 5.

8   Uwe Schweikert, 'Logbuch eines Verzweifelnden. Bernward Vespers "Die Reise"', *Frankfurter Rundschau*, 29 October 1977, p. 23.

autobiography here was the publication (in English), also in 1977, of a controversial journalistic history of the RAF: Jillian Becker's *Hitler's Children: The Story of the Baader-Meinhof Terrorist Gang*. Armed with Becker's book, whose title suggested a link between fascism and the urban terrorism of the 1970s, reviewers seized on Vesper's revolutionary fervour and on the facts of his biography – his father a fanatical Nazi, his fiancée a terrorist – as the co-ordinates of a biographical and psychological profile of urban terrorism in the Federal Republic. In *Der Spiegel* (11 July 1977), for instance, Christian Schultz-Gerstein labelled *Die Reise* the 'Bestandsaufnahme eines verhinderten Anarchisten'.[9] Alluding to the title of Jillian Becker's book, moreover, Peter von Becker in *Die Zeit* (11 November 1977) and Heinz Abosch in the *Neue Rundschau* (March 1978) presented Vesper's preoccupation with revolution as a psychological reversal of his father's right-wing extremism. Through the 'Erziehungsgewalt[...]' suffered at his father's hands, they argued, Vesper had internalised destructive patterns of behaviour which compelled him to re-enact, in other forms, the extremism of his father.[10] 'Was einst "Rasse" war, hieß jetzt modisch "Revolution"', claimed Abosch; or as von Becker put it: 'Einer von "Hitler's children", das war Bernward Vesper exemplarisch'.[11] Focusing on *Die Reise*'s explanatory value with respect to the phenomenon of urban terrorism, these reviews passed over the text's literary merits.

The more considered literary-critical response to *Die Reise* exhibits many continuities with the immediate reaction of the press. For many critics, Vesper's suicide provides the ultimate horizon for reading the text. In Jochen Vogt's 'Schwierigkeiten mit der Selbstentblößung. Versuch über "Die Reise" von Bernward Vesper' (1986), for instance, the text is interpreted as the account of an individual and generational failure.[12] Moreover, the problem of urban terrorism looms large in many other discussions, even those that do not take Vesper's relationship to it as their primary subject. Addressing questions of an aesthetic nature and placing the text in wider literary-historical contexts also, however, the literary-critical reception of *Die Reise* has considerably broadened the critical debate. We can divide the literary-critical reception of *Die Reise* into three categories: first, into discussions which pursue Vesper's

9   Christian Schultz-Gerstein, 'Deutscher Sumpf', *Der Spiegel*, 11 July 1977, pp. 146-48 (p.147).
10   Peter von Becker, 'Totgeboren ins deutsche Vater-Land. Bernward Vespers nachgelassener Roman-Essay "Die Reise"', *Die Zeit*, 11 November 1977, ('Literatur') pp. 11-12 (p. 11).
11   Heinz Abosch, 'Kein Weg ins Freie. Zu Bernward Vespers Buch "Die Reise"', *Neue Rundschau*, 89 (1978), 310-13 (p. 313); Peter von Becker, 'Totgeboren ins deutsche Vater-Land', p. 11.
12   Jochen Vogt, 'Schwierigkeiten mit der Selbstentblößung. Versuch über "Die Reise" von Bernward Vesper', *Diskussion Deutsch*, 17 (1986), 289-99 (p. 292).

relationship to urban terrorism; second, a formal analysis of the text; and finally, a set of reviews placing *Die Reise* in broader literary-historical contexts.

In the first category, Michael Schneider's 'Über die Außen- und Innenansicht eines Selbstmörders. Notwendige Ergänzungen zu Bernward Vespers "Die Reise"' (originally 1980) and Frederick Alfred Lubich's 'Bernward Vespers "Die Reise": Von der Hitler-Jugend zur RAF. Identitätssuche unter dem Fluch des Faschismus' (1988) explore the connections between Vesper's radicalism and his relationship to his father. Schneider ascribes to Vesper a sense of identity that oscillates between self-aggrandisement and self-contempt, an opposition amounting to a fascistic '"Endsieg"-' and '"Endlösung"-' mentality in which Vesper acts out 'gefühlsmäßig' the 'rassische Schema seines Vaters'.[13] Yet the contention that behind his apparent radicalism Vesper is a 'verkappte[r] Faschist[...]' is advanced most schematically by Lubich, who enumerates several parallels between Bernward Vesper's radicalism and his father's extremism: these include a shared paranoid 'Angst-Haß-Komplex' in which father and son respectively imagine a ubiquitous racial or class enemy; and a simplistic view of history in terms only of victors and vanquished.[14] For both Schneider and Lubich, Vesper's suicide represents his attempt to exterminate the 'versteckten "Faschisten"' within himself.[15] Another piece which belongs in this context is Emil Grütter's 'Faschistoide Sozialisation und Gesellschaftskritik in Bernward Vespers Autobiographie *Die Reise*' (1981). Grütter too ascribes to Vesper a 'faschistische Zerstörungslust' internalised through his relationship to his father.[16] Yet Grütter's more differentiated article goes further in its exploration of the psychological underpinnings of that relationship and of the mechanisms through which Vesper internalises the ideological dictates of his father. Noting Vesper's reception of Wilhelm Reich, Grütter highlights sexual repression amongst these mechanisms.[17]

---

13   'Über die Außen- und Innenansicht eines Selbstmörders. Notwendige Ergänzungen zu Bernward Vespers "Die Reise"' in Michael Schneider, *Den Kopf verkehrt aufgesetzt oder Die melancholische Linke. Aspekte des Kulturzerfalls in den siebziger Jahren* (Darmstadt and Neuwied, 1981), pp. 65-79 (p. 72).

14   Frederick Alfred Lubich, 'Bernward Vespers "Die Reise": Von der Hitler-Jugend zur RAF. Identitätssuche unter dem Fluch des Faschismus', *German Studies Review*, 11 (1988), 69-94 (p. 71 and pp. 81-88).

15   Michael Schneider, *Den Kopf verkehrt aufgesetzt*, p. 79; Lubich, 'Bernward Vespers "Die Reise": Von der Hitler-Jugend zur RAF', p. 94.

16   Emil Grütter, 'Faschistoide Sozialisation und Gesellschaftskritik in Bernward Vespers Autobiographie *Die Reise*', *Freiburger literaturpsychologische Gespräche*, 1 (1981), 63-77 (p. 74).

17   Grütter, pp. 68-69.

Schneider, Lubich and Grütter treat Vesper's autobiography unproblematically as a social-psychological case history, giving little consideration to *Die Reise* as text. A striking contrast, then, is Georg Guntermann's 'Tagebuch einer Reise in das Innere des Autors. Versuch zu Bernward Vespers "Romanessay" *Die Reise*' (1981). Guntermann abjures *Die Reise*'s perceived 'Schlüsselcharakter' in favour of a 'formale Analyse' which measures the text against the sketch contained in Vesper's letter of 11 September 1969 to his publisher (*DR*, 605-08).[18] Guntermann claims that the 'Verschmelzung' of the three narrative levels projected in this letter (the journey from Dubrovnik to Tübingen and the drugs trip, the account of Vesper's childhood and youth, and the present of writing) is not realised in the text. However, in the actual disposition of the three narrative levels in *Die Reise*, Guntermann observes a progressive stabilisation at odds with the fact of Vesper's suicide. Dividing Vesper's autobiography into three 'Schreibphasen' corresponding roughly to a third of the text each, he observes that the first narrative level (the journey and the trip) is concentrated mostly in the first phase. As the trip recedes in the second, the 'Einfacher Bericht', the narrative of Vesper's childhood and youth comes to the fore. In the text's final phase, reflections on the third narrative level become more coherent and issue into 'zusammenhängenden Berichten, kleinen Essays, [...] die Fragen der Psychologie, Politisches und Gesellschaftliches analysieren'. Concluding that *Die Reise* represents a 'Versenkung in das eigene Ich [als] die Bedingung für eine Öffnung gegenüber den Gegenständen der Welt', Guntermann offers a more positive appraisal of Vesper's autobiography than Schneider or Lubich. Nor does he offer any conjecture concerning Vesper's suicide, save noting that Vesper was apparently unable to realise the stabilising tendencies manifest within his autobiography in his social existence as '(politisch) bewußtes Subjekt'.

To date, the New Subjectivity of the 1970s has tended to provide the context for discussions seeking to place *Die Reise* within wider literary-historical horizons. For Bernd Neumann, in 'Die Wiedergeburt des Erzählens aus dem Geist der Autobiographie? Einige Anmerkungen zum neuen autobiographischen Roman am Beispiel von Hermann Kinders "Der Schleiftrog" und Bernward Vespers "Die Reise"' (1979), *Die Reise* refutes the view that a preoccupation with subjectivity in the literature of the 1970s implied a retreat from the political radicalism of the late 1960s. It proves, on the contrary, that the 'Problematik des "subjektiven Faktors" zu keiner Zeit

---

18 Georg Guntermann, 'Tagebuch einer Reise in das Innere des Autors. Versuch zu Bernward Vespers "Romanessay" *Die Reise*', *Zeitschrift für deutsche Philologie*, 100 (1981), 232-53 (p. 234). See pp. 246-51 for further references to Guntermann's article in the discussion above.

innerhalb der linken Szene gänzlich ausgeklammert [...] worden ist'.[19] In similar terms, the text shows for Klaus Hartung, in 'Die Repression wird zum Milieu. Die Beredsamkeit linker Literatur (Peter Schneider, Peter O. Chotjewitz, Inga Buhmann und Bernward Vesper)' (1979), that the 'autobiographische Wendung' of the 1970s did not simply constitute a 'Privatisierung', but could be highly political.[20]

Critics have related *Die Reise* to the 'Vater-Bücher' of the late 1970s too. Albert von Schirnding's descriptive 'Patre Absente. Eine Generation schreibt sich frei' (1980) fixes Vesper's autobiography as the first of a series of texts – including Härtling's *Nachgetragene Liebe* (1980) and Meckel's *Suchbild* (1980) – to conduct an 'Abrechnung mit der Vergangenheit in Form einer Auseinandersetzung mit dem Vater'.[21] More ambitiously, Michael Schneider's 'Väter und Söhne, posthum. Das beschädigte Verhältnis zweier Generationen' (originally 1980) seeks to account for the proliferation of such texts. Schneider links them to a specific 'Psychopathologie der deutschen Nachkriegsfamilie' in which antagonisms between parents and children were suppressed as the 'Väter-Generation' sought to repress its involvement in the Third Reich.[22] During the student movement, he claims, these antagonisms erupted as students asked questions about the role their parents played under Hitler. But the 'Väter-Biographien', the delayed treatment of these antagonisms, lack for Schneider real 'Verständnis für die Widersprüche [der] Väter'.[23]

Significantly, few treatments have as yet related *Die Reise* to literary traditions beyond the immediate context of New Subjectivity, let alone to more literary-theoretical questions. Identifying in the text 'ästhetisch-formale wie sozialpsychologisch-inhaltliche Aspekte der pikaresken Tradition', Frederick Alfred Lubich's 'Bernward Vespers *Die Reise* – der Untergang des modernen Pikaro' (1986) interprets Vesper's autobiography as a modern revival — and demolition – of the picaresque hero.[24] And most recently, Friedhelm

---

19 Bernd Neumann, 'Die Wiedergeburt des Erzählens aus dem Geist der Autobiographie? Einige Anmerkungen zum neuen autobiographischen Roman am Beispiel von Hermann Kinders "Der Schleiftrog" und Bernward Vespers "Die Reise"', *Basis*, 9 (1979), 91-121 (p. 98).

20 Klaus Hartung, 'Die Repression wird zum Milieu. Die Beredsamkeit linker Literatur (Peter Schneider, Peter O. Chotjewitz, Inga Buhmann und Bernward Vesper)', *Literaturmagazin*, 11 (1979), 52-79 (p. 79).

21 Albert von Schirnding, 'Patre Absente. Eine Generation schreibt sich frei', *Merkur*, 34 (1980), 489-97 (p. 490).

22 See 'Väter und Söhne, posthum. Das beschädigte Verhältnis zweier Generationen' in Michael Schneider, *Den Kopf verkehrt aufgesetzt*, pp. 8-64 (pp. 32 and 10).

23 Michael Schneider, *Den Kopf verkehrt aufgesetzt*, pp. 9 and 32.

24 Frederick Alfred Lubich, 'Bernward Vespers *Die Reise* – der Untergang des modernen Pikaro', in *Der moderne deutsche Schelmenroman – Interpretationen*, ed. by Gerhart Hoffmeister (Amsterdam, 1986) pp. 219-37 (p. 220).

Rathjen's 'Das andere Ende der Kerze: Bernward Vesper' (1994) has explored links between Vesper's autobiography and the work of Arno Schmidt.[25] However, a striking lacuna in the literature on *Die Reise* to date is an adequate treatment of the text as autobiography, with all the theoretical and literary considerations that this implies. Framed in the terms of the New Subjectivity debate, Neumann's 'Die Wiedergeburt des Erzählens aus dem Geist der Autobiographie?' never really raises the question of autobiography in *Die Reise*. Nor does Wolfgang Türkis, *Beschädigtes Leben. Autobiographische Texte der Gegenwart* (1990), whose conception of autobiography as social-psychological case history ignores questions about autobiography as text. The sub-Freudian psychologisms – 'Narzißmus', 'Zwangsgedanken', 'anal-sadistische Lustgewinnung'[26] – produced by Türkis's brief discussion of *Die Reise*, for instance, fail to enhance our understanding of Vesper's autobiography as a literary construction of the self. This issue is central to the discussion of *Die Reise* that now follows.

II   Bernward Vesper and the Revolution of the Bourgeois Subject

The fundamental fact about *Die Reise* which its critics fail adequately to consider is that it is both social document and autobiography. As such, it relates not only, as most critics recognise, to the historical circumstances of its composition; it also engages with the theoretical problem of autobiography, touching upon fundamental questions about the nature of autobiographical truth and self-invention. A recent instance of autobiographical theory that can help us to grasp both Vesper's reception of the discourses of the student movement and the conception of autobiography that underpins *Die Reise*, as well as the apparent disjunction between these, is Louis A. Renza's 'The Veto of the Imagination' of 1977.

Renza's 'The Veto of the Imagination' takes as its subject an 'epistemological ambivalence' at the heart of the autobiographical act.[27] Suggesting that 'the autobiographer of necessity knows as well as writes about his past from the limiting perspective of his present', Renza claims that 'the dynamics or drama of autobiographical cognition occurs in terms of the written performance itself'. Yet this performance always entails a 'tension between the act and object of signification' – a split between the autobiographer's written account of his life and that life as it was experienced

25   Friedhelm Rathjen, 'Das andere Ende der Kerze: Bernward Vesper', *Bargfelder Bote*, 185/186 (1994), 22-33.
26   Wolfgang Türkis, *Beschädigtes Leben. Autobiographische Texte der Gegenwart* (Stuttgart, 1990), pp. 157, 165 and 166.
27   Renza, p. 2. See pp. 2-9 for further references to Renza's article in the discussion above.

which represents the very structural principle of autobiography. Renza formulates this principle as a discontinuity in the act of self-reference between the autobiographer's intersubjective and present 'discursive intention' – to render public and accessible his experience – and precisely the private nature of that experience, which resists articulation in the publicly pregiven structures and forms used to apprehend it:

> The autobiographer's intentional act, however, aggravates the duality inherent in personal memory-acts. [...] Wanting to verbalize past events, one finds that they appear against a prelinguistic background, a gestalt of pastness, which is at once absent from these signifiable events and in contrast with the "present" orientation of the discursive intention.

What this distinction between the autobiographer's present-oriented 'discursive intention' and his private 'pastness' entails is that autobiographical discourse displaces the autobiographer's lived experience, shaping it according to the narrative structures and generic conventions of autobiography. Though autobiographical discourse is assumed to possess referential properties, it really precludes the writer's 'continuity with the "I" being conveyed through his narrative performance'. In the arbitrary link between the autobiographer and the subject position available within language, the first person pronoun with which the autobiographer seeks to assert his presence in the text continually dissolves into the anonymity of a 'de facto third-person pronoun', the sign of his absence from the text. Autobiography thus produces an 'empty or discursive "self"', an "I" never [the autobiographer's] own' because in it the specificity or truth of his experience is dissipated.

Although it is not always foregrounded equally, Renza identifies the split between the public intention to write, and the private, elusive nature of the past as central to all autobiographical writing. Here, Renza's distinction between the autobiographer's 'discursive intention' to 'bring his past into the intentional purview of his present narrative project' and a past that is constantly displaced provides a framework within which we can grasp the relationship between Vesper's radical intent in *Die Reise* and the autobiographical form in which it is articulated. But after the concept of intentionality has been contested as a means of interpreting literary texts, how do we speak of it here?

In a famous discussion of 1946, for example, W. K. Wimsatt, Jr. and M.C. Beardsley reject 'The Intentional Fallacy' on the grounds that the concept of intentionality rests on 'a biographical act of inference' which is unsound because an author's intentions cannot definitively be ascertained.[28] Moreover once written, they claim, a text 'goes about the world beyond the [author's]

---

28 W. K. Wimsatt, Jr. and M. C. Beardsley, 'The Intentional Fallacy', *Sewanee Review*, 54 (1946), 468-80 (p. 470).

power to intend about it or control it [...] It is embodied in language, the peculiar possession of the public, and it is [...] an object of public knowledge'.[29] Where for Wimsatt and Beardsley literature's public status militates against privileging authorial intentions in literary interpretation, Roland Barthes's 'The Death of the Author' (published in French in 1968) takes the critique of intentionality further. For Barthes, the author is less an empirical individual than an interpretative strategy in which the assumption of an authorial design assigns inflexible meanings to a text. Barthes thus proclaims 'the death of the Author' and the concomitant 'birth of the reader', the latter conceived as a locus 'without history, biography, psychology' where the polysemic character of 'writing' is activated.[30]

Whether the concept of author was, as Seán Burke puts it, ever quite the 'tyrannical deity' that Barthes suggests is questionable.[31] Yet what Barthes and Wimsatt and Beardsley do not consider is the relationship between texts and their historical contexts. Barthes reduces the literary text to pure textuality; and whilst Wimsatt and Beardsley acknowledge that a text 'goes about the world', they cannot recognise the implications of the 'worldliness' they ascribe to it.[32] For texts necessarily bear within them the signs of the historical context of their production. Put simply in *Die Reise*'s case, we cannot disengage Vesper's autobiography from the radical politics of the 1960s, in whose discourses its aspirations are grounded. By examining its reception of these discourses, we may ground an intentionality discursively in the text without recourse to any 'biographical act of inference'.

In Renza's theory of autobiography, the term 'discursive intention' describes how the autobiographer engages with language and literary convention to make his life publicly accessible. Renza relates it to the act of writing, outside any historical or ideological context. Yet the concept does not rule out that such an intention may be articulated within a specific ideological framework. Certainly, the intention informing the autobiographical act of self-reference in *Die Reise* appears unmistakably political. Critics have debated the representative significance of *Die Reise*. Yet with recurrent use of the first person plural 'wir', *Die Reise* already claims for itself exemplary significance and expresses an identification with the aims of the student movement. Vesper repeatedly describes, for instance, the collective socialisation during the 1950s and early 1960s of the generation from which the student movement arose.

---

29   Wimsatt and Beardsley, p. 470.
30   'The Death of the Author' in Roland Barthes, *Image, Music, Text*, trans. and ed. by Stephen Heath (London, 1977), pp. 142-48 (p. 148).
31   Seán Burke, *The Death and Return of the Author: Criticism and Subjectivity in Barthes, Foucault and Derrida* (Edinburgh, 1992), pp. 25-27 (p. 26).
32   See 'The World, the Text, and the Critic' in Edward Said, *The World, the Text, and the Critic* (London, 1984), pp. 31-53 (p. 32).

'Wir sind aufgewachsen im Kalten Krieg' (*DR*, 582), he writes; or, 'Adenauer und der Kalte Krieg hatten uns großgezogen' (*DR*, 568).

Furthermore, the 'discursive intention' motivating Bernward Vesper's autobiographical project is grounded in the theoretical discourses informing the student movement, and in particular the work of Reich and Marcuse, to whom *Die Reise* contains numerous references. (For references to Reich and his work see *DR*, 37, 46, 80, 287, 426-27, 679; and to Marcuse *DR*, 652, 683, 686, 693.) Let us examine Vesper's reception of this work, and the function that it fulfils in *Die Reise*.

The first function of Reich's and Marcuse's theories in *Die Reise* is to ground a critique of West German society during the 1950s and early 1960s. A 'Zeit des absoluten politischen Stillstandes' (*DR*, 568) according to Vesper, this period saw the consolidation of anti-democratic forces within the Federal Republic and the emasculation of the left. 'Eine Opposition gab es zwar de facto,' Vesper notes, 'aber seit sich die SPD von den letzten Resten einer sozialistischen Politik getrennt und zur "Volkspartei" geworden war, hatte sie [...] nach Godesberg 50 000 linke Mitglieder ausgesperrt' (*DR*, 582-83). In the 'Spiegel-Affäre' of 1962, twice mentioned in Vesper's notes to *Die Reise* (*DR*, 645, 679), the Adenauer government resorted to unconstitutional means to quash dissent – a sinister echo of the German past. And in 1966, finally, the loss of democratic vitality within the political institutions of the Federal Republic appeared to be institutionalised with the establishment of a CDU/CSU and SPD 'Große Koalition' (*DR*, 582) occupying 447 of 496 seats in the *Bundestag*.[33] In this context Marcuse's 'Der Kampf gegen den Liberalismus in der totalitären Staatsauffassung' (originally an essay of 1934) and his *One-Dimensional Man* of 1964 acquire a particular resonance for *Die Reise*.

First published in the Frankfurt School's *Zeitschrift für Sozialforschung*, 'Der Kampf gegen den Liberalismus in der totalitären Staatsauffassung' asserts a continuity between liberalism and forms of totalitarianism like fascism. Where the liberal state of the nineteenth century, Marcuse argues, was the social formation generated by a bourgeois 'Handels- und Industrie-kapitalismus', totalitarianism is the form of social organisation corresponding to a 'Monopolkapitalismus' superseding the economics of the free market.[34] Marcuse's *One-Dimensional Man*, by contrast, explores the function of technology as an efficient and even pleasant form of social control in advanced industrial society. In the medium of technology, Marcuse argues, opposition is neutralised, the spheres of social and private life are conscripted into the service of the status quo, and patterns of human thought and behaviour are

---

33   For an account of these processes see Burns and van der Will, pp. 1-11.

34   'Der Kampf gegen den Liberalismus in der totalitären Staatsauffassung' is reproduced in Marcuse, *Kultur und Gesellschaft*, I, 17-55 (p. 32).

assimilated to the requirements of prescribed technological norms. Human subjects are transformed, in short, into 'objects of total administration'.[35]

In *Die Reise* the perception derived from Marcuse's earlier essay that, as Vesper's notes put it, fascism represents 'eine notwendige variante des kapitalismus' (*DR*, 652) is conflated with an image of a society repressive in all its parts that owes more to *One-Dimensional Man*:

> Bild, Schrift, Ton: toute la 'réalité' ça veut dire: Produktionsformen, Kommunikationsformen, Produkte, Häuser, Straßen, Familien, Sprache – alles, um uns zu gut funktionierenden, weichen, gefügsamen Vegetables auszubilden.
>
> (*DR*, 264)

(A 'Vegetable', we should add, is Vesper's favoured term for a uniquely subservient and dehumanised individual: the 'faschistoiden Deutschen', *DR*, 54). Of the repressive agents of socialisation and domination listed here, the family occupies the central place in *Die Reise*. It is to a Reichian model of the family that Vesper most consistently appeals in his critique of repressive forms of social control.

For Reich, the family marks the site where the psychological and sexual needs of the individual are subordinated to the political and economic imperatives of the authoritarian state: exploitation and domination. Reich ascribes to the patriarchal nuclear family in capitalist societies the function of producing within individuals character structures that will sustain political domination. The family performs this task by means of sexual repression throughout childhood and adolescence, which inhibits healthy, outwardly directed 'genital impulses' expressing human needs for self-determination and leaves individuals crippled by an infantile dependence on authority. The energy attached to these stifled impulses (a tangible biological energy) is converted into fear and hatred and bound into a rigid character structure that Reich terms the 'character armour' ('die charakterliche Panzerung').[36] In the character armour the ideological imperatives connected to parental dictates confronted during the socialisation process are anchored physically within the individual.

Throughout *Die Reise* and his notes to the text, Vesper adopts a Reichian terminology of 'charakterlichen Strukturen', the character 'Panzer', and of 'autoritäre, [...] sexualverneinende Erziehung[...]' (*DR*, 46, 285, 679). In passages describing his adolescence, Vesper follows Reich in highlighting the moment of sexual repression in his socialisation (*DR*, 402-05, 407-18). He even cites a whole passage from Reich's *Die Massenpsychologie des*

---

35 Marcuse, *One-Dimensional Man*, p. 7.
36 Wilhelm Reich, *Die Funktion des Orgasmus. Sexualökonomische Grundprobleme der biologischen Energie* (Cologne, 1969), p. 106. This text first appeared in 1942.

Faschismus concerning the 'moralische Hemmung der natürlichen Geschlechtlichkeit des Kindes' within the 'autoritären Miniaturstaat der Familie, an deren Struktur sich das Kind zunächst anpassen muß, um später dem allgemeinen gesellschaftlichen Rahmen einordnungsfähig zu sein' (*DR*, 426-27).[37] A more subtle use of the work of Reich, however, is the way in which Vesper's 'Einfacher Bericht' circumscribes the domestic sphere of the family as the vehicle of ideological indoctrination. Here, paternal injunctions and prohibitions are frequently attached to ideological imperatives that fix themselves in Vesper's experience. The injunction imposed upon the young Vesper to eat clean his plate of 'Griesbrei' (*DR*, 330), for instance, is bound to his father's blood and soil ideology and the inviolability of paternal authority. Will Vesper admonishes his son, who disposes of the revolting pulp in the garden: "'[...] Wirf nie Brot auf die Erde! Brot ist etwas Heiliges in dieser Welt des Hungers und des Elends! Ich bin alt geworden und habe diese goldnen Regeln meines Vaters immer beherzigt. [...]'" (*DR*, 333). Or, in a striking reductio ad absurdum, Vesper's pet cat, Kater Murr, confronts him with his father's ideal of racial purity: "'"Katzen [...] sind eine fremde, unberechenbare Rasse. Sie passen nicht zu uns. Sie stammen aus dem Orient, aus Ägypten. [...] Man kann sie nicht erziehen. Sie ordnen sich in keine Gemeinschaft ein. [...] Irgendwie sind sie asozial. Die Deutschen lieben die Hunde. [...]'" (*DR*, 356). Will Vesper's praise for the faithful, teutonic virtues of the dog might appear comic if not starkly offset by his order that Kater Murr be done away with (he is shot). In *Die Reise* the father-son relationship is perceived as the vehicle through which repressive social demands, and the authoritarian ideologies subtending them, are internalised with all the physiological fixity of the Reichian character armour. The notion of a character armour built up through a series of prohibitions finds a striking metaphorical expression in the text in the barriers that Vesper describes around him at his family's estate near Gifhorn in North Germany:[38]

Die Grenzen des Gutes auf der kolorierten Generalstabskarte. Der Zaun des Parkes. Die Wände des Hauses. Meine Haut. Und immer wieder wird der Zaun verstärkt, damit Unbefugte nicht eindringen können.

(*DR*, 351)

Taking LSD on the 'realen Reise' from Dubrovnik to Tübingen helps Vesper to recognise the physical power of the internalised structures that connect him not only to his father, but also to altogether more sinister figures of authority:

---

37   Wilhelm Reich, *Die Massenpsychologie des Faschismus* (Cologne, 1971), p. 49. First issued 1933.
38   Compare Grütter, pp. 66-67.

Ja, ich wußte genau, daß ich Hitler war, bis zum Gürtel, daß ich da nicht herauskommen würde [...], seine gottverdammte Existenz hat sich an meine geklebt wie Napalm [...], ich muß versuchen, die brennende Flamme zu löschen, aber es ist gar nicht Hitler, ist mein Vater, ist meine Kindheit, meine Erfahrung BIN ICH...

(*DR*, 107)

Die Reise presents the mechanisms through which authoritarian structures and ideologies are internalised as seamless and monolithic. Blind to blatant contradictions in his father's anti-Semitic and nationalist tirades (*DR*, 449-53, 463-64, 482-87), Vesper campaigns zealously for the far-right *Deutsche Reichspartei* during the 1953 Federal elections (*DR*, 472-75). In Reich's theory of socialisation, individuals are conscripted willingly, even eagerly, into the support of a repressive social system. Yet the psychological cost of such support is debilitating. Indeed, cut off from 'die soziale Schönheit der Solidarität', Vesper is cast into 'die Eiseskälte der Isolation' (*DR*, 434): unable to imagine, let alone take steps toward the realisation of more humane forms of social existence. He remains a willing yet helpless object of the social process.

Vesper's vision of the repressive totality of social forces arrayed against the subject might appear to smother any possibility of transcendence. Yet Vesper draws on Reich's and Marcuse's work also to offer alternatives to this total system of domination. This is the second function of the theoretical discourses informing *Die Reise*. Here, the Reichian and Marcusean perspectives in the text intersect with another crucial element in Vesper's political thinking: hallucinogenic drugs.

Vesper's preoccupation with drugs has a range of literary and non-literary sources. These include the American Beat generation of writers of the 1950s and early 1960s, whose writings enjoyed great popularity in the Federal Republic during the 1960s. Vesper's autobiography refers, for example, to the poet Allen Ginsberg (*DR*, 9, 279, 588) and to the prose of William Burroughs (*DR*, 22, 217) and Jack Kerouac (*DR*, 290) in which the cycles of production and consumption dominating American society during the 1950s were filtered through the outsider's perspective of the addict and hobo. Vesper's correspondence with März also indicates his familiarity with the new ways of seeing propagated by Rolf Dieter Brinkmann in *ACID* – 'ein großartiges Buch', according to Vesper (*DR*, 604). However, what distinguishes *Die Reise* from these earlier texts is the theoretical insistence with which the consciousness-widening properties often attributed during the 1960s to drugs are harnessed to political ends. Indeed, the 'materialistische Beschäftigung mit LSD' (*DR*, 514) which Vesper advocates in a lengthy and important essayistic section of his autobiography on the relationship between 'LINKE UND LSD' (*DR*, 504) represents a polemic against the idealism implicit in received theories about drugs (for the whole section see *DR*, 497-516). For according

58

to Vesper the 'Politik der Ekstase' propounded by his polemical opponent, the American guru of drugs and psychedelia Timothy Leary, is politically naive:[39] it posits a 'psychedelische[...] Transformation der Wirklichkeit' obviating the need for social change (*DR*, 498). If Vesper derives from the work of Reich the concept of a rigid character structure formed within the family, he takes from Marcuse's *An Essay on Liberation* of 1969 the belief that hallucinogenic drugs like LSD can temporarily dissolve that character structure. A substantial part of *An Essay on Liberation* is devoted to exploring the idea that social and political revolution must be accompanied by a revolution in perception. It is in this context that both Marcuse's and Vesper's theories about the political implications of drugs must be viewed.

In *An Essay on Liberation*, Marcuse asserts that the '"trip" involves the dissolution of the ego shaped by the established society – an artificial and short-lived dissolution'; but significantly for Marcuse, this '"private" liberation anticipates, in a distorted manner', a broader 'social liberation'.[40] Putting this point in a more Reichian terminology, Vesper claims that LSD can achieve a 'vorübergehende Desintegration des neurotischen Zwangscharakters, der als Produkt und Stütze der autoritären Strukturen kapitalistischer Gesellschaften vorherrscht' (*DR*, 514). Yet where Reich and his doctrinaire advocates during the student movement (like *Kommune 2*) rejected taking drugs, Vesper follows Marcuse in ascribing them both critical and anticipatory functions. For Vesper, the 'trip' is critical in allowing the 'Drogenesser' (*DR*, 506) to perceive the social, economic and political relationships concealed beneath the smooth surface of the established social order. In *Die Reise*, Vesper's trip illuminates how insidiously even apparently private needs and tastes are regimented in the interest of sustaining political domination. Under the influence of LSD, for example, he recognises that innocently buying ice-cream and chocolate ensnarls him in a dynamic of '*Kapitalkonzentration und den unaufhaltsamen Untergang des Liberalismus*' (*DR*, 226). The anticipatory function of the trip resides in its capacity to project alternative, more fulfilling forms of human existence. The non-repressive, liberating alternative to the established social order prefigured by Vesper's LSD trip in *Die Reise* corresponds in fundamental ways to the aesthetic-erotic utopia elaborated by Marcuse in *Eros and Civilization* and *An Essay on Liberation*. Vesper's trip literally unlocks an 'aesthetic dimension', in which the beautiful and sensuous qualities of art are transformed into material reality.[41] The experience of the

39 Timothy Leary, *The Politics of Ecstasy* (New York, 1968). German: *Die Politik der Ekstase* (Hamburg, 1970).
40 Marcuse, *An Essay on Liberation*, p. 37.
41 Marcuse, *Eros and Civilization*, pp. 172-96; Marcuse, *An Essay on Liberation*, pp. 23-28.

trip is described using a 'tactile' vocabulary – for example, 'Teppiche' and 'sanft' below – and references to the visual arts:

> *Ich ging aber durch die Gefilde der Teppiche und über die sanften Grasbüschel ihrer zehntausend Knoten wie über ein renoirsches Feld, an einem Herbsttag in Saint-Prix, als wir über die Oise gingen, um das Grab van Goghs zu sehn.*

(*DR*, 101)

The erotic dimension of the trip too shows affinities with the liberated sensibility outlined in Marcuse's *Eros and Civilization* and *An Essay on Liberation*. The trip induces a regression to a state of primary narcissism, an erotic relation to the world prior to the 'antagonistic relation between ego and external reality'.[42] It achieves, put briefly, a dissolution of the boundaries between subject and object through which the subject is liberated from its isolation into a more free-flowing experience of the world and a more fluid sense of identity. Describing his trip, Vesper characterises himself as a '*Chamäleon-Mensch*' (*DR*, 263) able to shift between a plurality of possible selves. Yet above all, the temporary dissolution of the Reichian character armour affords a glimpse of relationships between self and other freed from the fetters of authority and domination. Crucially, the trip's climax projects an image of Vesper's son, Felix, whose warmth and intensity represents the negation of the coldness and brutality of his father. The boundaries between Vesper and his son appear to dissolve:

> *Ein neuer Strom von Tränen, von Glück, von Erschütterung. Die kleine Sonne!*
> *[In meiner tiefsten Verlassenheit.] Und plötzlich begriff ich, breitete meine Arme aus. Das Geheimnis, mein Geheimnis [unser Geheimnis: Felix].*
> FELIX IST DIE KLEINE SONNE.[43]

(*DR*, 110)

For Vesper, as for Marcuse, the trip is but a short-lived liberation. However, it generates an awareness of the discrepancy between the actual social order and possible alternatives to it that casts forward to the future realisation of these alternatives. Its political value is that, once the chemical effects have worn off, the memory of the trip impels the 'Drogenesser' towards its externalisation, the trip's re-establishment for society as a whole through transformative action. For Vesper, this is 'auf den phantastischsten Trip zu gehn: die Welt, die die gleiche geblieben war, während sich das Bewußtsein von ihr veränderte, nach den gemeinsamen Bedürfnissen zu verändern' (*DR*,

---

42   Marcuse, *Eros and Civilization*, p. 168.

43   In all editions of the text, square brackets mark words deleted in Vesper's original typescript. In citing from the text here, they are otherwise used to omit, and not to insert text for editorial purposes.

504). Here we encounter the third function of the theoretical discourses informing *Die Reise*. Vesper's autobiography draws on the theory of Reich and Marcuse not only for its critical force and for the alternatives to the status quo that it can offer. It draws on their work also to unlock or unblock the path to the realisation of these alternatives.

In the role it accords the individual's memory of the trip, Vesper's 'materialistische Beschäftigung mit LSD' (*DR*, 514) embodies a valorisation of the subversive potential of memory fundamental to Marcuse's own radical project. Memory implies an awareness of the contingent, historical and thus mutable character of social institutions that is the precondition of political action. Forgetting, or the failure of memory, by contrast strips human experience of its historical dimension, endowing the institutions and ideological imperatives of the status quo with the appearance of nature.[44]

But in practice it is through a Reichian discourse of character analysis that Vesper harnesses the radical potential of memory to a strategy of social transformation. In analogy with the method of character analysis, the LSD trip dissolves the character armour acquired during socialisation. As a result, the anxiety and hatred bound in the character structure, together with the memories attached to them, are released. By interpreting these memories, the 'Drogenesser' can recapitulate his psychological development:

> Zwangshandlungen, paranoide Zustände und Psychosen werden bewußt empfunden und können, vor allem dort, wo eine Anleitung besteht, bis auf ihren traumatischen Ursachen zurückverfolgt werden; der rasche Fluß von Phantasiebildern ermöglicht deren Analyse, die − wie die Träume − auf Verdrängungen verweisen.
>
> (*DR*, 514)

Vesper claims, in short, that drugs like LSD set in motion a process of self-interpretation through which 'ursprüngliche Fehlentwicklungen' may be partially rectified, and character structures alterable only as a result of the 'Sturzes der herrschenden Klasse' identified (*DR*, 515). Following this process of self-analysis, the partially reconstructed subject stands poised to engage in the revolutionary action that brings complete self-realisation. Following Reich, Vesper identifies the hatred released by the dissolution of the character armour as the motor of social action.[45] He asserts: '$E = ERFAHR\text{-}UNG \bullet HASS^2$/Das ist unsre Einsteinsche Formel' (*DR*, 13). Critics like Michael Schneider and Lubich have viewed such formulations as the expression of a

---

44 Martin Jay, *Marxism and Totality: The Adventures of a Concept from Lukács to Habermas* (Cambridge, 1984), pp. 220-40 (p. 224).

45 Wilhelm Reich, *Die sexuelle Revolution* (Frankfurt am Main, 1966), p. 94. First published in 1936 under the title *Die Sexualität im Kulturkampf. Zur sozialistischen Umstrukturierung des Menschen*.

blind hatred.[46] However, it is proper to assert that Vesper's belief in 'die nützliche funktion des hasses' (*DR*, 634) – whatever the forms it takes in *Die Reise* – must be understood also in terms of the theoretical framework of his radical project. If Vesper's revolutionary hatred is destructive, it turns the sublimated violence of the agencies of repressive socialisation back onto themselves.

Significantly, Vesper's views on the political implications of hallucinogenic drugs are mirrored in the very structure of his autobiography. The passage 'LINKE UND LSD' formulates a movement from an initial trip, through the awakening and interpretation of memories, to a readiness for political action which corresponds to the stabilising tendencies that Guntermann notes within *Die Reise*.[47] Vesper's description of his LSD trip comes largely at the beginning of the text (indeed, the title, *Die Reise*, plays on the hallucinogenic meaning of the English 'trip'). This description then gives way to a review and interpretation of childhood memories, many revolving around the figure of Vesper's father: the 'Einfacher Bericht', Vesper's account of his repressive socialisation. As the 'Einfacher Bericht' progresses, reflections of a political nature come to the fore. These include, beside 'LINKE UND LSD', an analysis of the 'BAUELEMENTE DES ZWEITEN DEUTSCHEN FASCHISMUS' (*DR*, 431-32), an account of '*Guerilla-Ausbildung*' in the Middle East (*DR*, 435-38), and an excursus on the false consciousness of the writer (*DR*, 543-46). In subject matter and form these passages exhibit a programmatic and pamphlet-like character which prefigures direct political action and systemic upheaval. Returning to the terms offered by Renza's theory of autobiography, we might formulate the 'discursive intention' at the heart of Vesper's text as follows. Combining them with ideas of his own, Vesper draws on the theories of Reich and Marcuse to ground the narrative of his transformation from the middle-class son of a fascist poet into a revolutionary subject – a role reserved for the proletariat in orthodox Marxism. The autobiographical act becomes a political act: the writing of what we might describe as a revolutionary case history, in whose course Vesper asserts both his self-presence in the medium of autobiographical discourse and his subject status within the historical process. He writes: '*Ich fing an, meine Möglichkeiten zu überdenken* [...]. *ICH war vorhanden, ein Subjekt, das der Welt nicht hilflos ausgeliefert war*' (*DR*, 254).

Faced with the fact of Vesper's suicide, the idea that *Die Reise* could be constructed as a revolutionary case history may seem astonishing. This interpretation is consonant, however, with other documents of the student movement, like the *Kommune 2*'s *Versuch der Revolutionierung des*

---

46   Michael Schneider, *Den Kopf verkehrt aufgesetzt*, p. 76; Lubich, 'Bernward Vespers "Die Reise": Von der Hitler-Jugend zur RAF', p. 79.
47   Guntermann, pp. 248-51.

bürgerlichen Individuums of 1969, which presses Reich's theoretical discourses into the service of a comparable process of collective radicalisation. Though it does not reflect upon a loss of working-class radicalism so much as upon its author's middle class origins (for example, *DR*, 445-46), Vesper's projected narrative of personal radicalisation aligns him with the crisis of revolutionary subjectivity within the discourses of anti-authoritarianism outlined in Chapter 1 of this study. *Die Reise* too can be read as a response to *Kommune 2*'s question: 'Wie können bürgerliche Individuen ihre bürgerliche Herkunft und ihre davon geprägte psychische Struktur soweit überwinden, daß sie zu einer kontinuierlichen Praxis befähigt werden?'.[48]

III   Political Limitations and Autobiographical Considerations

Where *Kommune 2*'s collective radicalisation failed, losing itself in microstructural processes of change, could Vesper's own projected radicalisation prove more successful? Demonstrably, the exemplary self-presence which Vesper asserts in his text as a subject of both autobiographical discourse and the historical process is doubly undermined: first, by 'theoretical' or political limitations in the way his revolutionary case history is formulated; and further, by the conception of the autobiographical act that underpins *Die Reise*. When we read *Die Reise* for what it tells us about the problematic of autobiographical writing, we seem to be reading another story entirely.

In order to grasp the 'theoretical' problems that bedevil Vesper's revolutionary case history, we will turn to comments on the student movement made by Jürgen Habermas. These comments, moreover, can help us to consider whether *Die Reise* offers the explanation of the phenomenon of urban terrorism which critics suggest. In a series of interventions into its debates over its aims and strategies, Habermas drew attention to the problematic relationship between theory and practice within the student movement. Addressing the SDS's 1967 'Bedingungen und Organisation des Widerstands' conference (whose proceedings appeared in the *Voltaire Flugschrift*), he argued that the student movement embodied a compensatory function within the political culture of the Federal Republic, restoring substantive political debate to a depoliticised public sphere. Two of the dangers which, for Habermas, jeopardised this function are of particular interest here: a tendency on the part of the theorists of anti-authoritarianism, first, toward theoretical

48   Kommune 2, p. 11.

oversimplification; and a related tendency, second, to collapse theory into practice – 'Aktionismus'.[49]

For Habermas, mistaken assumptions about the relevance of Marxist theories of revolution to late capitalism and misplaced identifications with revolutionary movements in the Third World led the theorists of anti-authoritarianism to a false analysis of the scope for radical change within the Federal Republic. (Arguably, Habermas himself failed to appreciate the extent to which the theorists of anti-authoritarianism were already questioning Marxist theories of revolution.) And false analyses, he claimed, led to inappropriate forms of action, promoting amongst the protesters, as the introduction to his *Protestbewegung und Hochschulreform* (1969) put it, the illusion of a phantom revolution in which '[die Rebellen] wähnen sich als revolutionäre Kämpfer gegen faschistische Unterdrückung, während sie tatsächlich nichts anderes tun, als unvermutete liberale Spielräume ausnutzen'.[50] At worst, incorrect analyses and inappropriate strategies, Habermas argued, could terminate in violent forms of provocation which became an end in themselves. It was to warn against this extreme form of 'Aktionismus' – a practice detached from any theoretical presuppositions – that Habermas at the 'Bedingungen und Organisation des Widerstands' conference coined the notorious term 'linke[r] Faschismus' (a term which he later conceded had been infelicitous).[51]

In their discussions, both Lubich and Michael Schneider invoke the concept of a 'linken Faschismus' to support their assertion of a relationship between the virulent anti-Semitism of his father and Vesper's own support for revolutionary violence.[52] Yet where Habermas coined the term to circumscribe an imbalance in the relationship between theory and practice, Lubich and Michael Schneider take it in a psychological direction to describe the perceived internalisation on Vesper's part of 'fascistic' patterns of thought and behaviour through his relationship with his father.

Certainly, the case put by Michael Schneider and Lubich finds support in the text – for instance, where Vesper asserts in his notes that 'meine klasse hat mich gelehrt, daß man nur mit gewalt etwas erreichen kann, und ich bin bereit, diese lehre gegen sie anzuwenden' (*DR*, 631). But if we can link a

---

49   Jürgen Habermas, untitled, in *Bedingungen und Organisation des Widerstands. Der Kongreß in Hannover. Protokolle Flugblätter Resolutionen*, ed. by Bernward Vesper, *Voltaire Flugschrift*, 12 (1967), 42-48 (pp. 46-47).

50   Jürgen Habermas, *Protestbewegung und Hochschulreform* (Frankfurt am Main, 1969), p. 29.

51   See Habermas's 'Diskussionsbeitrag', in *Bedingungen und Organisation des Widerstands. Der Kongreß in Hannover. Protokolle Flugblätter Resolutionen*, ed. by Bernward Vesper, *Voltaire Flugschrift*, 12 (1967), 100-01 (p. 101).

52   Michael Schneider, *Den Kopf verkehrt aufgesetzt*, p. 71; Lubich, 'Bernward Vespers "Die Reise": Von der Hitler-Jugend zur RAF', p. 71.

preoccupation with violence on Vesper's part to his relationship with his father, we cannot offer that relationship itself as a psychological explanation of urban terrorism as some critics of *Die Reise* do. The fact remains that Vesper himself, unlike his fiancée Ensslin, never turned to political violence. This alone makes a reading of his autobiography as a psychological document of urban terrorism problematic; indeed, it would be as pertinent to ask why Vesper did not follow this path. Moreover, the pitfalls of attempting to grasp the character of urban terrorism in such reductive psychological or biographical terms are amply demonstrated by Becker's *Hitler's Children*, the 1977 history of the RAF whose title too has fed the claim that Vesper's radicalism represents a psychological reversal of his father's extremism. Far from demonstrating the connection suggested by its title, Becker's book in fact indicates that many terrorists, often women like Ensslin and Ulrike Meinhof, came from liberal, even progressive backgrounds. In short, treating urban terrorism as an affective phenomenon is dangerous because this ignores its ideological determinations. What is crucial to understanding Vesper's relationship to urban terrorism is that, like groups such as the RAF, Vesper took to an extreme views widely held in the anti-authoritarian student movement. These included a mistrust of an apparently complacent working class and its organisations; a conviction that peaceful protest represented a weak and unsatisfactory means of achieving social change; and a stylised view of the role of intellectuals in a strategy of constant confrontation with a repressive state.[53] Thus the original terms of Habermas's analysis, focusing on the movement's tendencies toward theoretical oversimplification and 'Aktionismus', arguably offer a more fruitful approach both to the problematic manner in which Vesper's revolutionary case history is constructed, and to the connections between *Die Reise* and the urban terrorism of the RAF.

Die Reise certainly exhibits a tendency toward theoretical oversimplification. Marcuse's analysis of indefinite capitalist stabilisation in *One-Dimensional Man*, his thesis on the continuity of liberalism and authoritarianism, and Reich's theory of repressive socialisation doubtless provided Vesper with useful conceptual tools with which to articulate a concern over authoritarian tendencies within politics and society within the Federal Republic. However, *Die Reise* conflates them into a seamless model of repression and domination – a social theory itself of 'one-dimensional' proportions – that equates the Federal Republic of Germany with a fascist state and altogether fails to recognise the resources for critique and social action available within it.

The totalising perspectives at work in *Die Reise* engender in turn a reductive conception of politics and political practice. This is nowhere more

53   Markovits and Gorski, p. 65.

clear than where Vesper berates the liberal establishment – journalists, doctors, writers, and teachers (*DR*, 249-51, 294-96, 500, 536-43 respectively) – for its adherence to a project of political enlightenment. Advocating progress through enlightenment and debate, this liberal establishment is for Vesper the unwitting guardian of the status quo. The 'Argumente des Liberalen', he asserts, 'haben aber sowieso nie etwas mit der Wirklichkeit zu tun; deswegen braucht er sie auch nie zu verändern' (*DR*, 500). Yet Vesper's own political universe, inhabited by counter-revolutionary liberals, reactionary 'Vegetables' (*DR*, 54), brutal 'Bullen' (*DR*, 98) and committed revolutionaries hardly evidences a more pragmatic relation to political reality.

Vesper's reductive politics assume terroristic forms where he uncritically accepts the applicability to the Federal Republic of the strategies of guerrilla organisations outside Europe. With the escalation of the student movement and the forces arrayed against it after 1967, the turn to guerrilla strategies was admittedly widespread within anti-authoritarianism. In *Die Reise*, certainly, it is stripped of the emphasis on enlightenment that marked, say, Dutschke and Krahl's 1967 paper, 'Das Sich-Verweigern erfordert Guerilla-Mentalität'. Vesper's autobiography reveals a particular admiration for the *Al Fatah* ('*Guerilla-Ausbildung*': *DR*, 435-38), a Palestinian guerrilla organisation with whom RAF members Horst Mahler and Petra Schelm trained, and militant black organisations in the USA like the Black Panther Party ('*Nachtrag*': *DR*, 440-44), to whom Vesper had devoted an edition of his *Voltaire Flugschrift* in 1968.[54] In *Die Reise*, Vesper's reductive politics and his preoccupation with militant struggle converge in a sympathy for the practitioners of 'revolutionäre Gewalt' (*DR*, 249) in the Federal Republic: the RAF.

Die Reise certainly sheds interesting light on the origins of urban terrorism in the Federal Republic in the late 1960s. However, it does so through what it reveals about the theoretical and ideological influences shaping the theory and practice of the anti-authoritarian currents within the student movement. It is instructive in this respect to compare Michael 'Bommi' Baumann's *Wie alles anfing* (originally 1975), the autobiography of a member of the urban terrorist group the *Bewegung 2. Juni*. Like Vesper, Baumann identifies the Federal Republic as a fascist state and advocates revolutionary violence based on the models provided by militant struggles elsewhere:

> Wenn [der Staatsapparat] irgendwo angeknackt wird, kommt sofort wieder das faschistische Gesicht hervor. Auf der anderen Seite war es die Erkenntnis, daß Revolution ohne Gewalt nicht erreicht wird. [...] Wir haben Bücher gelesen wie

---

54 *Black Power. Ursachen des Guerilla-Kampfes in den Vereinigten Staaten. Zwei Analysen*, ed. by Bernward Vesper, *Voltaire Flugschrift*, 14 (1967).

[...] Robert Williams "Stadtguerilla", [...] oder Che Guevaras "Schaffen wir, zwei, drei viele Vietnams" — das war die zentrale Losung.[55]

Baumann's demotic autobiography confirms that the anti-authoritarian tendencies toward theoretical oversimplification and 'Aktionismus' identified by Habermas illuminate better the relationship between *Die Reise* and the origins of urban terrorism in the Federal Republic than do the psychological speculations of critics like Michael Schneider and Lubich. Unlike Baumann, Vesper never engaged in terrorist activity; thus instead of dwelling further on Vesper's sympathy towards urban terrorism, it will prove more fruitful here to examine how *Die Reise* as a revolutionary case history is undermined by what we have signalled as its 'theoretical' flaws.

Despite the hope he invests in drugs like LSD, Vesper's totalising vision of human domination constantly threatens to crush his radical project. Confronted with the monolithic force of the established social order and its institutions, self-realisation for Vesper becomes truly possible only through total revolution:

> die Revolution ist gerechtfertigt [...]. Die *Massen* werden siegen. Wir werden siegen. [...] "Wir werden Menschen sein. Wir werden es sein oder wir werden die Welt dem Erdboden gleichmachen bei unserem Versuch, es zu werden."
>
> (*DR*, 122)

Arguably, Vesper's perception of a monolithic and seamless context of domination allows only the alternatives of complete integration into the established social order or absolute emancipation from it. He ascribes the subject no capacity for resistance within its parameters. The absence of total revolution – '*Zehn Jahre lang habe ich versucht, die Verhältnisse zu verändern. Aber sie haben sich nicht geändert*' (*DR*, 237), Vesper laments – is thus nothing short of disastrous for his revolutionary case history. In the very act of shaping his autobiography as a revolutionary case history, Vesper inscribes the failure of his projected radicalisation into the text. For failing the revolutionary transformation that brings complete self-realisation, Vesper leaves himself no alternative but to conclude that he remains enslaved to the authoritarian character structures internalised through his repressive socialisation. Worse, he must conclude that his behaviour amounts to an acting out of an infantile relationship to authority even where already oriented towards future liberation. In *Die Reise*, Vesper frankly characterises his politicisation in the student movement as part of an 'autoritätsfixierten Halluzination' (*DR*, 34), and suggests that his fiancée, Ensslin, with whom that

---

55   Bommi Baumann, *Wie alles anfing. Mit einem Vorwort von Heinrich Böll und einem Nachwort von Michael Sontheimer* (Berlin, 1991), pp. 52-53.

politicisation was intimately connected, represented for him above all a surrogate for the authority of his domineering father:

> Meine Geschichte zerfällt deutlich in zwei Teile. Der eine ist an meinen Vater gebunden, der andre beginnt mit seinem Tod. Als er starb, flüsterte ich ihm noch den Namen "Gudrun" ins Ohr, die ich gerade kennengelernt hatte.
>
> (*DR*, 39)

Yet nowhere is Vesper's radical intent more poignantly undone than where his son is concerned. It is in an image of Felix that Vesper's trip affords him a glimpse of more liberated forms of human relationship. The more shocking, then, for Vesper's admission of culpability, is his subsequent abandonment of Felix to foster parents and a childhood as wretched as his own:

> Felix. (Warum bin ich diesem Thema so lange ausgewichen?) *Felix ist nicht mehr bei mir.* Er lebt auf der Schwäbischen Alb. Ja, es stimmt, ich habe ihn selbst dort hingebracht. [...] Der Gedanke, daß er genauso durch die Scheiße waten muß wie ich, aus den Tiefen eines Dorfes, ist mir unerträglich.
>
> (*DR*, 164-65)

Failing both the revolutionary upheaval that enables true self-realisation and a concept of subjectivity permitting meaningful political action within the limits of the status quo, suicide looms large as a possible act of resistance in *Die Reise*. Throughout the text, reflections on suicide offer a resigned counterpoint to the revolutionary case history inscribed in the text. 'Die Wahrheit sieht so aus: [...]', Vesper writes, 'Verzweiflung und Chancenlosigkeit treiben Tausende in den *Frei*tod, weil der Tod das einzige ist, was ihnen wirklich "frei"steht' (*DR*, 249-50; also 18, 21, 559, 665). It is in such reflections, rather than in the revolutionary case history, that *Die Reise* most accurately anticipates its author's subsequent fate.

Yet Vesper's revolutionary case history is not just undermined by what we might regard as its 'theoretical' flaws. It is also rendered problematic in more subtle ways by Vesper's conception of the autobiographical form in which it is articulated. Against his 'discursive intention' to construct his autobiography as a narrative of personal radicalisation, Vesper's understanding of the nature of the autobiographical act pulls the text in another direction. According to Renza, the autobiographical act hinges on a 'split intentionality', a disjunction between a present-oriented 'discursive intention' and an elusive autobiographical truth which is dissipated in the technical armoury of rhetorical devices, conventions and forms to which the autobiographer must turn in order to fix it. In *Die Reise*, the exemplary self-presence which Vesper simultaneously asserts in the text and in the social process – 'ICH *war vorhanden, ein Subjekt, das der Welt nicht mehr hilflos ausgeliefert war*' (*DR*,

254) – is undercut by precisely this 'split intentionality'. A fragmentary meta-narrative in the text concerning the impossibility of self-knowledge merges into passages which thematise a disjunction between autobiographical discourse and Vesper's sense of the elusive truth of his experience. In addition to examining this meta-narrative, we can interrogate also the silences of the text – probing what it omits or represses – to elicit how this for Vesper himself ungraspable experience nonetheless decisively shapes his autobiography.

According to *Die Reise*'s fragmentary meta-narrative about self-knowledge, it is first of all the physiological organisation of the human cognitive apparatus that precludes the attainment of reliable knowledge about the self. For Vesper, the impossibility of reliable self-knowledge clearly renders any act of self-assertion or self-reference provisional and arbitrary. As Vesper puts it:

> Ich klopfte an mein Schienbein, aufs Brustbein, an die Schläfe, noch spannten sich Haut, Sehnen, Muskeln darüber. Wo war "ich"? War "ich" in diesem Körper? Und wo dort? Im Kopf liefen die paar Organe zusammen, die ich hatte: Nase, Ohren, Augen, Hirn. Wenig genug. Viel zu wenig, um auch nur das geringste wirklich zu begreifen.
>
> (*DR*, 172)

Where the autobiographical act is concerned, the unreliable character of self-knowledge is compounded by the constraints which language imposes upon self-expression. With its 'völlig im System verhafteten, jedem andern Ausdruck unzugänglichen Wort- und Syntax-Fossilien' (*DR*, 47), first, Vesper identifies language as one of the mechanisms of social control that oppose his radical project. Assigning inflexible meanings to concepts, language, for Vesper, militates against transcendence of the status quo. Second, language imprints its linear structure on the lived experience of the subject and presses it into syntagmatic forms possessing an alien cogency: 'Niemand, der schreibt, kann sich dem Zwang der Linie entziehen. Immer entstehen Zeilen, Geschichten, ohne daß zugleich Gegen-Zeilen, Gegen-Gegen-Geschichten sichtbar würden. [...] Der inner space hängt ja schließlich nicht auf einer Linie' (*DR*, 17). Finally, the process of deformation to which experience is submitted in language is aggravated by the generic conventions of the autobiography. Vesper notes near the start of *Die Reise*:

> Jetzt versuche ich schon die ganze Zeit mir klarzumachen, wie das eigentlich mit dem Buch damals war. Vorhin, nach dem Bad mit Felix, war es *fast* schon da, auf jeden Fall wollte ich endlich mal auspacken, abrechnen, es den Leuten zeigen, "Schonungslose Autobiographie etc."
>
> (*DR*, 24)

The authentic transcription of experience in autobiographical discourse, in short, is impossible when the forms of self-expression available to the autobiographer – 'auspacken, abrechnen' – are always already figurative. The very notion of "'Schonungslose Autobiographie'" is a well-worn rhetorical topos. Thus for Vesper, autobiography is at best an exercise in fabrication or fiction, and at worst, a form of lying. It is telling that Vesper should directly follow his remark on "'Schonungslose Autobiographie'" with the comment: 'Ich erinnere mich auch genau, daß ich "einflechten" wollte, ich wäre ein "notorischer Lügner" usw.' (DR, 24-25).

Admittedly, the meta-narrative in *Die Reise* that thematises the cognitive, linguistic, and formal strictures shaping the autobiographical act, attempts, through articulating these strictures, to transcend them. The text's multi-layered narrative structure too represents an endeavour to break open the perceived linearity and conventionality of autobiographical discourse. To this end, it also suggests alternative representations of experience using Vesper's jagged illustrations (DR, 68, 111, 165, 175, 191) and references to cinema (DR, 203-04, 434). Yet at base, Vesper remains acutely aware of a disjunction (precisely Renza's 'split intentionality') between the act of self-presentation and the actual lived experience that it seems to exclude. Vesper puts it thus:

> "Die Geschichte", meine "Geschichte", die ich, mit den Kategorien meines Hirns, mir "gemacht" habe, zur Deckung bringen mit dem, was ich wirklich bin. [...] Das ist das Ende des Berichts. Das ist die Aufhebung des Abstands.
>
> (DR , 283)

Apparently committed to a concept of personal experience that pre-exists the autobiographical act, such an 'Aufhebung des Abstands' remains for Vesper a utopian horizon. In practice, Vesper can only lament the futility of attempting to surmount the limitations of autobiographical discourse: 'Es ist sinnlos, die Wahrheit in einen Kampf mit Stil, Metapher usw. eintreten zu lassen' (DR, 69). Autobiographical discourse, for Vesper, signifies only his absence from and discontinuity with the text, in which the 'Ich' that he writes continually reverts into 'ein andres' (DR, 126) and the history that he writes for himself 'ist nicht meine eigene Geschichte' (DR, 18).

If self-knowledge is perceived as impossible in the autobiographical act, then it follows that the ungraspable experience of the autobiographer is unmasterable too. As a revolutionary case history, *Die Reise* is premised on mastering the past in analogy with Reich's method of character analysis. Yet for all the scrutiny to which Vesper submits his past in his 'Einfacher Bericht', there is clearly something about it which evades him, a power that it continues to exert over him in the present of writing. This becomes clearer when we turn to the silences and lacunae punctuating the surface of *Die Reise*.

A first such lacuna appears in Vesper's representation of his father. The father-son relationship constitutes the centre of the 'Einfacher Bericht'. Yet despite the role which Vesper accords his father in his socialisation, the figure of Will Vesper remains elusive throughout *Die Reise*. Descriptions of Will

Vesper in the text, for instance, consist in little more than fragmented details –
his 'mächtige Stimme' and 'die Adern an seinen Schläfen' that protrude as he
shouts (*DR*, 142) – which stand metonymically for him and his paternal
authority and yet resist organisation into a whole portrait. And in the notes to
Die Reise, Vesper's final attempt to pin down the memory of his father is lost
behind a screen of historical analysis concerning 'die maximierung der profite,
[...] die entrechtung der arbeiterklasse, [...] die ausbeutung des volkes, zu
ehren der banken, der monopole' (*DR*, 672). Far from promoting a
confrontation with his past in the interest of future liberation, Vesper's appeal
to the Marxist rhetoric of the student movement seems calculated here as an
evasive manoeuvre designed to spare him from confronting his father's power
over him. Put briefly, Vesper's memory of his father is simply too highly
charged for him to grasp:

> ÜBER DEN VATER, ÜBER DIE MUTTER SCHREIBEN können wie über
> den Teekessel auf dem Gasherd: Aber sie sind nicht der Teekessel, sie haben
> mich in die Welt gesetzt, das habe ich ihnen inzwischen verziehen, aber sie sind
> auch 23, 26 Jahre mit mir umgesprungen, auf eine feine Weise, da ist was
> hängengeblieben.
>
> (*DR,* 285)

Yet precisely because it so insistently resists articulation, Vesper's memory of
his father holds him in thrall, repeatedly drawing him back towards it as he
writes; '*mein vater*', he writes at the start of the description in his notes,
'(noch einmal, und zum letzten mal, und ganz von neuem)' (*DR*, 668). In the
face of the obsessive fascination that speaks from such remarks, it is clear that
his father, though long dead at the time of writing *Die Reise*, still represents
for Vesper something of 'des mannes, der uns am kinderbett nicht nur als der
mann überhaupt erschien, sondern als der magier, der gott, der mit
unsichtbaren kräften kommunizierte' (*DR*, 668).

A similar pattern of simultaneous absence and influence emerges in the
comments *Die Reise* devotes to Vesper's fiancée, Gudrun Ensslin. The text
provides little insight into Vesper's life with Ensslin before she left him in
1967 for Andreas Baader. But her name haunts *Die Reise* with an almost
incantatory power, its presence always at the same time signalling her absence
in the present of narration:

> Gudrun war *da*. Ich konnte immer zu ihr zurückgehn und sie nahm mich auf,
> wir liebten uns und: "Immer?" "Ja, immer!" Wunder, daß sie es eines Tages satt
> hatte, und mich heute *haßt*? Aber das ist vorbei.
>
> (*DR,* 276)

Vesper's claim here that his troubles with Gudrun are 'vorbei' is strangely
hollow. Remarks about his subsequent sexual encounters with other women –
notably a Petra and Ruth (Gudrun's sister) – demonstrate that his efforts to put

Ensslin behind him infallibly return him to her. Vesper writes of his liaison with Ruth:

> Gudrun hatte völlig recht, wenn sie aus dem Gefängnis schrieb "Konvulsionen mit Ruth". Das wird immer so bleiben, immer. Als es anfing, hatte es wirklich nichts mit Deiner Schwester Gudrun zu tun, aber im Bett bist Du halt genauso, das ist es, ist ja viel schlimmer als "Rache", "Assoziation" usw.
>
> (DR, 89)

In *Die Reise*, these comments about Vesper's father and fiancée not only signal their absence from the present of narration. They also testify to a powerful sense of loss or lack which repeatedly drags the autobiographical act back into their orbit. The way in which these crucial figures both elude Vesper's grasp and force his autobiography to circle around them represents the most fundamental sense in which the revolutionary case history inscribed in *Die Reise* is undermined. Fed by a concept of autobiographical writing that assumes the impossibility of self-knowledge, the autobiographical act traps Vesper between the irretrievability of his past and the sheer power which it exerts over his present. Autobiography offers Vesper less the opportunity to reappropriate his past (the precondition of his revolutionary case history) than it allows his unmasterable past to strengthen its hold over him. Near the end of *Die Reise*, Vesper expresses this using the metaphor of an insect trapped by a carnivorous plant:

> Ich war naiv: aufgeputscht von der Lust, mich in vergangene Zustände zu versetzen, übersah ich ihre Fangarme [Fangvorrichtungen], die sich über mir schlossen wie die Fäden des Sonnentaus über dem Insekt, das sich auf dem [Fang-] Teller der Pflanze niedergelassen hat. [Oder anders: Anfangs glaubte ich, ich könnte von "heute" aus mühelos ein paar Beiträge zu dem alten Thema "Zittern vor Deutschland" liefern, jetzt merke ich, daß ich alle Stationen ganz von neuem durchlaufen muß. Und keinesfalls sicher sein kann, die alten Türen, die mir das Entkommen aus dem faschistischen Ghetto ermöglichten, auf Anhieb wiederzufinden. Pitch and toss:]
>
> (DR, 501)

Vesper's revolutionary case history is undeniably already rendered problematic by what we have termed the political or 'theoretical' flaws in the way it is formulated. But more fundamentally it is subverted also by its apparent incommensurability with the autobiographical form in which it is articulated. Vesper's ideal of a revolutionary case history and his conception of the autobiographical act pull in different directions. Where *Die Reise* as a revolutionary case history is predicated on the radical potential of memory and on the mastering of the past, the cognitive, linguistic and formal pressures of the autobiographical act on the contrary render that past for Vesper irretrievable and unmasterable. Where the revolutionary case history seeks to liberate him into a new experience of solidarity, Vesper's engagement with the autobiographical act seems to drive him into precisely the monadic isolation which he seeks to transcend: 'Schreiben: Harakiri, ich ziehe meine Gedärme heraus. Dazu die totale *ISOLATION*. Konfrontiert mit den Tasten, der Walze, der kahlen Wand. Gefängnissituation.' (*DR*, 116). Indeed, the opposition between Vesper's radical intention and his understanding of the autobiographical act appears so great that *Die Reise* fixes them as irreconcilable:

> Aber, verflucht, im Grunde möchte ich wirklich lieber ganz was andres machen, da mit der Veränderung der Wirklichkeit fortfahren, wo ich aufgehört habe, statt diese Wirklichkeit in das Hintereinander der Buchstaben zu zwängen, wo sie getrost veröden kann, angenehm für jeden, der seine geilen Augen die Linotype entlanghuschen läßt.

> (*DR*, 298)

Writing autobiography and changing society appear here as activities that are mutually exclusive.

IV   From Autobiographical Truth to Self-Invention

Taking as its point of departure a notion of autobiography that revolves around the concept (and the impossibility) of self-knowledge, *Die Reise* corroborates Renza's assertion of a discontinuity at the heart of the autobiographical act between the autobiographer's 'discursive intention' to make present his life and the private nature of his past experience, which eludes him. Is it not possible, however, that the opposition between Vesper's politics and the autobiographical act upon which *Die Reise* hinges might represent a misunderstanding of the possibilities of autobiography as a genre?

This question touches upon issues still being worked out within the theory of autobiography. Vesper holds fast to what we might term a common-sense view that the autobiographical act involves knowing and representing a self and a past which pre-exist the moment of writing. This view of autobiography provides Vesper with his measure for autobiographical truth, for in *Die Reise* the perceived impossibility of reliable self-knowledge helps to ruin his revolutionary case history. However, this stress on knowing and representing a self that pre-exists the autobiographical act flies in the face of much recent theory. Increasingly, critics of autobiography, from Roy Pascal in his *Design and Truth in Autobiography* of 1960 to John Paul Eakin, in his *Fictions in Autobiography* of 1985, have come to regard the genre as a form of 'self-invention' in which the autobiographer constructs a self through the act of writing. Moreover, studies informed (like Eakin's) by a structuralist conception of the role of language in the production of meaning tell us that the

self is precisely the product of the rhetorical tropes and formal conventions that Vesper so mistrusts. In other words, is it not possible that, despite conceiving *Die Reise* as a revolutionary case history, Vesper's radical intent is thwarted by a failure to grasp autobiographical discourse as the vehicle of an act of self-invention that is in any case already implicit in the text? Jean Starobinski's 'The Style of Autobiography' of 1971, which touches upon the role of language in autobiography, can illuminate this question.

Starobinski's article elaborates a concept of 'style' in autobiography that seeks to transcend the discontinuity between lived experience and its representation which for critics like Renza (and autobiographers like Vesper) lies at the heart of the autobiographical act. Dismissive of the claim that the autobiographer's 'contemporary self-reference may appear as an obstacle to the accurate grasp and transcription of past events',[56] Starobinski argues that theories of the genre stressing the discontinuities in the autobiographical act are predicated on a misunderstanding of the function of style. It is a wrong, he suggests, to view style as a '"form" (or dress, or ornament) superadded to a "content"' anterior to it, or as an 'instrument' applied to a 'material of another sort'. Thus conceived, style appears 'more than an obstacle or screen, it becomes a principle of deformation and falsification'. Precisely the apparent 'redundancy' of style over and against the autobiographer's experience, Starobinski claims by contrast, is autobiography's most 'individualizing' feature. Understood as an individual act or as a 'system of revealing indices, of symptomatic traits', style produces autobiographical truths that transcend questions of verisimilitude with respect to the transcription of experience. Starobinski may not invoke the fully fledged notion of autobiography as self-invention that characterises more recent theory, but in marking out autobiographical truth as a product of language he surely takes a step in that direction. However, faced with Vesper's understanding of autobiography as a futile 'Kampf mit Stil, Metapher usw.' (*DR*, 69), how can we make Starobinski's concept of style, and even the notion of self-invention productive for *Die Reise* as an autobiographical text? Two points require consideration here.

A first point concerns Vesper's hostility towards the aesthetic questions raised by the autobiographical act and the process of literary production generally. The reader of *Die Reise* must treat this hostility with caution. It is coloured, surely, by Vesper's revolutionary absolutism, which leaves the subject in revolt only the alternatives of total emancipation from or complete integration into the established social order. Moreover, it is shaped by the cultural politics of the late 1960s too, when Hans Magnus Enzensberger's 'Gemeinplätze, die Neueste Literatur betreffend' (*Kursbuch*, 1968) famously

---

56 Starobinski, p. 286. See pp. 286-87 for further references to Starobinski in the above discussion.

declared that literature fulfilled no useful social function. Measured against the total integration or emancipation of the subject on the one hand, and against its direct capacity for social change on the other, it is not hard to see why Vesper should regard the act of writing as an aesthetic irrelevance – as 'papierene[...] Onanie' or as 'individuelle Scheiße zwischen zwei Pappdeckel zu spritzen!' (*DR*, 298).

A further point to consider is the irrepressible literariness of *Die Reise* itself. Contrasted with Vesper's anguished utterances about the elusiveness of autobiographical truth, this quality points to the fundamental role played by language, style and metaphor in the construction of human experience. Vesper's reflections on questions of metaphor and literary style only ever consider them from the point of view of literary production, that is, the act of writing itself. However, *Die Reise* contains a striking number of literary allusions and clearly begs examination from the perspective of what it indicates about the reception, appropriation and transformation of literary metaphors in human subjectivity. (Indeed, in addition to Kerouac and Burroughs, *Die Reise* is replete with references to authors as diverse as Hemingway, Grass, Peter Weiss, Kipling and Hamsun: *DR*, 28, 208, 272, 388, 525.) *Die Reise* is arguably most radical where, against Vesper's preoccupation with a personal truth which cannot ultimately be grasped in the autobiographical act, it confronts the way in which literary discourses shape and determine the experience of a subject always already constructed within the discourses historically available to it. Here, Vesper's 'style' and his often inventive use of metaphor come into their own. *Die Reise* best serves Vesper's intention of writing his autobiography as a revolutionary case history where it exploits the rhetorical armoury at his disposal to dismantle and reconstruct a concept of subjectivity constructed in language and grounded in metaphorical notions of self. We can illustrate this with what one critic has referred to as the text's 'Reisemetaphorik'.[57]

The motif of the journey is central to Vesper's autobiography because, as his letter of 11 September 1969 to his publisher puts it, 'auf verschiedenen Ebenen gereist wird' (*DR*, 606). *Die Reise* not only recounts a journey in the literal sense (the 'reale[...] Reise' from Dubrovnik to Tübingen). It also exploits more figurative ideas of travelling: the process of '*Rückerinnerung*' as a journey into the past, and Vesper's LSD trip as a 'psychedelische Reise' (*DR*, 606). Exploring travel and its metaphors in this way, *Die Reise* engages with a notion of selfhood which, far from pre-existing language and discourse, was

---

57 Anil Bhatti, 'Wozu Schreiben? Bemerkungen anläßlich der Lektüre von Bernward Vespers "Die Reise"', in *Erzählung und Erzählforschung im 20. Jahrhundert. Tagungsbeiträge eines Symposiums der Alexander von Humboldt-Stiftung Bonn-Bad Godesberg, veranstaltet vom 9. bis 14. September 1980 in Ludwigsburg*, ed. by Rolf Kloepfer and Gisela Janetzke-Dillner (Stuttgart, 1981), pp. 309-17 (p. 312).

discursively produced by the philosophical and literary discourses of the eighteenth century, when travel became a privileged metaphor for human experience.[58] The motif of travel represents a paradigmatic encounter between self and world through which the relations between subject and object, self and other, the known and the unknown are organised. In *Die Reise*, it is part of a set of temporal and topographical metaphors embodying Vesper's process of personal radicalisation.

In his 'Einfacher Bericht', for example, Vesper emerges from his socialisation as a monadic entity isolated and discrete in both time and space. In temporal terms, the 'Einfacher Bericht' runs as a chronological narrative from Vesper's birth until he completes an apprenticeship at the Westermann press; after this point, at which the 1977 edition of *Die Reise* ends, Vesper's account of his history becomes more fragmentary (*DR*, 565). In topographical terms, the monadic fixity of the Reichian character armour built up through the socialisation process is represented by the barriers surrounding Vesper at the family estate: 'Die Grenzen des Gutes', 'Der Zaun des Parkes', 'Die Wände des Hauses' and 'Meine Haut' (*DR*, 351). Closed off from its surroundings, the estate becomes a figure for Vesper's impoverished ego. It is this state of fixity and isolation which the motif of the journey serves to dismantle.

The monadic isolation produced by the process of repressive socialisation is unsettled already in a series of youthful travels that Vesper undertakes as a teenager. These trips – holidays spent throughout Europe on the trail of writers, and in the company of other young travellers (*DR*, 524-28, 529-30) – introduce an element of fluidity into his 'Einfacher Bericht'. Returning from them, his family's estate in North Germany appears 'geschrumpft', its power over him briefly diminished: 'aber dann bemerkte ich, daß [...] das Leben in den festgefahrenen Bahnen des Tagesplans mich wieder veränderte, so daß nach einiger Zeit von der Freiheit der Straße nur noch eine Erinnerung zurückblieb' (*DR*, 526). Significantly, Vesper's temporary sense of release finds expression in a flurry of literary activity, 'Kurzgeschichten, kleine, romantische mysteriöse Stücke, die ich anonym an Provinzzeitungen verschickte' (*DR*, 527).

These early trips anticipate the greater freedom of the 'Bericht der realen Reise' (*DR*, 606), which introduces an altogether different dimension into Vesper's experience of self in time and space. This journey lasts only a matter of days and hours. Yet during it, Vesper's subjective experience of the linear flow of time is opened out by a host of personal recollections and associations. For instance, driving through the Alps with his travelling companion as far as Munich, an American Jew named Burton, reminds Vesper of an earlier trip

58 Hermann Schlösser, *Reiseformen des Geschriebenen. Selbsterfahrung und Weltdarstellung in Reisebüchern Wolfgang Koeppens, Rolf Dieter Brinkmanns und Hubert Fichtes* (Vienna, Cologne and Graz, 1987), p. 13.

when he crossed the Gotthardt pass with Gudrun Ensslin (*DR*, 39). And in contrast to the linearity of the 'Einfacher Bericht', Vesper's account of the 'realen Reise' is freer, frequently proceeding by association as an interior monologue or a stream of consciousness. On this journey, the psychological immobilism symbolised by his family's North German estate is unravelled by the fluidity of rapid movement.

The climax of the journey from Dubrovnik to Tübingen is Vesper's LSD trip. This 'trip' altogether explodes the concept of a subject fixed in relation to time and space, and to the world of objects. Vesper's account of his LSD trip begins: '*die* Dinge *kommen auf uns zu, die* Dinge *sind da, treten in uns ein, erfüllen uns, sprengen uns, vernichten uns, breiten sich aus, werden zu Ländern, Zeitaltern* [...]' (*DR*, 52). Put briefly, the trip temporarily liberates Vesper into a utopian space, utopian in its original etymological sense of being beyond time and space, in 'no place'. Vesper's description of the trip evokes this new dimension of experience through references to floating in time and space – for instance, '*Ich schwebte losgelöst von der Vergangenheit*' (*DR*, 109) – and through a language replete with exotic, oriental, and mythological allusions, from '*den Tempelplateaus in den Dschungeln Mexikos*' to '*Diana von Ephesos*' and the kingdoms of '*Thrakien*' (*DR*, 107, 158). Set against the impenetrability of the barriers between self and world symbolised by his family's estate, the fluid sense of self into which Vesper's trip releases him is characterised also by images of flowing and water (for example, *DR*, 53, 75, 169).

Notwithstanding Vesper's mistrust of the metaphorical and stylistic tools at his disposal, his autobiography adeptly takes up the motif of the journey and exploits the temporal and spatial metaphors of the self organised around it. To be sure, the journey is a well-worn motif, with Vesper's most conscious models including Dennis Hopper's 1969 film *Easy Rider* (*DR*, 148), and given his acquaintance with the work of Jack Kerouac (*DR*, 290), surely also Kerouac's *On the Road* of 1957. Yet the force of Vesper's engagement with the motif of the journey in *Die Reise* lies in the way that the spatial and temporal metaphors of selfhood associated with it are filtered through the present of writing – the associative and diaristic level of '"momente Wahrnehmung"' (*DR*, 607). Here, they are played out against one another to produce a complex and multi-layered simulacrum of human experience. At some points in the text the tension between them is exploited for aesthetic effect in a self-conscious form of textual play. Explicitly contrasted, for example, with the brutal realities of Vesper's upbringing – the passage following the beginning of Vesper's LSD trip describes 'DER SCHLEIM, DIE MATTIGKEIT, die ganze Unklarheit des Dorfes' (*DR*, 53) – the exotic allusions and flowing images of the trip surely acquire a political resonance. Elsewhere, Vesper's present of writing becomes a site where his past and his anticipated future are folded into one another, the past remoulded to meet the demands of that future. The parallel that *Die Reise* draws between Vesper's relationship with his father, Will, and his son, Felix, provides a good example. Recounting how he intercepted a letter from his school to hide his poor performance from his father, Vesper writes:

> Lieber Felix, [...] Diese Briefe wurden uns in der Schule vorher angekündigt. Ich wußte, an welchem Tag er auf die Post gegeben, mit welcher Post er bei uns ins Haus kam. Ich fing ihn ab, [...] um ihn, wenn ich mal eins hätte, ihn meinem Kind zu geben, wenn es mal einen kriegte. Ich habe ihn noch. Für Dich.

(DR, 428-29)

It is precisely in the autobiographical performance itself, in short, in the self-conscious play of metaphor and style, that *Die Reise* most successfully carries through Vesper's radical aims. It is in the convergence of the text's narrative strands in the present of writing that Vesper comes closest to reconciling his past, present and anticipated future; and it is through exploiting the spatial and temporal metaphors of selfhood organised around the motif of the journey that *Die Reise* most effectively dismantles the monadic subject position into which Vesper's repressive socialisation forces him. Indeed, given the richness of *Die Reise* precisely as text, it seems astonishing that Vesper should tend to present the autobiographical act as a futile struggle with style and metaphor, rather than grasp within it the basis for a more productive aesthetics of resistance or, better still, the vehicle of a potentially liberating act of self-invention. To the extent Vesper's radical project is undone by his conception of the autobiographical act, surely this amounts to a misunderstanding of the possibilities of autobiography as a genre?

We might formulate the disjunction between Vesper's radical intent of writing his autobiography as a revolutionary case history on the one hand and his conception of autobiography on the other as a mismatch between his 'practice' and his 'theory' of autobiography in *Die Reise*. But the text's engagement with the problematic of autobiography is more complex than this formulation would suggest and, for reasons regarding the relationship between textual and social practice, it is not ultimately possible to convict Vesper of misunderstanding the aesthetic possibilities of the genre. What is at stake in *Die Reise* is less an inability to grasp autobiography as a form of self-invention than a preoccupation with the limits of autobiographical self-invention.

In a revealing passage that occurs in his description of his LSD trip, Vesper unashamedly entertains the idea of self-invention — not only in the freedom provided by the trip but also in the medium of the autobiographical act. Vesper writes:

Ich habe mir nicht darum gebeten, Europäer werden zu dürfen, geboren als Deutscher im Jahre 1938 in einer Klinik in Frankfurt an der Oder, als Kind von Mittelklasseeltern, die einem vertrottelten Traum vom Tausendjährigen Reich anhingen. Ich werde mir die Freiheit nehmen, die man mir vorenthalten hat, ich werde mich verwandeln [...]

(*DR*, 238)

Yet Vesper does more than simply invoke the idea of autobiographical self-invention. Some shorter passages in the text openly experiment with it. For example, a schematic chronology in which Vesper reviews his life year by year – from '1: Das Jahr der Geburt' to '32: Das Jahr der Festigung und der Arbeit' (*DR*, 231-33) – is followed by a much more bold exercise in self-invention. Vesper continues: 'MIT ZWÖLF HOLTEN MICH die Franzosen als Geisel in den Steinbruch. Mit vierzehn steckte mich mein Vater nach Stuttgart in die Lehre, die Stadt war eine einziges Trümmerfeld. [...] Dann bin ich acht Jahre zur See gefahren. Außer Asien kenne ich alle Erdteile. Jetzt geht es mir gut.' (*DR*, 233). But herein lies Vesper's problem with the concept of self-invention. To be sure, Vesper's preoccupation with a personal truth beyond the autobiographical act flies in the face of the ideas of self-invention increasingly central to recent autobiographical theory. Equally, however, Vesper's autobiography poses a considerable challenge to theoretical conceptions of the autobiographical act as a form self-invention. For if we accept the concept of self-invention, Vesper is asking, where do we set its limits? If we accept the suggestion that ultimately the autobiographical act represents the fictional production of the self, what it is to stop the autobiographer from breaking what Vesper describes as the '*Kausalitätskette*' (*DR*, 214) that binds him as subject to the material, physical conditions of his socialisation, of his origins? The problem with autobiographical self-invention is for Vesper precisely that it is potentially limitless, a slippery slope that leads beyond what the autobiographer might reasonably regard as truthful about himself. It is arguably for this reason that in *Die Reise* Vesper ultimately prefers to commit himself to a pre- or extra-textual ideal of autobiographical truth. As Vesper puts it: 'Warum kann man nicht genau so legitim ein Neuseeländer sein. (Ich *erinnere mich* und dann ist es mir verdammt klar, warum ich kein andrer sein kann.)' (*DR*, 70). If the act of self-invention, in other words, were to sever the cords connecting the autobiographical text to the material realities of Vesper's social and political experience, this would surely make a mockery of his ultimate desire to engage with and transform the social and political structures and institutions that surround him.

We suggested above that *Die Reise* hinges on a split between Vesper's 'discursive intention' to write a revolutionary case history and his grasp of the autobiographical act as the struggle to pin down an elusive personal truth. This is certainly true, but it is a conclusion which we should qualify. Considered as a social document and as a literary text, *Die Reise* undeniably pivots on a disjunction between Vesper's radical intent and his understanding of autobiography. At the same time, and more subtly, the text also poses substantial questions about the aesthetic possibilities and limitations of autobiography as a literary genre. Is autobiography, as common sense might dictate, a faithful representation or depiction of a subjective truth anterior to it? Or is it a form of self-invention, an active process of shaping and constructing a self? In other words, *Die Reise* revolves also around a tension between seemingly diverse views of autobiography: between a common-sense view of autobiography as a referential discourse about a life anterior to it, and a more constructive view of autobiography as a form of self-invention. As a revolutionary case history, *Die Reise* is premised on the very possibility of self-invention; yet in the text, a commitment to a truth anterior to the autobiographical act goes hand in hand with an insurmountable suspicion of the limits of this same self-invention. Perhaps it is this unresolved tension between competing conceptions of autobiography as a referential discourse and as an act of self-invention that Vesper himself expressed when, in a letter dated 23 August 1969 to his publishers, he labelled *Die Reise*, in a term that became its subtitle, a 'Romanessay' (*DR*, 603).

CHAPTER 3

Mass Media and Autobiography:
Rolf Dieter Brinkmann's *Erkundungen für die Präzisierung des Gefühls für einen Aufstand*

I   The *Erkundungen* and the Problem of Rolf Dieter Brinkmann in
     Recent Literary Criticism

Rolf Dieter Brinkmann's *Erkundungen für die Präzisierung des Gefühls für einen Aufstand* represent one of the most unusual autobiographical texts written in the Federal Republic during the early 1970s.[1] A sprawling collection of diaries, collages and autobiographical materials, the *Erkundungen* were written as notes towards a second novel that Brinkmann planned to write, a novel more explicitly autobiographical than his earlier *Keiner weiß mehr* (1968). This autobiographical novel remained unwritten at the time of Brinkmann's death in a traffic accident in 1975. The plans relating to it have only appeared posthumously. The brief 'Notizen und Beobachtungen vor dem Schreiben eines zweiten Romans' (written in 1970, amended in 1974), were published by Rowohlt in 1982.[2] The *Erkundungen*, which comprise the bulk of the materials for the autobiographical novel were published in 1987, when they appeared as part of Rowohlt's project to issue Brinkmann's unpublished and unfinished manuscripts.

Critics have disputed whether Brinkmann intended the materials comprising the *Erkundungen* for publication. Sibylle Späth suggests that he did; Michael Zeller, by contrast, has expressed the hope that he did not.[3] Our claim here is that the *Erkundungen*'s relationship to the political and subcultural concerns of anti-authoritarianism on the one hand, and the projected autobiographical novel on the other make them a fascinating historical and literary document. Relating them to the culture and politics of

---

1   Rolf Dieter Brinkmann, *Erkundungen für die Präzisierung des Gefühls für einen Aufstand: Reise Zeit Magazin. (Tagebuch)* (Reinbek, 1987). Further references are provided in the main body of the study using the abbreviation *E*. In citing from the *Erkundungen*, we have neither altered the many typing errors in the facsimile typescript of the published text nor, given their number, marked them as such.

2   Rolf Dieter Brinkmann, *Der Film in Worten. Prosa. Erzählungen. Essays. Hörspiele. Fotos. Collage. 1965-1974* (Reinbek, 1982), pp. 275-95.

3   Sibylle Späth, *Rolf Dieter Brinkmann* (Stuttgart, 1989), p. 94; Michael Zeller, 'In den Haß emigriert. Ein Einsamer auf dem "Idiotenschlachtfeld": Rolf Dieter Brinkmanns Tagebuch ist das Protokoll einer Selbstzerstörung', *Die Zeit*, 28 August 1987, p. 39.

anti-authoritarianism, this chapter argues that Brinkmann's *Erkundungen* pose a challenge to the very premises of autobiography as a genre.

Despite reviewers' initial perception that they are indeed an important cultural document, the *Erkundungen* have received comparatively little attention since their publication in 1987. This is in part because of the fragmented form of the text, and the rebarbative materials that it contains. Edited posthumously by Brinkmann's widow Maleen, the facsimile typescript that makes up the published text of the *Erkundungen* comprises three sections. The first section ('1971 Notizen'), composed between September and November 1971, consists of collages made up by Brinkmann from his typed notes (often arranged in parallel columns across the page) and photographs, as well as articles and images taken from the press (*E*, 5-182). The second section, confusingly entitled 'Notizen (Fakten) Tagebuch, 3. Teil' contains Brinkmann's typed diary from the same period, and documents a visit which he made in that November to Freyend, a painter living in the Hunsrück village of Longkamp (*E*, 183-370). It contains the greater part of Brinkmann's autobiographical reflections, and includes also letters to Maleen (*E*, 268-69 and 274-75; 297-301) and to his friend Hermann Pieper (*E*, 207-11; 343-48; 349-51; 363-67; 368-70). The final part of the text (*E*, 371-410), entitled '5. Mai 73, Köln', comprises notes and collages made by Brinkmann during a break in 1973 from his stay in Rome as a writer in residence at the Villa Massimo, the fruits of which were published posthumously in *Rom, Blicke* (1979).

Yet the scant critical attention paid to the *Erkundungen* also reflects Brinkmann's awkward position within the literary-historical discourses about the anti-authoritarian student movement. We must clarify Brinkmann's relation to anti-authoritarianism and the left before examining the reception of the *Erkundungen*, as the issues raised will resurface throughout the chapter.

Brinkmann's literary career began with the publication of *Ihr nennt es Sprache*, a volume of poetry, in 1962. However, it is with the reception of American pop and underground writing that Brinkmann is most often associated, having translated and presented to a West German readership the work of Ed Sanders, Frank O'Hara, Michael McClure and others in a series of texts of the late 1960s. These included *ACID. Neue amerikanische Szene* (co-edited with Ralf-Rainer Rygulla), *Silverscreen. Neue amerikanische Lyrik*, and Frank O'Hara's *Lunch Poems und andere Gedichte*, all published in 1969. Moreover, Brinkmann also developed in his own poetry of the time – *Godzilla* (1968), *Die Piloten* (1968) and *Gras* (1970) – a German variant of pop.

Brinkmann's role in the West German reception and development of a pop literature certainly aligns him with the cultural currents of anti-authoritarianism. As Andreas Huyssen has noted, the West German reception of pop at the height of the student movement entailed a more widespread view of 'Pop as critical art' than in the United States.[4] Used interchangeably with terms like 'Subkultur', the term 'pop' has indeed become a catch-all for the aesthetic and life-style impulses of anti-authoritarianism.[5] Brinkmann's work of the late 1960s (especially the volumes he edited) stands at the leading cultural-revolutionary edge of these impulses. *ACID* combined aesthetic, sexual and technological motifs in the proclamation of a 'neuen Sensibilität' (the text was dedicated among others to Marcuse); and in *Silverscreen*, Brinkmann advocated a turn to 'alltäglichen Dinge' (like the objects of mass culture) to produce democratic cultural forms able to close the gap both between "'hohe[...] Kulturleistungen" für eine kleine Elite und "niedere[...]" Unterhaltungsprodukte'.[6]

To be sure, Brinkmann aligned himself with the student movement more as the embodiment of a 'New Sensibility' than for its theoretical analyses or political objectives. (His work is indeed remarkable throughout for its anti-theoretical bias.) Nonetheless, his relationship with the movement was harmonious until 1969. For his part, Brinkmann read critical literature ranging from Marcuse to the left-wing monthly *konkret*; and the *Erkundungen* record his participation in demonstrations as late as 1969 (*E*, 233).[7] As for the left, Klaus Briegleb's study of the literature of anti-authoritarianism has suggested that *ACID* found a resonance well in excess of its comparatively modest sales (Vesper, for one, termed it 'ein großartiges Buch', *DR*, 604).[8]

Some commentators have theorised the decline of the student movement as an separation of its political and cultural currents which culminated in a 'proletarische Wende', a turn from the politics of anti-authoritarianism toward a more orthodox class politics around 1969.[9] We can trace this separation of culture and politics within the movement within many documents of the period. In 1970, for instance, 'Die Kinder von Coca Cola' (*kürbiskern*) attacked the tone of subjective 'Eskapismus' at the heart of what Michael

---

4   See the chapter on 'The Cultural Politics of Pop' in Andreas Huyssen, *After the Great Divide: Modernism, Mass Culture, Postmodernism* (Basingstoke and London, 1988), pp. 141-59 (p. 142).

5   Gundel Mattenklott, 'Literatur von unten – die andere Literatur', in *Gegenwartsliteratur seit 1968*, ed. by Klaus Briegleb and Sigrid Weigel (Munich, 1992), pp. 153-81 (pp. 160-63); Huyssen, p. 141

6   Brinkmann and Rygulla, eds., *ACID*, pp. 418-19; Rolf Dieter Brinkmann, 'Notizen 1969 zu amerikanischen Gedichten und zu dieser Anthologie', in *Silverscreen. Neue amerikanische Lyrik*, ed. by Rolf Dieter Brinkmann (Cologne, 1969), pp. 7-32 (pp. 11 and 22).

7   See Brinkmann, 'Notizen 1969 zu amerikanischen Gedichten und zu dieser Anthologie', p. 28; and Rolf Dieter Brinkmann, 'Sex und Politik', *konkret*, June 1966, p. 8.

8   Klaus Briegleb, *1968. Literatur in der antiautoritären Bewegung* (Frankfurt am Main, 1993), p. 301, note 25.

9   Rainer Bieling, *Die Tränen der Revolution. Die 68er zwanzig Jahre danach* (Berlin, 1988), pp. 77-78.

Buselmeier and Günter Schehl perceived as an affirmative pop 'Subkultur'; and Enzensberger's 'Baukasten zu einer Theorie der Medien' (*Kursbuch*) seemingly accepted the separation between the student movement and an apolitical subculture as a *fait accompli*.[10] If the cultural and life-style impulses of anti-authoritarianism were previously inseparable from its political currents, they were after the 'proletarische Wende' consigned to the realm of subculture.

Social and political theorists have since grasped the student movement as part of a shift in political discourse extending beyond its turn to a more orthodox class politics. But for Brinkmann, the immediate 'proletarische Wende' marked a turning point in his relationship with the left. His *Erkundungen* outline how he regarded it as a betrayal of the movement's most vital impetus:

> Der Betrug: <u>Jetzt gehts los</u>, dachte ich, als die ersten wilden Aufstände anfingen/Kölner KVB Streik/angehaltene Straßenbahnen/Wasserwerfer später/sich duckende Gestalten/jetzt gehts los, überall, auf allen Gebieten eine Bewegung neue Filme neue Bücher, neue Malerei, neue Musik würde entstehen, [...] der ganze muffige Angstüberbau [würde verschwinden...] /jetzt bricht endlich barbarisch die verschüttete Vitalität hervor/aber die zärtlicheren wilden Gefühle, die die Gegenwart übernehmen sollten, gingen in entsetzlichem politischen Geschwätz unter/mit der Abrichtung auf Politische Fragen, sind sie alle kaputt gegangen/keine Schönheit mehr/ zerredete Träume/einkasernierte Gedanken/verwaltetes Bewußtsein durch Begriffe/ein Krümel!
>
> (*E*, 135)

For the left in turn, the anti-theoretical character of Brinkmann's enthusiasm for American pop in *ACID* and *Silverscreen* made him a privileged target for critics of 'subculture'. Yaak Karsunke's 1970 review of *Gras* labelled Brinkmann the affirmative 'Vorgarten-Zwerg der US-Pop-Szene'; and in 'Über die Neueste Stimmung im Westen' (*Kursbuch*, 1970) Martin Walser attacked the psychedelic and sexual concept of revolt advanced in *ACID*, labelling Brinkmann's work, alongside that of Handke, as 'Bewußtseinspräparate für die neueste Form des Faschismus'.[11] Indeed, the posthumous publication of *Rom, Blicke* in 1979 subsequently reinforced Walser's alignment of Brinkmann with the right, and even with fascism. The record of Brinkmann's stay at the Villa Massimo in 1972 and 1973, *Rom, Blicke* caused critical consternation on account of its invocations of hatred and

---

10 Michael Buselmeier and Günter Schehl, 'Die Kinder von Coca Cola', *kürbiskern*, 1 (1970), 74-89; Hans Magnus Enzensberger, 'Baukasten zu einer Theorie der Medien', *Kursbuch*, 20 (1970), (pp. 165-66).

11 Yaak Karsunke, 'Ins Gras gebissen. Rolf Dieter Brinkmanns Gedichtband', *Frankfurter Rundschau*, 27 June 1970, p. 21; Martin Walser, 'Über die Neueste Stimmung im Westen', *Kursbuch*, 20 (1970), 19-41 (p. 36).

its tirades against the left. In *Der Spiegel* (17 September 1979), Hermann Peter Piwitt even went so far as to describe Brinkmann as a would-be 'D'Annunzio aus Vechta/Oldenburg'.[12] The perception of *Rom, Blicke* as a rightwards shift has not, however, found universal acceptance.[13]

We have suggested that Brinkmann's work of the late 1960s belongs to the wider moment of anti-authoritarianism, before the separation of its political and cultural impulses. Yet how does this make his position in the literary-historical discourses about the student movement problematic as we suggested? According to Gerhard Lampe, in a monograph of 1983, Brinkmann's work has fallen victim to a literary historiography of the student movement already premised on a differentiation between the progressive 'political' and the retrogressive 'subcultural' currents that originated with the 'proletarische Wende'.[14] Already Brinkmann's alignment with the subcultural face of anti-authoritarianism has thus made him a marginal figure within the received critical narratives of a literature in revolt. Further, the antagonism that developed between Brinkmann and the left has arguably cast a long shadow over the subsequent reception of his work, leaving scholars interested in the radical politics of the late 1960s suspicious of him. Brinkmann's effort to develop an anti-elitist pop literature has been well documented.[15] But in the absence of critics willing to explore his relationship with anti-authoritarianism, issues raised by his work have been flattened into a set of popular myths and clichés circulating within the West German feuilletons: Brinkmann's euphoric 'Anknüpfung an die amerikanische Beat- und Pop-Generation'; Brinkmann the 'Achtundsechziger' turned 'Reaktionär mit "faschistoiden Zügen"'; Brinkmann as an outsider in the 'Literaturbetrieb', 'ein Verbannter'.[16] Given the role played by the popular myths of mass culture in the art and literature of pop, it is ironic that Brinkmann has in his own right acquired something of the discursive status of a popular myth. Yet fascinating as this is, it does not help us to answer the questions raised by his work. What does Brinkmann's work tell us about the relationship between political and cultural currents within the anti-authoritarian student movement? Did Brinkmann's work really undergo a shift to the right? Only comparatively

12 Hermann Peter Piwitt, 'Rauschhafte Augenblicke. Hermann Peter Piwitt über Rolf Dieter Brinkmann: "Rom, Blicke"', *Der Spiegel*, 17 September 1979, pp. 252-57 (p. 252).
13 Schlösser, pp. 120-23; Späth, *Rolf Dieter Brinkmann*, pp. 1-3 and 102-07.
14 Gerhard Lampe, *Ohne Subjektivität. Interpretationen zur Lyrik Rolf Dieter Brinkmanns vor dem Hintergrund der Studentenbewegung* (Tübingen, 1983), pp. 14-29 (p. 29).
15 See Harald Hartung, 'Pop als "postmoderne" Literatur. Die deutsche Szene: Brinkmann und andere', *Neue Rundschau*, 82 (1971), 723-42.
16 Michael Braun, 'Finsterer Alptraum Gegenwart. Aus dem Nachlaß von Rolf Dieter Brinkmann', *Badische Zeitung*, 12/13 December 1987, ('Magazin') p. 4; Hans-Jürgen Heise, 'Einer nennt es Sprache. Der überschätzte Rolf Dieter Brinkmann. Pop-Poesie mit Klischees aus zweiter Hand', *Rheinischer Merkur*, 5 December 1980, p. 37.

recently has Brinkmann's place within (and his reception of) the discourses of anti-authoritarianism become the subject of closer critical scrutiny, in monographs of 1983 and 1989 by Lampe and Späth respectively, and in Klaus Briegleb's *1968. Literatur in der antiautoritären Bewegung* of 1993. For its part, this study will argue that the *Erkundungen* belong in the context of a disjunction between the discourses about the mass media within the movement's political and subcultural streams.

Contrasted with that of *Rom, Blicke*, the critical reception of the *Erkundungen* in 1987 suggests a conciliatory revaluation of Brinkmann's legacy. Indeed, the implication of right-wing leanings surfaces only in some pointed references towards a profound 'Haß' expressed in the text.[17] Reviews stress rather Brinkmann's links with the anti-authoritarian culture and politics of the 1960s and 1970s. Some reviewers even ascribed to the *Erkundungen* the exemplary status of a historical document. In *Merkur* (1987), for example, Genia Schulz interpreted them as a map of the desolate 'Gefühlslage einer Generation', namely 'der um 1940 geborenen Initiatoren, Träger und Anhänger der Beat-, Pop- und Protestbewegung'.[18] Others, though, stopped short of such claims for the text's exemplary status. For Hermann Peter Piwitt in *Der Spiegel* (3 August 1987), the *Erkundungen* charted rather Brinkmann's flight from the radical upheavals of the 1960s into a solipsistic 'Ich-Bessessenheit'.[19]

Most critics to review the *Erkundungen* measure them against Brinkmann's stated plan in the text to write an autobiographical novel. Piwitt asserts that measured against this project, the *Erkundungen* are found wanting. The work of a 'fanatischer Registrator', he suggests, they represent at best the 'ungeheueren, aber fast immer geheimgehaltenen Schlamassel, dem sich große Kunst in der Regel verdankt'.[20] Others reach a more positive conclusion, though. In the *Rheinischer Merkur* (28 August 1987), for instance, Klaus-Peter Philippi claims that in 'gewisser Weise *sind* die "Erkundungen" die Form des intendierten "Romans", der sich allen herkömmlichen Erwartungen an die Gattung entzieht'.[21]

The initial critical response to the *Erkundungen* is useful insofar as it relates them to the social and historical context of their composition and to Brinkmann's projected autobiographical novel. However, it only addresses

---

17   Michael Zeller, 'In den Haß emigriert', p. 39.

18   Genia Schulz, 'Kein Zugeständnis. Rolf Dieter Brinkmanns "Erkundungen"', *Merkur*, 41 (1987), 916-21 (p. 916).

19   Hermann Peter Piwitt, '"Die ganze Häßlichkeit der Welt bin Ich." Hermann Peter Piwitt über Rolf Dieter Brinkmanns Nachlaßband "Erkundungen"', *Der Spiegel*, 3 August 1987, pp. 143-45 (p. 143).

20   Piwitt, '"Die ganze Häßlichkeit der Welt bin ich."', pp. 143 and 145.

21   Klaus-Peter Philippi, 'Ohne Sinn wird die Kultur zur Müllkippe. Ein nachgelassenes Tagebuch von Rolf D. Brinkmann', *Rheinischer Merkur*, 28 August 1987, p. 18.

these twin horizons in reductive terms. Schulz, for example, is correct to assert that the *Erkundungen* be aligned, not with the right, but with the frustrated hopes of the student movement. But in assimilating the 'Beat-, Pop- und Protestbewegung' unproblematically to one another, she smooths over Brinkmann's difficult relationship with the left. The links that critics forge between Brinkmann's projected novel and the *Erkundungen* likewise simplify the relationship between the two, ignoring how the planned autobiographical novel functions as a shifting discursive horizon within the text.

In truth, the initial reception of the *Erkundungen* often does little more than reproduce the popular Brinkmann 'myth' outlined above. Reviews consistently dissolve the questions raised by the *Erkundungen* as a historical document and a literary text into a string of clichés and generalisations about Brinkmann as the 'zornige junge Mann der deutschen Literatur', the 'Gallionsfigur der sogenannten Pop-Lyrik'.[22] Indeed, Piwitt is more astute than many when he refers to a Brinkmann 'Legende' circulating within the 'Szene': a 'Bild jener irren, bekifften Type Brinkmann'.[23] The reception of the *Erkundungen* illustrates the enduring fascination of such a Brinkmann 'Legende' on the feuilletons of the West German press.

To judge, moreover, from contributions to a recent issue of Rowohlt's *Literaturmagazin* (1995), it would not be unreasonable to claim that Brinkmann still holds a similar fascination for elements of the literary-critical establishment today.[24] Indeed, Sibylle Späth's 1989 monograph on Brinkmann and her 'Gehirnströme und Medientext. Zu Rolf Dieter Brinkmanns späten Tagebüchern' (1992) arguably represent the only scholarly accounts to date to take up the questions raised by the *Erkundungen*.

In her monograph, Späth argues that the *Erkundungen* represent a confrontation not only with their author's life history, but also with a slice of German history extending from the Second World War to the aftermath of the student movement. She also points to the problem of autobiography within the text. Following the initial critical responses, she assimilates Brinkmann's notes to his planned autobiographical novel. Yet the *Erkundungen*, she suggests, negate the traditional attributes of autobiography:

Sie vertreten weder den Anspruch auf Wahrheit der Aussage, Dauer oder universelle Gültigkeit des Werks noch den auf Originalität. [...] Nicht die Darstellung des Lebens als kontinuierliche Ich-Entwicklung bildet mehr den

22   Zeller, 'In den Haß emigriert', p. 39; Thomas Groß, '"...jetzt, jetzt, jetzt ad infinitum!" Zum neuen Materialband aus dem Nachlaß von Rolf Dieter Brinkmann', *taz*, 10 July 1987, pp. 15-16 (p. 15).

23   Piwitt, '"Die ganze Häßlichkeit der Welt bin ich."', p. 145.

24   See A. Leslie Willson, 'Der schöne, einzigartige Brinkmann', *Literaturmagazin*, 36 (1995), 38-40.

Strukturrahmen des Textes, vielmehr steht das Subjekt selbst in diesen Texten selbst in Frage.[25]

Within the context of her monograph, Späth's reflections on the *Erkundungen* as an autobiographical text are necessarily general. Clearly there is much more that needs to be said, and in more detail, about Brinkmann's engagement with the autobiographical act. Späth's 'Gehirnströme und Medientext' offers a fuller examination, but it contains a tension that we must resolve if we are to grasp the complexity of the *Erkundungen* as a discourse about the mass media and the self. This essay identifies the 'Prägung der Gesellschaft wie des Bewußtseins durch Medientechnik' as the key to the *Erkundungen*.[26] Yet Späth's reading elides without reflection the view that the text acts as a repository of experience uncontaminated by the representations of the mass media – an 'Archiv unmittelbar erlebter Gegenwart' – with a contrary claim that it lays bare a reality that is always already a product of the mass media, a 'Medienrealität'. Consequently, Späth leaves us unclear as to how the text construes the relationships between media and subjectivity. Does subjectivity pre-exist, and require shielding from the media? Or is it discursively produced within a network of media technologies?

Späth's readings of the *Erkundungen* are often incisive. However, if the text's engagement with autobiographical discourse remains to be examined more thoroughly, so too does its confrontation with the discourses about human subjectivity and the media in circulation within the student movement. For what Späth does not address is that the text pivots throughout on a contradictory construction of the relationship between the media, subjectivity and autobiography. In 'Baukasten zu einer Theorie der Medien' of 1970, Enzensberger outlined a distinction between the media theories of, on the one hand, the more strictly political and, on the other, the wider cultural or subcultural moment of anti-authoritarianism. Where theorists of anti-authoritarianism, Enzensberger argued, elaborated a simplistic view of the media that hinged substantially on the concept of 'Manipulation' (a concept derived largely from Marcuse), its subcultural currents had through the work of Marshall McLuhan come to a more differentiated, if apolitical, understanding of the 'technischen und ästhetischen Möglichkeiten' of the media.[27] In the *Erkundungen*, in short, the autobiographical act is suspended precariously between the Marcusean and McLuhanite discourses informing these respective positions. For the work of Marcuse provides the grounding in them for a deep pessimism about the destructive impact of the media on the

25 Späth, *Rolf Dieter Brinkmann*, pp. 91-92.
26 Sybille Späth, 'Gehirnströme und Medientext. Zu Rolf Dieter Brinkmanns späten Tagebüchern', *Literaturmagazin*, 30 (1992), 106-17 (p. 111). See pp. 109-11 for further references to this piece in the discussion above.
27 Enzensberger, 'Baukasten zu einer Theorie der Medien', pp. 163-66 (p. 166).

human subject – and by extension also on the autobiographical act. Yet at the same time the *Erkundungen* display a more utopian, and McLuhanite emphasis on the transformative power of the technical media. Let us continue with a brief discussion of the relevant aspects of Marcuse's theory, and their partial translation into autobiographical theory in Bernd Neumann's *Identität und Rollenzwang* of 1970.

II   Autobiography in Flight from the Mass Media

In his *Eros and Civilization* of 1955, his *One-Dimensional Man* of 1964 and 'The Obsolescence of the Freudian Concept of Man' (a lecture of 1963 initially), Marcuse contends that in contemporary society the classical Freudian account of identity formation has become obsolete. Two basic developments are involved in Marcuse's account of this process: the rise of monopoly capitalism, and of the mass media.

For Marcuse in 'The Obsolescence of the Freudian Concept of Man', the classical Freudian model of the 'father-dominated family' as the 'agent of mental socialization' is not a universal feature of human society.[28] Specific, rather, to the social formation of free market capitalism, it is the mechanism that produces individuals equipped with the mental attributes necessary to participate in the entrepreneurial activity of the free market. The formation of the subject through conflict with the father (after the prototype of the Oedipus conflict) is a repressive procedure, in which the father's authority is powerfully underwritten by his economic status. Yet the ego thus formed acquires the capacity for autonomous action: 'rebellion and the attainment of maturity are stages in the contest with the father' also. While the autonomy of the bourgeois subject is a psychological prerequisite of free market capitalism, it may also be mobilised against it.

Marcuse argues, however, that the historical trend toward the monopolisation of capital undermines the father's authority by reducing his economic status. The result is a diminution of the conflict that goes into the formation of the ego:

> the ego that has grown without much struggle appears as a pretty weak entity, ill equipped to become a self with and against others, to offer effective resistance to the powers that now enforce the reality principle, and which are so very different from father (and mother).

---

28   Marcuse, *Five Lectures*, p. 47. See pp. 46-51 for further references to 'The Obsolescence of the Freudian Concept of Man' in the discussion above.

For Marcuse, the father's role in the socialisation process is further eroded by the ascendancy of the mass media. Bypassing the family as the site where social values are internalised, the media inaugurate 'society's direct management of the nascent ego'. In *Eros and Civilization*, Marcuse describes this as the 'technological abolition of the individual':

> the ego seems to be prematurely socialized by a whole system of extra-familial agents and agencies. As early as the pre-school level, [...] radio, and television set the pattern for conformity and rebellion [...]. The experts of the mass media transmit the required values, they offer the perfect training in efficiency, toughness, personality, dream and romance.[29]

Significantly, the 'direct management' of the ego goes hand in hand with the mobilisation of unconscious needs. Where the earlier *Eros and Civilization* had argued that the human sexual drives uphold a desire for gratification incompatible with a social order based on repression and domination, *One-Dimensional Man* introduced the term 'repressive desublimation' to describe the 'mobilization and administration of libido' whereby the media and advertising industries bind individuals into the cycles of consumption and waste through which capitalist society reproduces itself.[30]

Within the broader framework of his theory, Marcuse's account of 'technological abolition of the individual' is balanced against more utopian tendencies, like the proclamation of a 'New Sensibility' in *An Essay on Liberation* of 1969. Yet for us here, it suffices to observe that Marcuse's account of the impoverishment of the ego and the manipulation of unconscious needs by the mass media amounts to a closing off of the conscious and unconscious resources of human subjectivity, such as critical reason or sexual desire, that transcend the status quo. Individuals are turned into objects of domination before any project of social transformation can even take root. In 'The Obsolescence of the Freudian Concept of Man', Marcuse suggests that individuals can offer resistance only through a near superhuman '"power of negation"': in practice meaning precarious (and doomed) attempts on the part of the ego 'to build and protect a personal, private realm with its own individual needs and faculties'.

In 1970, Bernd Neumann's *Identität und Rollenzwang* transposed aspects of Marcuse's account of the evolving patterns of human socialisation into the terms of autobiographical theory. In essence, Neumann reformulates the obsolescence of the classical bourgeois processes of identity formation outlined by Marcuse as the historical obsolescence of autobiography as a genre. This is because, for Neumann, autobiography is pre-eminently a bourgeois genre associated with the emergence of a particular historical subject: the free

29   Marcuse, *Eros and Civilization*, pp. 96-97.
30   Marcuse, *One-Dimensional Man*, pp. 56 and 75.

economic subject of market capitalism. The autonomy of the bourgeois subject springs, Neumann claims, from an 'optimales und konfliktfreies Zusammenspiel [der] drei psychischen Instanzen [Es, Ich, Über-Ich]' that he terms 'Identität': this represents the matrix through which the autobiographer mediates his status as both 'Subjekt wie auch Objekt seiner Lebensgeschichte' and 'Subjekt und Objekt der Gesellschaft' into a meaningful totality.[31]

The assertion of a correspondence between bourgeois subjectivity and autobiography is hardly unique amongst theorists of the genre. But Neumann argues that under the pressures of capital concentration and the rise of the mass media the 'Identität' associated with classical autobiography implodes into a mechanical and conformist 'Rollenzwang'. This amounts to a slippage of autobiography into memoir. Autobiography, for Neumann, articulates 'das persönliche und psychische Ergehen' of its author, and brings into play a constellation of dynamic and synthetic faculties and activities that include 'Erinnern', and 'Erzählen'. Memoir, by contrast, is concerned only with the 'das Ergehen eines Individuums als Träger einer sozialen Rolle'; the vehicle of a vacuous 'Belegen' and 'Zitieren', it represents the inscription of socially prescribed roles and performances.[32] Significantly, though, Neumann's study barely extends its critical gaze beyond the nineteenth century, raising the spectre of socialisation by the media only as the vanishing point toward which the autobiography of the twentieth century is heading. Let us now return to Brinkmann's *Erkundungen*.

It is simply not true that Brinkmann's *Erkundungen* refuse, as Späth suggests, all claims to universal significance. Brinkmann himself unequivocally affirms the wider significance of his autobiographical notes, declaring to an interviewer from the local press: '"Ich versuche, den gegenwärtigen Bewußtseinsraum zu erkunden."' (*E*, 106). However, he never articulates the premises, methods or aims of this project except by way of what Gerd Pickerodt describes (with regard to *ACID*) as an elliptical series of 'Zitatfetzen und Zitatcollagen';[33] we must consequently elicit them for ourselves.

The *Erkundungen* are driven foremost by a forceful documentary impetus. Circumscribing his project as a 'Grundlagenforschung der Gegenwart' (*E*, 129) and as 'Feldstudien' (*E*, 264), Brinkmann appears to conduct his examination of contemporary consciousness in a dispassionate manner closer to empirical observation than to the theoretically grounded critique of Vesper's *Die Reise*.

---

31   Neumann, *Identität und Rollenzwang*, pp. 20, 1 and 21.
32   Neumann, *Identität und Rollenzwang*, pp. 10, 25, 60 and 83.
33   Gerd Pickerodt, '"Der Film in Worten." Rolf Dieter Brinkmanns Provokation der Literatur', *Weimarer Beiträge*, 37 (1991), 1028-42 (p. 1035).

The objects of Brinkmann's empirical gaze are twofold: both Brinkmann himself and his environment. The *Erkundungen* record first a minutious process of self-observation. In the third part of the text, he elaborates: 'dränge danach, jeden Gedanken, jede Erfahrung, jeden körperlichen Zustand in den vergangenen 3 Jahren aufzuschreiben!!!' (*E*, 230). At the same time, Brinkmann directs his gaze (and the lens of the camera that he takes with him) out toward his home city of Cologne, which he dubs his 'elektrisches Versuchslabyrinth' (*E*, 77). The *Erkundungen* record many itineraries through the city. For example: '30. Sept 1971, Donnerstag: Um anzufangen machte ich die Fotografen-Tour durch die zerfallne Teile der Stadt, *schoß* 60 Bilder mit der Instamatic Schwarz/Weiß.' (*E*, 57).

Piwitt rightly recognises in the *Erkundungen* the work of a 'fanatischer Registrator [...von] Wirklichkeit'.[34] Yet we should not allow the manifest preference for observation over reflection at work in the text to obscure a crucial theoretical input into it. The *Erkundungen* attest to the powerful influence of Wilhelm Reich, to whom they allude several times (for example: *E*, 179, 211, 229). Moreover, although they do not expressly refer to Marcuse, it is demonstrably his work that shapes them in more far-reaching ways, and so provides also a more useful purchase on the text. Marcuse's influence becomes palpable when we examine the diagnosis reached by Brinkmann's 'Versuch, den gegenwärtigen Bewußtseinsraum zu erkunden'.

For Brinkmann, contemporary society is characterised by a state of 'psy-chischen Notstand' (*E*, 231). In a passage recalling the vision of a repressive social totality invoked in Vesper's autobiography (*DR*, 264), Brinkmann sees the subject confronted by a battery of repressive institutions and agents of socialisation:

> Bewußtsein: IMMER geschunden, verkrüppelt, beschnitten, verboten, ritualisiert, schließlich verseucht von Familien, Vater, Mutter, ganzen Generationen, von Staatsformen, Gesellschaftsformen, Handelsformen, [...] von Schule in Wort und Bild — grauenhaft!
>
> (*E*, 58)

However, Brinkmann's autobiographical notes reveal a striking shift of emphasis against *Die Reise*. In Vesper's autobiography, a resolutely Reichian discourse privileges the family as the primary site of socialisation. But in the *Erkundungen*, the family is stripped of all formative significance for the subject. In marked contrast to the figure of Will Vesper, Brinkmann's father recedes into anonymity in his recollections of his childhood in Vechta in North Germany:

---

34   Piwitt, '"Die ganze Häßlichkeit der Welt bin Ich."', p. 143.

[es] taucht eine blaue leichte Sommerjacke auf eines Vormittags zwischen den Baumstämmen außerhalb Vechtas, und man sagt mir, das sei mein Vater, was ist das?

(*E*, 168)

Moreover, Brinkmann's own familial relationships as he writes are hardly foregrounded by the *Erkundungen*. His wife Maleen and his handicapped son Robert, often abbreviated to their initials, are relegated to minor parts of the inventories of events and activities recorded in the third part of the text: '/M. packt Roberts Geschenke ein/'; or '/M. & R., die gerade aus der Straßenbahn steigen/'(*E*, 188, 237).

Put briefly, in Brinkmann's autobiographical notes familial relationships forfeit pride of place in the discourses of subjectivity and subject formation. Rather, the text takes up the problematic of socialisation by the mass media outlined by Marcuse. For just as the skyline of Cologne is dominated by the towers of 'IBM und WDR' (*E*, 18; for photographs of IBM, *E*, 18 and 58), subjectivity is constructed for Brinkmann within a social and cultural space – a consumer wasteland – delimited by the American or Americanised corporations of monopoly capitalism and the mass media.

In the *Erkundungen*, the corporations of monopoly capitalism symbolised by IBM represent the motor propelling contemporary society to the edge of desolation. Photographs of detritus and decay mounted into the text testify to the havoc wreaked by an aggressive economic need for expansion (*E*, 21, 38, 46). Yet the text is most compelling where it illuminates the mechanisms through which individuals are conscripted into the service of destructive processes of production, consumption and waste. Here, the *Erkundungen* foreground an insidious 'Bewußtseins=Redaktion' conducted by 'Rundfunk, Zeitung, Fernsehen', an invasive and pervasive 'Kontrolle durch Massenmedien' (*E*, 265, 112).

The *Erkundungen*'s conception of the operation of the mass media on the subject appears highly monolithic. For Brinkmann, the pages of the Cologne tabloid *Express*, the images transmitted on the '1. Programm' and the broadcasts of the 'WDR' merge into a single, repressive 'Bewußtseinsindustrie' (*E*, 23, 18, 85). Coined by Enzensberger in 1962 in analogy to Adorno and Horkheimer's 'Kulturindustrie', the term 'Bewußtseinsindustrie' appears to have enjoyed wide currency on the left.[35]

Brinkmann's *Erkundungen* register the manipulative power of the 'Bewußtseinsindustrie' above all in a series of exclamations that belie the dispassionate objectivity which the text claims for itself. Invectives abound: against the 'Großen Kontrollmaschine Fernsehen' (*E*, 34); the 'lebende Abfall

---

35   See the essay 'Bewußtseins-Industrie' in Hans Magnus Enzensberger, *Einzelheiten* (Frankfurt am Main, 1962), pp. 7-15; see also Neumann, *Identität und Rollenzwang*, p. 144.

der Massenmedien' (*E*, 266); and the 'peinigende Idiotenschau im Fernsehen und Kino' (*E*, 94). But probing beyond these anguished utterances, we can glean from the *Erkundungen* a penetrating account of the impact of the media on the human subject.

Broadly speaking, what is at stake in the text is quite literally an invasion or colonisation of the human subject. The subject is bombarded by an unrelenting barrage of 'Zeichen und Chiffren' (*E*, 232) that relentlessly wears down the ego. As Brinkmann puts it: 'Mit einem elektrischen Bildgestöber wollten sie ihn verheizen. Wen? Das selbstbewußte Ich' (*E*, 172). More than this, however, the media reach into and anchor themselves within the deepest recesses of the subject: 'Und da sah ich, was los war: sie drangen immerzu neu in den wortlosen Traumbereich ein' (*E*, 172). Here, the *Erkundungen* clearly presuppose a core or substratum of human subjectivity which pre-exists language and culture; Brinkmann derives this notion from Reich and arguably also from his reading of William Burroughs.[36] Framed by this conception of the colonisation of the subject by the media, however, is a concern influenced by Marcuse rather than Reich: the closing off of the human faculties and needs that point to alternatives to the status quo. Let us examine the text's treatment, first, of critical reason and, second, of human sexuality.

In an allusion to the critical theory of the Frankfurt School, the *Erkundungen* single out a reduction in the scope of human reason as a central aspect of the contemporary consciousness that they set out to chart. However, though the text refers to a 'Reduzierung der Vernunft auf rein praktische Fragen' (*E*, 107), it does not so much record the ascendancy of instrumental reason in the sense of the Frankfurt School as simply register the atrophy of critical reason.

The *Erkundungen* use the technique of montage to point to the decline of critical reason at the hands of the media. Brinkmann's use of montage has neither the theoretical grounding nor the critical force that we find in a contemporary like Alexander Kluge. This is not to say, however, that it altogether lacks critical impetus: on the contrary, juxtaposing image and text, and columns of text, the *Erkundungen* mimic the newspaper page to suggest how the media erode the capacity to perceive crucial differences between events. Collages in the first part of the text, for example, show how, far from encouraging critical awareness, the reports of violence circulated within the press actually naturalise aggression and destruction. Side by side, images of Northern Ireland or Vietnam, articles about riots in Japan, assaults on celebrities ('Revolverheld suchte Liz Taylor'; *E*, 22) and car crashes hamper the subject's ability to perceive events within their proper socio-political context (*E*, 7-27). Violence appears simply as a fact of life, universal and

36 See 'Spiritual Addiction. Zu William Seward Burroughs' Roman Nova Express' (originally 1970) in Brinkmann, *Der Film in Worten*, pp. 203-06.

inevitable. In addition, the media's penchant for the trivial – 'Zeitungsüberschrift Express: Blauer Bruder vom Flugkapitän entdeckt!: Was ist das für eine Nachricht?' (*E*, 232) – clouds judgement further. It becomes difficult, in Marcuse's words, to 'distinguish between the media as instruments of information and entertainment, and as agents of manipulation and indoctrination'.[37] The subject is finally left unable to process the undifferentiated flood of information confronting him. Brinkmann describes his own predicament:

> Massenmedien: egal ob ein sogenannter Report über katastrophale Wohnverhältnisse gezeigt wird oder ein Bericht über Müllhalden/nie kann ich darin sehen, warum das gezeigt und berichtet wird, immer nur ein Wusel hin und her.
>
> (*E*, 231)

Above critical reason, however, the *Erkundungen* circumscribe human sexuality as the site where the subject is most effectively enmeshed within a set of destructive and exploitative social relations. Here, the text exhibits a shift in Brinkmann's views on the subversive potential of the sexual drives comparable to, and surely influenced by, Marcuse's concept of 'repressive desublimation'.

In 'Der Film in Worten', his epilogue to *ACID*, Brinkmann ascribed to the increasingly sexual images of advertising an erotic charge capable of exploding the ideology of the market.[38] The *Erkundungen*, by contrast, offer a more sombre vision of the reduction and manipulation of human sexuality in contemporary society. In this latter text, the apparent liberalisation of sexual imagery and of the public discourses about sexuality is seen to mask an augmentation of the mechanisms of control and domination arrayed against the subject. As Brinkmann puts it: 'Sex und Polizei gehören auch zusammen: in beidem steckt Kontrolle!' (*E*, 232). The *Erkundungen*'s vision of sexuality as an instrument of control has two components. First, sexual needs are increasingly available to regulation from without in contemporary society. Sex becomes 'ferngesteuert[...]' (*E*, 126): and the proliferation of 'Nackte[...] Bilder[...]' (*E*, 231) within the audio-visual and print media does not so much cater to existing sexual needs as force them along prescribed pathways. This external regulation of sexuality is related, second, to a reduction in its scope. The sexual drives are deprived of the qualities which transcend the status quo. Brinkmann laments the fact that 'Lust nur als bloße Sex-Ausübung gesehen wird' (*E*, 207).

The manipulation and reduction of the sexual drives provide the precondition for what Marcuse terms the 'inclusion of libidinal components

---

37 Marcuse, *One-Dimensional Man*, p. 8.
38 Brinkmann, 'Der Film in Worten', p. 382.

into the realm of commodity production and exchange'.[39] What this means becomes clear when we turn to a further instance of montage in the text: an article about a motor show in London (*E*, 162). Mounted into the *Erkundungen*, the article, which bears a photograph of two naked women mounting a car and the headline 'Londons Motor Show: Mehr nackte Haut als neue Autos', makes a simple, yet powerful point.[40] Far from exploding the ideology of the market, sexual desire is mobilised to provide individuals with the incitement that binds them, both as consumers and as producers, to a repressive and destructive social order. Further, sexual desire itself becomes, in analogy to the products that it promotes, commodified: locked into mechanisms of production and consumption and regulated by laws of supply and demand. Negating Marcuse's claim in *Eros and Civilization* that the so-called 'perversions' embody a 'revolt against the performance principle in the name of the pleasure principle', Brinkmann asserts that even the transgressive appetites of his homosexual friends offer no purchase for resistance to the manipulation of sexual needs.[41] He writes: '(<u>Anm.</u>: Auch dieser Staat wird, mittels Gesetzgebung und verbaler Manipulation die Homosexualität einzäunen und sich dienlich machen!)' (*E*, 252).

With the erosion of critical reason and the manipulation of sexuality, then, the media shut down those aspects of human subjectivity incompatible with the status quo. This is true also for Brinkmann's treatment of phantasy (also accorded radical potential in Marcuse's *Eros and Civilization*),[42] which features in the text only in a series of anguished and fragmentary exclamations: 'Aus den Arbeiten ist die Fantasie verschwunden'; or 'konditioniertes Bewußtsein!/: Erledigte Fantasie!/' (*E*, 107, 225). What is important, however, is that, for Brinkmann as for Marcuse, the loss of these faculties effectively marks the dissolution of a subject – 'Das selbstbewußte Ich' (*E*, 172) – endowed with the capacity for autonomous and creative selfhood.

Broadly speaking, this process of dissolution has two aspects: the first objective, the second subjective. Stripped of the capacity for autonomous action, first, the subject becomes a malleable object of the social process, and is enmeshed in ungratifying and repressive performances and processes of production: 'Rabotti, Rabotti, Wirtschaft, IBM, ohne Rücksicht auf den Aufbau eines eigenständigen Bewußtseins' (*E*, 250). For Brinkmann, this subject can grasp its needs only within the terms prescribed by the global capitalist order symbolised by corporations like IBM. The endpoint of this development is its assimilation of freedom to a free choice between a wide

39 Marcuse, *One-Dimensional Man*, p. 75.
40 Compare Späth, *Rolf Dieter Brinkmann*, p. 99.
41 Marcuse, *Eros and Civilization*, p. 50.
42 Marcuse, *Eros and Civilization*, p. 14.

variety of goods and services. As Brinkmann puts it: 'Freiheit ((übersetzt: die Freiheit zwischen Colgate oder Blendax zu wählen, aber ist das eine Wahl? Ist das eine tatsächliche Differenzierung?))' (E, 251).

In subjective terms, the transformation of the subject into an object of the social process is experienced as a dislocating process of 'Ich-Auflösung' (E, 117):

> Mit einem elektrischen Bildgestöber wollten sie ihn verheizen. Wen? Das selbstbewußte Ich. Also tastete ich mich weiter durch diesen Wirbel aus Wörtern und Bildern, die zu einer elektrischen Suppe sich vermischten, und schneller, und immer schneller um mich herum zu wirbeln begannen. [...] //Wer war ich und was?
>
> (E, 172)

We can grasp this experience of fragmentation in terms of what Fredric Jameson has theorised as a loss or 'crisis of historicity'.[43] The concept is useful because it points to a crippling cognitive inability on the part of the subject to apprehend its position in the social and historical space in which it is embedded. In the passage above, the use of words like 'tasten' or 'Wirbel' convey a powerful sense of indeterminacy; this is intensified throughout the text as Brinkmann dissolves the concrete historical setting of his autobiographical notes – '/BRD 1971/' (E, 21) – into a diffuse, but monolithic 'Gegenwart' (for example: E, 19, 155, 266). The notion of a loss of historicity is suggestive also in a manner that touches upon the Erkundungen as a literary construction of subjectivity. It highlights an incapacity on Brinkmann's part to set himself, as autobiographer, in relation to his own life history. His ruptured relationship to his own history finds expression in the metaphor of a broken mirror:

> Ich taste mich durch einen undeutlichen, zum Teil zerbrochenen Spiegel von mir selber, losgelöste autobiografische Fetzen, halb verwischte Ereignisse und Vorgänge.
>
> (E, 360)

This metaphor has a counterpart in the formal composition of the text. The technique of montage certainly displays a critical thrust in the Erkundungen; but mostly, it tends to reproduce the dissolution of the subject in the face of the barrage of signs and images emanating from the mass media. In the Erkundungen, the linear anamnesis of conventional autobiographical discourse is broken open in favour of a more spatial arrangement of material: a synchronic juxtaposition of image and text; and of parallel and unrelated columns of text (there are as many as four typed columns on E, 144). The arrangement

---

43   Fredric Jameson, *Postmodernism; or, The Cultural Logic of Late Capitalism* (London and New York, 1992), p. 25.

of these pictorial and textual elements is in no sense a stable one. Just as the media assault the subject with a barrage of different stimuli, the *Erkundungen* are constructed as a chaotic and unpredictable collision between a range of different discourses: from comics to postcards; from journalism to autobiographical self-reflection; and from film transcripts to popular songs. Confronted at every turn with such a 'Wirbel aus Wörtern und Bildern' (*E*, 172), what chances does the subject have? Or as Brinkmann puts it: 'Bilder und Dialoge der Gegenwart. Es gibt daraus kein Entkommen?' (*E*, 144).

Surprisingly, perhaps, the *Erkundungen*'s emphasis on the stupefying and manipulative force of the mass media strike a new note in Brinkmann's work. In marked contrast to them, for example, 'Der Film in Worten', Brinkmann's conclusion to *ACID* in 1969, had seen in the proliferation of electronic media (in 1970, 70% of West German households had television sets as against 17% in 1960)[44] the possibility of an 'effektiven Erweiterung des menschlichen Bewußtseins'.[45] If the new stress on the manipulative power of the media signals a break with some of Brinkmann's own preoccupations of the late 1960s (we will bracket for now the question of continuities in his work), it aligns him more closely with positions formulated by theorists of anti-authoritarianism during the same period. For Brinkmann's vision of a pernicious 'Kontrolle durch Massenmedien' (*E*, 112) bears a definite resemblance to the 'Manipulationsthese' widely held by the student protesters of the 1960s. According to Gerd Langguth, this represented less a clearly articulated theoretical position than the

> Grundidee [...], daß infolge der Manipulation das eigentliche revolutionäre Subjekt, das Industrieproletariat, nicht mehr in der Lage sei, seine eigenen objektiven sozialen und politischen Interessen zu erkennen. Die Industriegesellschaft verhindere nämlich die freie Selbstentfaltung der Menschen durch Manipulation, Repression und Konsumterror.[46]

There are distinct contiguities between the *Erkundungen*'s account of a 'Kontrolle durch Massenmedien' and the anti-authoritarian 'Manipulationsthese'. These include a common grounding in the work of Marcuse, especially *One-Dimensional Man* and subsequent texts; and the shared conviction that advanced capitalist societies stifle dissent by binding individuals into repressive cycles of production and consumption. (In the Federal Republic the theory and practice of the student movement in this respect increasingly focused on the reactionary Springer press.) There are

---

44 Ingo Helm, 'Literatur und Massenmedien', in *Gegenwartsliteratur seit 1968*, ed. by Klaus Briegleb and Sigrid Weigel (Munich, 1992), pp. 536-56 (p. 540).

45 Brinkmann, 'Der Film in Worten', p. 381.

46 Langguth, pp. 37-38

crucial differences also, however, and these arise in part from Brinkmann's difficult relationship with the left upon the decline of the student movement. The *Erkundungen* offer in effect a radically individualised version of the 'Manipulationsthese', closer perhaps to the initially individual focus of *Subversive Aktion* than to the student movement's full-blown opposition to Springer. That is to say, they concentrate above all on the crippling subjective effects of the mechanisms through which the individual is integrated into the consumer society, giving no space to the discourses of class struggle, false consciousness, or revolution. Indeed, Brinkmann's notes frequently express suspicion and even antipathy towards the ever more orthodox left's political ambitions, deriding its glib talk of 'Marxismus, Weltrevolution usw.' (*E*, 236). Moreover, in their representation of the subject being taken over by the mass media, the *Erkundungen* are infused with a horror and an anguish uniquely their own.

In view of Brinkmann's rift with the left, how do the *Erkundungen* resist the destructive effect of the media on the subject? Brinkmann's antipathy toward the left surely blocks off the path toward the cultural, social or political emancipation of the self through transformative action. Rather, the *Erkundungen* contest the media in a spirit of resignation and retreat. They fall back on the '"power of negation"' outlined by Marcuse and relinquish the universal claims inherent in the project of studying contemporary consciousness.

The *Erkundungen*'s attempt to claw back from the mass media 'a personal, private realm' comprises two moments.[47] The first hinges on a concept of somatic experience that eludes the enculturating grasp of the media and issues into a second moment – the endeavour to disengage a sphere of autonomous selfhood from the control of the media; Brinkmann's projected autobiographical novel acquires a central importance here.

The *Erkundungen* oppose the media first with a retreat to the body. Against the nightmare of the colonisation of the subject, they set the perception (or perhaps the hope) that the physical and cognitive organisation of human subjectivity is ultimately irreducible to the intervention of the media, whatever its force. Governed by its own 'innere[...], vegetative[...] Rhythmen' (*E*, 304), Brinkmann suggests, the intentionless materiality of the body affords subversive moments. 'Die tatsächlich gefährlichen Momente', he writes, 'passieren auf den verschiedendsten Ebenen des menschlichen Körpers, und alle diese Momente sind sprachlos' (*E*, 51).

Further, the body furnishes the basis in the text for a concept of experience whose absolute singularity appears inalienably private. Take, for example, Brinkmann's brief description of autumn in Cologne:

47 Marcuse, *Five Lectures*, p. 51.

ein Wirbel nasser Blätter, Straßenbahngeklingel, schwere, drückende nebelige
Feuchtigkeit im Oktober über dem Rudolfplatz abends um halb sieben/

(*E*, 89)

The uniqueness of this experience is affirmed not only by its location in time and space ('Rudolfplatz', 'abends um halb sieben'), but also through an appeal to the physical senses: sight ('ein Wirbel'), hearing ('Straßenbahngeklingel') and touch and smell ('drückende nebelige Feuchtigkeit').

According to Späth, Brinkmann's use of photography enjoys a privileged relationship to personal experience in the *Erkundungen*. Photographs have a dual function in the text, she argues. Revealing 'der radikal subjektive Blick des einzelnen auf seine Umwelt', they point to an unmediated experience of the object world; and in so doing they open up 'Realitätsbezirke, die von der offiziellen Repräsentation [durch die Massenmedien] ausgeschlossen werden'.[48] Thus the dereliction depicted in Brinkmann's own photographs ruptures the seamless representation of reality in, for example, a postcard of Cologne cathedral (*E*, 166). Much the same is true of the language with which Brinkmann endeavours, as in the evocation of Cologne in autumn above, to grasp and reproduce his experience. This is not to say, as Späth seems to imply, that Brinkmann ascribes a complete transparency to images (or words) in the representation of his experience, or ignores the fact that the purportedly immediate experience presented by the text is in fact mediated through linguistic and photographic representations. What is at stake here is rather an attempt to wrest the production of meaning from the control of the mass media for a private usage that institutes the subject as its source.

In the *Erkundungen*, the assertion of a private usage of language and images belongs in the context of a wider endeavour to disengage the self from the repressive social relations in which it is embedded. This endeavour begins with an act of 'totale Absage' (*E*, 217), as if Marcuse's 'Great Refusal' – a refusal to participate in socially required performances – is thrown onto an individual plane:[49] 'schaffe Bücher weg/Platten weg/kein TV mehr, keine Filme mehr/' (*E*, 217). During Brinkmann's visit to his painter friend, Freyend, at Longkamp (near Bernkastel), this initial refusal issues into wholesale withdrawal. Underwritten by a belief in an originary harmony between man and nature, the sections of the *Erkundungen* written at Longkamp in November and December 1971 tentatively assert a process of self-realisation (*E*, 268-367).

The antithesis of the garish spectacles manufactured by the media, the natural colours and sounds around Longkamp promote for Brinkmann a sense

48   Späth, *Rolf Dieter Brinkmann*, p. 108.
49   Marcuse, *One-Dimensional Man*, p. 257.

of physical well-being. He elaborates: 'Blau, das rötliche Buchenlaub, die gelben Lerchen, die grünen Tannen, die leichte, klare, nach Wald riechende Luft, ich fühle mich körperlich wohl' (*E*, 312). This harmony between nature and the body provides fertile ground for the cultivation of a sense of self whose hallmarks are plenitude and self-presence. 'Und werde ich, werde ich!', Brinkmann exclaims (*E*, 285). Crucially, Brinkmann's retreat to Longkamp is marked also by a new-found autonomy that is expressed in a symbolic power to name: 'Ich müßte einen völlig neuen Namen mir eigentlich zulegen' (*E*, 285).

In the *Erkundungen*, Brinkmann's retreat to nature is linked to a further strategy aimed at carving out a personal space for the self: his autobiographical novel. Typically, Brinkmann articulates his plans for it only in fragments. Significantly, though, he places his projected novel in the tradition of the *Bildungsroman*:[50]

> Den Roman als ein heutiger Entwicklungsroman schreiben. (:zieht in die Welt hinaus, in die elektrifizierte, kontrollierte, von ständigen gleichen Impulsen als künstliches Labyrinth angelegte Tag- und Nachtwelt!)/:
>
> (*E*, 285)

Elsewhere, he suggests that while this projected text might be fragmented in form, its *telos* remains conventional:

> Wenn Roman, dann ein total freier, aufgesplitterter in Einzelszenen und Gesamtszenen, mit Reflexionen, Zusammenbrüchen, Delirien, und am Schluß: das selbstbewußte Ich.//
>
> (*E*, 193)

There are compelling reasons for accepting the critical commonplace that the *Erkundungen* already represent Brinkmann's projected autobiographical novel. They certainly resemble the 'freier, aufgesplitterter' text outlined above. Moreover, the *telos* of a 'selbstbewußte Ich' appears to find expression in Brinkmann's exclamations of self-presence at Longkamp. However, a careful reading of the passages of the text devoted to (and composed during) Brinkmann's trip to Longkamp suggests two reasons why the self-presence asserted in the text is illusory; with this, the perceived identity of the *Erkundungen* and the projected novel collapses. First, Brinkmann's vision of a pristine nature beyond the reach of the media is untenable. The destructive technologies of modern society make their insidious presence felt especially here: the sky over Longkamp is crossed by 'Düsenjäger', its silence is pierced by the noise of an 'Auto-Radio' (*E*, 360, 335). Second, the very idea of a pristine natural world in which Brinkmann grounds his sense of self is itself

50 Compare Späth, 'Gehirnströme und Medientext', p. 109.

surely a representation that is deeply ideological. Brinkmann intuits this in an anecdote about a visit to a country snack bar; the waiter reports there is no fresh meat:

> Er müsse eine Dose aufmachen. Da merkte ich, daß ich von einer falschen Vorstellung ausgegangen war, wieder, nämlich: Land, gutes Fleisch, kräftiger Fleischspieß.

$(E, 283)$

We should therefore consider the relationship between the *Erkundungen* and Brinkmann's projected novel less in terms of an identity than a discontinuity between the two. Brinkmann himself disavows any identity between them: '((ist das hier schon der Roman, den ich schreiben will??//Nein [...]))//' (*E*, 229). Moreover, the composition of the novel is deferred in the *Erkundungen* across a series of 'Romananfänge' – a series of attempted openings that never develop into the novel itself (for example, *E*, 233, 266, 284, 308). In short, what the *Erkundungen* dramatise is Brinkmann's failure to write his autobiographical novel.

The reasons for this return us to Neumann's theory of autobiography in *Identität und Rollenzwang*. For Neumann, classical autobiography represented the means by which the bourgeois subject negotiated his position in the world, mediating his role as subject and object in the historical process through his status as subject and object of his own life history. With the rise of monopoly capitalism and of extra-familial agents of socialisation, he argues, autobiography slides into memoir, the inscription of a repressive 'Rollenzwang'. Though the *Erkundungen*'s empirical impetus embodies something of the zeal for 'Belegen' and 'Zitieren' that Neumann associates with memoir,[51] the *Erkundungen* dramatise the fragmentation of the subject in the face of the mass media rather than a slippage into role-play. Neumann's account of the implosion of the psychological, socio-historical and literary preconditions of the autobiographical act is nonetheless suggestive. Two points are relevant here.

First, Brinkmann's failure to write his autobiographical novel points to the disappearance of an subject able to mediate its status within the historical process through the autobiographical text. Given the *Erkundungen*'s vision of the decline of the subject's critical faculties, it is significant that Brinkmann ultimately adduces his failure to write his novel to an inability to synthesise his materials. He writes to his friend Helmut Pieper:

> Ja, ich schreibe seit ganz langer Zeit an einem Buch, aber ich bin so hilflos, daß ich nicht weiß, wie ich alle die Sachen, die Einzelnen Fotos, Erlebnisse,

---

51   Neumann, *Identität und Rollenzwang*, pp. 60 and 83.

Gedanken, Projektionen, Halluzinationen, Ängste zusammenbündeln kann:
eben wie gebündeltes Licht=Laserstrahlen/

(E, 209)

This inability makes itself felt above all in Brinkmann's failure to draw a central figure for his novel: 'ich wollte immerzu schreiben, schreiben, dieser furchtbare Druck, sich beweisen zu wollen, der mich erledigte, eine Figur darstellen zu müssen' (E, 292). It is ironic in this respect that the *Erkundungen* should have been edited and published by his wife after his death.

Second, Neumann's theory of autobiography helps us to grasp how, in the *Erkundungen*, the very social and historical matrix of autobiography has collapsed. Subject to the 'direct management' of the mass media, the need for the autobiographer to negotiate his (or her) situation in the world by means of the autobiographical act simply does not arise. In the *Erkundungen*, the recovery of some notion of selfhood or self-determination appears possible only through a flight from the media – into the materiality of the body, or into the realm of nature. The notion of an autobiographical text outside any social, historical or linguistic determination is an impossibility. Nonetheless, autobiography, conceived not as an attempt to define the self in relation to the world but rather as a retreat from it, provides Brinkmann with an ultimate point of flight in the *Erkundungen*. Brinkmann's projected autobiographical novel founders; but in this failure the project is thrown onto another plane. It becomes a utopian horizon, an imaginary point of flight for a subjectivity that cannot be accommodated within an inimical reality. Riddled with typing errors, the manuscript reads:

//NEIN/: ich WILL meinen Roman über die Erfahrungen schreiben, die ich hoer
für mich skizzieren! Intensiv! Denn ich habe sie in tensiv erfajren! Radikal,
demn ich habe sie radikal für mich erfahren! Ohne kompromiß.

(E, 241)

Brinkmann's autobiographical novel takes the notion of a truly private language to its conclusion: for it is a truly private 'text', unwritten and unwriteable.

III   The Media and the Transformation of the Autobiographical Subject

In the *Erkundungen*, then, autobiography figures as a flight from the 'Bewußtseinsindustrie' that is the mass media. We suggested above that Brinkmann's conception of the mass media as 'Bewußtseinsindustrie' aligned him in several respects with the anti-authoritarian 'Manipulationsthese'. At any rate, the *Erkundungen* share with the 'Manipulationsthese' also a marked tendency toward oversimplification.

In his 'Baukasten zu einer Theorie der Medien' of 1970, Enzensberger attacked what he saw as a 'Medien-Feindschaft' on the left that reduced political questions about the media to the term of 'Manipulation'; the 'Schreckbild einer monolithischen Bewußtseins-Industrie', he argued, was 'undialektisch und obsolet'.[52]

Brinkmann's conception of the 'Bewußtseinsindustrie' certainly appears monolithic. Operating with totalising concepts, it confronts the 'totalen Notstand' of the subject with the sheer manipulative force exercised by the media (*E*, 222). Indeed, given the repressive force that Brinkmann ascribes to the media, it seems surprising that the *Erkundungen* can countenance any resistance at all. Whether in a retreat to the body or into nature, Brinkmann's opposition to the media is ultimately grounded in the assertion of a will that appears immunised against them: '<u>ich ziehe mich in den Traum zurück!</u>'; 'Ich WILL meinen Roman über die Erfahrungen schreiben [...]' (*E*, 225, 241). It is not immune, though, and collapses into hatred – a final negation, with every last fibre, of an oppressive reality: 'bleibt zuletzt nur noch ein wilder, geisterhafter Haß übrig?' (*E*, 135). Oscillating between voluntaristic self-assertion and hatred, Brinkmann's *Erkundungen* prefigure the dialectic of self-aggrandisement and contempt which found full expression in *Rom, Blicke*.

Viewed in context, it is curious that Brinkmann should adopt an individualised version of the 'Manipulationsthese' just as the left began to elaborate a more differentiated critical discourse on the media than the emphasis on 'Manipulation' allowed. Enzensberger's initial intervention into the debate, an essay entitled 'Bewußtseins-Industrie' in his *Einzelheiten* of 1962, viewed the media largely in terms of manipulation. His 'Baukasten zu einer Theorie der Medien' of 1970, though, reformulated his own concept of the 'Bewußtseins-Industrie' to take account of a contradiction between the egalitarian productive forces of the media themselves and the hierarchical relations of production in which they were embedded – a contradiction that could be mobilised by the left. And in *kürbiskern* in 1970, Horst Holzer's 'Massenmedien oder Monopolmedien?' stressed the responsibility of socialist intellectuals working within the media for generating a 'systemkritischen Widerstand' that could lead to the eventual 'Demokratisierung der Massenkommunikation'.[53] Brinkmann's totalising perspectives, though, seem to admit no compromise. Mocking as 'Massenmedienaffen' (*E*, 222) writers willing to work with the media (Jürgen Becker, Hans Werner Richter and Günter Grass are targets; *E*, 247), Brinkmann intones that their 'Job ist Bewußtsein zu verwalten!' (*E*, 222). Given these words of censure, we are surprised to learn that Brinkmann too has recently written radio plays of his

52   Enzensberger, 'Baukasten zu einer Theorie der Medien', pp. 163-64 and 161.
53   Horst Holzer, 'Massenmedien oder Monopolmedien?', *kürbiskern*, 4 (1970), 622-37
     (pp. 630-32).

own: 'Auf der Schwelle', written in 1970 and broadcast in mid 1971; and 'Der Tierplanet', written in 1971 and broadcast in 1972 (E, 363, 366, 368).

It would be wrong, however, to dismiss the *Erkundungen*, in Enzensberger's words, as undialectical. Against his opposition to the media – 'Gegen Etwas zu sein, was da ist, ist reinster Blödsinn' – , Brinkmann signals another possibility: 'die zweite Einstellung ist: Mit dem zu sein, worauf man sich bezieht und auf das, worüber man sich bezieht, hinausgehen' (E, 228-29). Put briefly, these elliptical comments herald a textual strategy directed at pressing the colonisation of the subject by the media to a point where it yields new freedoms. What Brinkmann terms his 'Methoden, technische Sachen der Selbstbefreiung' (E, 278) must be seen in the context of his involvement with the cultural and subcultural streams of anti-authoritarianism during the late 1960s – and especially his reception of the media theorist Marshall McLuhan.

We noted above that in the literary-historical discourses about the 1960s, the concept of subculture, like the term 'pop', covers a range of aesthetic and life-style impulses. In 'Baukasten zu einer Theorie der Medien', Enzensberger suggested that the subcultural currents within anti-authoritarianism had understood 'die technischen und ästhetischen Möglichkeiten' of the electronic media better than the left – Benjamin and Brecht excepted – ever had.[54] At any rate, one feature that links writers associated with the development of a pop literature in the Federal Republic is an interest in the relationship between the development of the media and the production of cultural forms. Texts like Peter Chotjewitz's *Vom Leben und Lernen. Stereotexte* (1969), Helmut Salzinger's 'Das lange Gedicht' (1969), and Bazon Brock's *Bazon Brock, was machen sie jetzt so? Die 'Blaue Illustrierte' – eine Autobiographie* (1968) all attempted to rethink the nature of literary production (and concepts like 'work' and 'author') in an age of media, advertising and serially produced consumer goods.

The relationship between technology and cultural production received an aggressive formulation also in Brinkmann's 'Der Film in Worten' in *ACID*. Admittedly, Brinkmann's interest in this relationship predated his reception of pop: already *Le Chant du Monde* (1964) and *Raupenbahn* (1966) adumbrated the transposition of photographic and cinematographic techniques into poetry and prose respectively. However, it was his reception of McLuhan that gave his understanding of the effects of the electronic media a fresh impetus in the late 1960s.

McLuhan's *Understanding Media* of 1964 offered very different perspectives on the media from Marcuse's *One-Dimensional Man* of the same year. Marcuse barely distinguished between the various media. Proclaiming that 'the medium is the message', McLuhan by contrast explored how the technical structure of a given medium (any technological 'extension' of man

---

54 Enzensberger, 'Baukasten zu einer Theorie der Medien', pp. 166 and 175-76.

from the typewriter to the radio) impacted on the human subject prior to any question of usage – like manipulation.[55] McLuhan saw a double process at work. The technical media, he argued, extended the central nervous system into the space around the human subject. At the same time, they worked back on the subject, transforming human cognitive functions and creating 'new ratios or new equilibriums among the other organs and extensions of the body'.[56]

In *ACID*, McLuhan's notion of a technological reorganisation of the subject converges with a radical iconoclasm derived from the American literary critic Leslie Fiedler.[57] For in 'Der Film in Worten', Brinkmann perceived 'die Verwendung technischer Apparate' as crucial not only to an 'effektiven Erweiterung des menschlichen Bewußtseins', but also to an assault on the 'Abrichtungscharakter, der in tradierten [literarischen] Ausdrucksformen steckt'.[58] It was precisely this technological assault on literary tradition that Brinkmann had admired in American pop and underground writing, and which he aspired to in his own work in the late 1960s – in the poems of *Die Piloten* and *Godzilla*, for example, and in the novel *Keiner weiß mehr* (all published in 1968). The *Erkundungen*'s conception of the media as a monolithic 'Bewußtseinsindustrie' admittedly strikes a new note in Brinkmann's writing. However, the McLuhanite discourse of cognitive transformation through the media (and the iconoclastic twist that Brinkmann gives it) persists in his work also, finding expression in his radio plays of the early 1970s and in the *Erkundungen*.

The *Erkundungen* acknowledge few forebears. Brinkmann's 'Lektüre' (*E*, 258) includes: Karl Philipp Moritz and William Burroughs (*E*, 175, 35). However, his preoccupation with the impact of technical media on cultural forms is not without precedent, neither with respect to aesthetic practice nor to its theoretical formulation. In the 1920s, Dadaists like Grosz and Heartfield, for example, deployed photographic and cinematographic montage techniques in an attack on the concept of the organic artwork; and in 1936, Walter Benjamin's 'Das Kunstwerk im Zeitalter seiner technischen Reproduzierbarkeit' theorised the implications of electronic reproduction for cultural and revolutionary practices. Moreover, Brinkmann's endeavours to apply cinematographic techniques to prose – though less his own 8mm experiments of 1968 (*Atomic Man, Tod, Porträt*) – aligns him with a whole 'tradition' of filmic representation in literature: from Döblin's *Berlin Alexanderplatz* (1929) to more recent work like Wellershoff's *Die*

---

55 McLuhan, pp. 7-8.
56 McLuhan, pp. 3 and 45.
57 See the defence of Fiedler in Rolf Dieter Brinkmann, 'Angriff aufs Monopol. Ich hasse alte Dichter', *Christ und Welt*, 15 November 1968, pp. 14-15.
58 Brinkmann, 'Der Film in Worten', pp. 382, 381 and 398.

Schattengrenze of 1969. Questions of originality lose their force when we confront the implications of mass reproduction techniques for literary works. But even given this, the *Erkundungen*'s exploration of the ramifications of the electronic media for the autobiographical act make them a remarkable literary document.

Wolfgang Adam has argued that in *Rom, Blicke* the use of montage has fundamental aesthetic consequences for the text:

1. Die klassische Definition des Autors als Schöpfer sui generis wird ersetzt durch die Rolle des Arrangeurs von Materialien.
2. Das neuentstandene 'Kunstwerk' besitzt keine *Aura* im Sinne Benjamins, es ist für jeden herstellbar und im 'Zeitalter der Abbildungen' beliebig zu vervielfältigen.[59]

We might argue by analogy that in the *Erkundungen* the autobiographer becomes an 'Arrangeur von Materialien'; and that the autobiographical text is robbed of its 'aura', its singularity. However, Brinkmann's preoccupation with the impact of the media on the subject gives the *Erkundungen* a radical spin that Adam's approach to *Rom, Blicke* misses. Manfred Schneider's *Die erkaltete Herzensschrift* of 1986, by contrast, provides us with a more useful perspective.[60]

The transformative power of the media is central to Schneider's study. Where McLuhan examines how the technical media transform the human cognitive apparatus, Schneider argues that they appropriate the functions and reorganise the tropes of autobiographical discourse. For Schneider, the subject is constructed within a range of anthropological discourses (like autobiography), which are in turn produced at a historically attained level of the deployment of material channels of communication. Classical autobiography, he suggests, arose within a culture of the written and printed word that forged a unity between the interiority of the bourgeois subject and script (a unity materialised in Rousseau's metaphor of the 'Herzensschrift').[61]

According to Schneider, the technical and electronic media challenge the 'Charakterologie', the 'Einheit von Subjekt und Buchstaben' on which classical autobiography is predicated.[62] For in the twentieth century, he argues, new mechanised and electronic forms of cultural memory take over from autobiographical discourse the function of producing and recording individual

59   Wolfgang Adam, '*Arkadien* als *Vorhölle*. Die Destruktion des traditionellen Italien-Bildes in Rolf Dieter Brinkmanns *Rom, Blicke*', *Euphorion*, 83 (1989), 226-45 (p. 235).
60   Manfred Schneider's study is briefly invoked to assert a 'Semiotik der Unmittelbarkeit' at work in Brinkmann's autobiographical writings in Späth, *Rolf Dieter Brinkmann*, p. 92.
61   Manfred Schneider, *Die erkaltete Herzensschrift*, pp. 9-10 (p. 10).
62   Manfred Schneider, *Die erkaltete Herzensschrift*, p. 16.

and anthropological truths. As the interiority of the subject is erased in a process of 'mechanische[...] Transkription' and 'Speicherung', Schneider suggests that the technical media effect a metaphorical displacement within the genre: autobiography capitulates to the pre-eminence of the technical media by inscribing its own 'ruinierte Wahrheit' in the 'Metapher eines technischen Mediums'.[63] This is not a negative development, however. For Schneider, the burden of truth borne by classical autobiography is in any case a dubious one, as concerned with prescribing normative codes of behaviour as with the revelation of personal truths. Freed by its loss of function from the 'symbolische Territorium der Wahrheit', the autobiographical text is able by contrast to dramatise a self-reflexive and liberating play of 'Schaltungen'.[64]

It is doubtful how legitimately Schneider can make such universal claims for twentieth-century autobiography using so few examples. Yet the main points of his thesis (regarding autobiography's loss of function vis-à-vis the technical media, a metaphorical displacement within the genre, and a conception of recent autobiography as a play of 'Schaltungen') are very pertinent to Brinkmann's *Erkundungen*.

Like Brinkmann's collage of photographs of his home in 'Wie ich lebe und warum (1970)'[65] the *Erkundungen* acknowledge the pre-eminence of the technical media in recording and storing information about the subject. The *Erkundungen* contain a number of photographic self-portraits, mostly taken with the camera held at arm's length (*E*, 20, 21, 68, 86, 97, 135, 152), that fix the features of Brinkmann's physiognomy more accurately than any passage of self-description could. Yet their accuracy also deprives Brinkmann, as autobiographer, of a crucial moment of self-recognition or self-reflection (perhaps this is why he describes the process of autobiographical writing as groping his way along 'einen undeutlichen, zum Teil zerbrochenen Spiegel meiner Selbst'; *E*, 360); and their serial, 'mug shot' quality denies him the interiority which such a moment might afford. Brinkmann's inscrutable face becomes a signifier to which the text is unable to provide a signified.

The *Erkundungen* also corroborate Schneider's assertion of a metaphorical displacement within the genre. Their privileged metaphors of self-cognition are precisely those furnished by the technical media. The *Erkundungen* apprehend the workings of autobiographical memory in cinematographic metaphors such as 'Flashback: (Erinnerung)' or the image of a reel of film – 'Ich mußte die Zeit um eine Woche zurückdrehen, bis ich das genaue Bild fand rasiermesserscharf' (*E*, 221, 151); and in metaphors deriving from photography, like the 'langen Kette aus einzelnen Blitzlichtfotos, die in mir

---

63   Manfred Schneider, *Die erkaltete Herzensschrift*, p. 28, 15 and 247.
64   Manfred Schneider, *Die erkaltete Herzensschrift*, pp. 13 and 43.
65   In *Trivialmythen*, ed. by Renate Matthaei (Frankfurt am Main, 1970), pp. 67-73.

aufflammen' (*E*, 145); and from the technology of sound-recording, such as the 'Magnetfelder des Ichs', or the 'Wort- und Gedankenschleifen, die bei mir im Kopf ablaufen' (*E*, 20, 345).

These technical metaphors make a nonsense of Brinkmann's endeavours to disengage a self from the control of the media, or to institute a pristine autobiographical language. The subject is imbricated with the technical media not only with respect to the content of experiences or memories – such as popular music on the radio: Harry Belafonte's 'Banana-Song', 'Cliff Richard im WDR', 'Charles Mingus-Musik' (*E*, 176, 250, 227). More than this, the processes of self-cognition and autobiographical memory are themselves dependent on the technical media for their very structure and form. In short, the subject is constructed, as Schneider suggests, within the framework of a given historical constellation of media technologies. Brinkmann's plan for his second novel may aspire toward the attainment of a 'selbstbewußte Ich', but the constellation of media technologies that provides the framework for his attempts to write proves inimical to this goal. Caught between the reproduction of the image in the media of film and television, the reproduction of sound by gramophone, tape recorder and radio, and the mechanical reproduction of script by the typewriter (a medium in the McLuhanite sense) the authority of the subject is expunged, its interiority eradicated.

In a 'Kaleidoskop der Geschichte des Sehens' of 1984, Christoph Wulf has identified sight as the dominant sense of modernity. Citing Goethe's 'anschauende[s] Denken' and Foucault's analysis of the 'kontrollierende Blick' of the eighteenth century, Wulf argues that the gaze has occupied a privileged place in the discourses of human knowledge.[66] In Brinkmann's *Erkundungen*, the human eye is assimilated, via a McLuhanite discourse of the technological transformation of human cognition, to the operation of the camera. The imperious gaze through which the subject of modernity confronts, controls and appropriates the world is dissolved into the technical manipulation of the play of light on a receptive surface:

> Das Auge. Film und Licht ermöglicht Ihnen, diese Realitäten umzupacken und in eine Form zu bringen, die leicht zu behandeln ist und leicht zu gebrauchen [...] Licht und Film arbeiten präzise zusammen über jede Begrenzung von physischer Manipulation hinaus.
>
> (*E*, 13)

In short, the autobiographical 'I' is displaced in the *Erkundungen* by a cinematographic 'eye' that transforms the text into a kind of 'Drehbuch'

---

66 Christoph Wulf, 'Das gefährdete Auge. Ein Kaleidoskop der Geschichte des Sehens', in *Das Schwinden der Sinne*, ed. by Dietmar Kamper and Christoph Wulf (Frankfurt am Main, 1984), pp. 21-45 (pp. 25 and 27).

operating 'exakt nach Filmtechniken [...], mit Rückblende, Überblendung, Szeneneinfärbung, Schnitte, Gegenschnitte, Ton gemischt, ausgefilterten Geräuschen, Gesamtszenen und Details, Schwenks, Rundschwenks usw.' (*E*, 13, 261).

Further, the reproduction of sound by the radio, tape recorder and gramophone plays a part in the transformation of the subject by the media. The coding of sound as electromagnetic signals severs the production of the voice from the human body, destroying the bond forged in Western thought between identity and the voice.[67] In the *Erkundungen*, the Brinkmann's inner voice – the token of his self-presence as subject – has been destroyed. He writes: 'Ich hörte in mich rein. Ein paar differenzierte gluckernde Geräusche waren nicht die Botschaft' (*E*, 144). Rather, the reproducibility of the human voice casts Brinkmann into a polyphony of 'gespentische Stimmen' (*E*, 143) that he seems to tune in to as if at random: '"Das ist hier ein Millionenspiel, verspielen Sie nicht die Millionen!"'; '"Sie sind hier im Dienst, junger Mann, da wird nicht geträumt."'; '"Du, Heidi, ich glaub, der Spinat steht da an einer zu feuchten Stelle, was meinst Du?"' (*E*, 28, 30, 40). It is unclear who speaks here; these voices inhabit a no-man's-land neither inside nor outside the subject.

Finally, the rhythmic, mechanical operation of the typewriter undoes the unity of subject und script that Schneider identifies in the characters of the written word. The typewriter at which Brinkmann works generates an unrelenting 'Tipp-Rhythmus' (*E*, 268) whose repetitive action – exemplified in the slashes that puncture the flow of the text – destroys the rhetorical patina of an individual style. The result is a telegraphic, staccato type in which the first person singular pronoun 'ich' is mostly omitted:

> /Winter 1970: lebe allein, trinke, wandere nachts lange allein rum, gehe in Kneipen/sehe: Die Verrottung/kann nicht mehr nach oben/kriege die Panik [...] /halte eine Lesung in Duisburg (Anfang 1971)/schreibe Hörspiel, brauche Geld, verkaufe Bücher, gehe schwimmen, esse Weizengehl, magere ab, /lese Burroughs.
>
> (*E*, 267)

According to Friedrich Kittler, the standardised keyboard of the typewriter illustrates a truth about the production of all meaning (in any medium): namely, that meaning arises from the selection of differential marks from a reservoir that allows limitless (even if nonsensical) combination.[68] Brinkmann's frequent typing errors evidence just how precarious this process

---

67 Michael Wimmer, 'Verstimmte Ohren und unerhörte Stimmen', in *Das Schwinden der Sinne*, ed. by Dietmar Kamper and Christoph Wulf (Frankfurt am Main, 1984), pp. 115-39 (pp. 122-24)

68 Kittler, *Aufschreibesysteme. 1800/1900* (Munich, 1985), pp. 200-02.

is. Occasionally, his attempts to wrest meaning from his typewriter break down altogether. The technical construction of the medium takes over, producing a typographical jumble that contradicts Brinkmann's belief that he could control the production of meaning, let alone constitute its source:

> /:::(bin wie der vor der Schreibmaschine)///::::/Unterbrechung, nicht?!/:::::////:away & beyond X?!/:wer und was istX?/:eine verwischte Hand, die in jeden reinlangt un die Bilder mixt???//:::(ein Wort?)/:in einem bestimmten Schnittpunkt?)//::: ("and I get drunk")/
>
> (*E*, 197)

To suggest, as Adam does in respect of *Rom, Blicke*, that the *Erkundungen* enact the reduction of their author to the status of an 'Arrangeur von Materialien' is inadequate. We have examined some of the metaphorical displacements, to use Schneider's term, effected within the *Erkundungen* by the media of film, the radio and the typewriter. These all converge in the text within a single grounding metaphor: that of the autobiographer transformed into a machine. This metaphor is underwritten by a mechanistic and cybernetic concept of the brain, with its synapses and motor functions, that Brinkmann derives from his reading of neurological texts by W. Grey Walter, and Rudolf Bilz (*E*, 263, 252). (Brinkmann's interest in neurology arose, Späth claims, from a need to understand the condition of his brain-damaged son Robert.)[69]

In *Understanding Media*, McLuhan observes that in 'this electric age we see ourselves being translated more and more into the form of information, moving toward the technological extension of consciousness'.[70] The *Erkundungen* offer a striking extension of this observation: with the figuration of the autobiographer as a machine, the autobiographical act becomes a form of information processing. This notion of information processing arguably underwrites the powerful documentary impulse of the *Erkundungen* that we highlighted earlier in our discussion. The typed protocols of Brinkmann's activities that make up much of the third part of the *Erkundungen* represent nothing less than the transcription and recording of human experience as discrete units of data: 'Montag, 1. November 1971: fahle, bleigraue Helligkeit, 1/4 vor 1 mittags durch M. geweckt wegen Kino-Gang/gekochtes Ei, 1 Scheibe mit Wurstaufschnitt, 2 Tassen Kaffee, 1 Zigarette (von M. ans Bett gebracht)' and so forth (*E*, 189). By analogy, autobiographical memory is recast as the retrieval of information. Take Brinkmann's recollections of childhood in Vechta:

> Erinnerung: Doofe Dirk, Eiserne Birbaum, Amtmannspult, Galgenberg, Kapunier, Poggenburg, Klingenhagen, [...] Ostendorf, Oythe, Tante Lissi,

---

69   Späth, 'Gehirnströme und Medientext', p. 111.
70   McLuhan, p. 57.

Lohne, Langförden, [...] Gymnaium Antonianum, Rhetorika, Ezra Pound, Gottfried Benn, Sartre, Beat, Hillbillie Musik, AFN, BFN, die roten Lichter zu Allerseelen.

(E, 233)

The assimilation of autobiography to information processing does not stop at the transcription, storage and retrieval of data. Forced by a monthly budget of 500 DM (E, 253) to monitor his expenses closely, Brinkmann's records of his expenditure assume a properly computational aspect. 'Wie ne Rechenmaschine' (E, 253), he types:

> 5 Uhr in die Stadt, Illustrierte gekauft (Stern und Penthouse/9.80), im Schnellimbiß Pommes frites u. 1 Mettwurst, [...] 1 Heft gekauft 15.85 + Postkarte Köln 60Pfg. + 11 Stuyvesant/1 DM/weiter in eine anderes Geschäft:Kladden 20.85/Buchhandlung Gonski 2 Hörspielbücher 16. -DM/in Café:1 Kaffee + Weinbrand=5DM/

(E, 187)

Brinkmann's redaction of autobiography as information processing takes Neumann's hypothesis about the obsolescence of the genre to an extreme conclusion. Roy Pascal has written that autobiography is defined as a genre by the organic imprint of a subjectivity that transcends all questions of facticity.[71] By contrast, the Erkundungen dissolve human subjectivity into the cataloguing of facts. From this perspective, even the momentary perceptions (such as the evocation of Cologne in the autumn discussed above) that we characterised as Brinkmann's most subjective experiences appear as little more than the transcription of sensory data. Here, experience no longer means that which is given shape, or sense, by the autobiographer in the retrospective gaze of the autobiographical act; rather, it designates the discrete and serial impressions imprinted upon the subject by its random encounters with the object world, as if it were a kind of 'Nerven-Orgel' (E, 54).

Yet precisely where the metaphor of the machine most insistently converts the subject into information, it possesses also a productive aspect that yields new ways of writing about the self. This must be understood in the context of a deep ambivalence toward autobiography that runs through the Erkundungen. It is correct that, especially in the parts of the text devoted to Brinkmann's stay at Longkamp, autobiography is conceived as a flight from the forces of the mass media arrayed against the subject; and that the autobiographical novel remains a utopian horizon even when it cannot be written. But like ACID's onslaught on the 'Abrichtungscharakter' embodied within established literary forms, the Erkundungen exhibit a deep suspicion towards conventional forms of autobiographical discourse. For Brinkmann, the linear narrative identity of

---

71   Pascal, p. 1.

conventional autobiographical forms amounts to little more than a discursive straitjacket that condemns the subject to accept an identity in which the past weighs intolerably on the present: 'Die verdammte Vergangenheit, dieses Zufällige und das Festgesetztwerden durch diese zufällige Vergangenheit als Identität' (*E*, 307).[72] Surrendering the autobiographical act to the metaphors provided by the technical media comes into its own here. The assimilation of the autobiographer to a machine activates, as Brinkmann puts it, a series of 'Schaltkreise' (*E*, 265) through which autobiographical material is accessed and arranged according to different principles and in limitless combinations. A 'Kurze Montage von Eindrücken und Gedanken, die mir im Lauf der Woche passiert sind', for example, organises material according to the temporal proximity of its occurrence (*E*, 170-71). By contrast, a 'Rasche Erinnerungsmontage an Weihnachten' arranges memories in a more 'thematic' or associative manner (*E*, 339). Mostly, however, memories and facts are subject to arrangements which appear randomly generated (for example: *E*, 257).

In short, the machine's capacity for generating infinite combinations provides the basis for a concept of self invention that, for Brinkmann, explodes the strictures of the autobiographical act. Or, to put it another way: the grounding metaphor of the machine quite literally produces the subject as a fiction. Where in *Die Reise*, Vesper cannot commit himself wholesale to such a notion, Brinkmann's *Erkundungen* elaborate a concept of autobiography as a form of self-invention that is able to undo the hold that his past exerts over him: 'Ich mußte lernen die Vergangenheit endgültig hinter mich zu lassen./ Ich lernte das, indem ich sie zuerst einmal als geschehen sehen lernte. So konnte ich sie fiktiv nehmen.))' (*E*, 108). In the *Erkundungen*, Brinkmann perceives this concept of autobiographical self-invention as liberating precisely because it grasps the subject as continually remade in the act of writing. As Brinkmann puts it:

> Also: (der TRICK, und das ist doch nur die METHODE, VERSTEHEN SIE? mit der man das eigene konditionierte Bewußtsein überlistet, ist HIER NATÜRLICH das Zusammenstellen von gerade im Augenblick des Schreibens mir einfallenden ZUFÄLLIGEN REISEstrahlen, WENN Sie VERSTEHEN können, WAS Ich meine)[73]
>
> (*E*, 15)

Arguably, all autobiography constructs its subject in the writing process. But the *Erkundungen* go further: in analogy to the infinite permutations generated by the machine, the figuration of the autobiographer as a writing machine

---

72 Compare Späth, *Rolf Dieter Brinkmann*, p. 101.
73 This passage is read as the evocation of a drugs trip in Späth, *Rolf Dieter Brinkmann*, p. 98.

(literally, a 'Schreibmaschine') releases Brinkmann from a single narrative into a plurality of possible selves, each equally valid and equally contingent: 'Ich sind viele, und so gehe ich, eine Melodie, durch viele ichs' (*E*, 101). Here, Brinkmann's inability to produce a central character for his projected autobiographical novel is made productive for the *Erkundungen*. Nowhere does the ideal of a plurality of possible narratives, a simultaneity of selves without central focus, find a clearer embodiment than in the 'Romananfänge' running through the text:

> Forts.: ANFANG ROMAN: Noch einmal rufen und schreien die Jungen, draußen, und ich höre sie rufen und schreien, draußeb, vor dem Haus. Kommste mit? He, kommste mit?/: (szene 1949, Kuhmarkt)/
>
> (*E*, 233)

> Roman!: ich bin der Gastwirtschaft Zum Stern, in Longkamp und esse ein Brot mit HausmacherBlutwurst und Leberwurst.
>
> (*E*, 288)

These 'Romananfänge' transpose into autobiographical terms an insight that Brinkmann gains from an unspecified 'englischen Unterhaltungsroman': 'Eine Geschichte hat keinen Anfang und kein Ende. Man wählt [...] aus der Kette der Erlebnisse ganz willkürlich jenen Augenblick aus, von dem man entweder [...] rückwärts oder vorwärts zu schauen gedenkt' (*E*, 171). The *Erkundungen*'s conception of the self as a fictional construct that could 'begin' with any point forces us to address once more the relationship between the *Erkundungen* themselves and the projected novel. We argued previously that Brinkmann's project for his autobiographical novel constitutes a utopian horizon within the text. Equally, this planned novel figures as a template against which the *Erkundungen* deploy the metaphors provided by the technical media to deconstruct the autobiographical subject. Autobiography is dissolved into an elaborate textual mechanism for exfoliating discourses about the self.

But is it ultimately possible to view the contradictory constructions of the relationship between the mass media, subjectivity and autobiography in the text as part of a single cohesive textual strategy? Pitting a Marcusean critique of the mass media against a McLuhanite exploration of their technical and aesthetic possibilities, Brinkmann's *Erkundungen* undeniably pivot on a contradictory conception of the relationship between the media and the autobiographical act. To the extent that they are informed by a Marcusean pessimism regarding the destructive impact of the mass media on the human subject, they fix the autobiographical act as a site of resistance against a pervasive 'Bewußtseinsindustrie'. Yet faced with the monolithic force that Brinkmann ascribes to this 'Bewußtseinsindustrie', the endeavour to preserve the integrity of the autobiographical act appears precarious, to the point that it can embody only a utopian horizon within the text. At the same time, the *Erkundungen* take up a McLuhanite discourse of the transformation of human experience through the media, using metaphors taken from the media to provide the basis for a radical concept of self-invention. Grounded in the metaphor of the machine, this concept proceeds in analogy to the processing of information, and without a sovereign consciousness to guide it. Both the 'Marcusean' and 'McLuhanite' discourses within the *Erkundungen* share a historical grounding in the discourses of anti-authoritarianism. Moreover, they are certainly linked in the text by the perception that the mass media's power over the human subject ultimately marks the end of an autonomous autobiographical subjectivity conceived, say, in the sense of Neumann's 'Identität'. An ambiguous literary document, however, Brinkmann's *Erkundungen* both contest and embrace this loss of autonomous selfhood at the hands of the media and their technologies. In the final analysis, this makes it hard to see the Marcusean and McLuhanite discourses about the mass media and the autobiographical act within them as part of a single cohesive textual strategy. Rather they are set awkwardly side by side, as if to testify to the rift that opened up after 1968 between the political currents of anti-authoritarianism and its cultural and subcultural streams – the very rift that had shattered Brinkmann's own cultural-revolutionary aspirations.

CHAPTER 4

Life History, History and Autobiography:
Karin Struck's *Klassenliebe*, Inga Buhmann's *Ich habe mir eine Geschichte geschrieben* and Verena Stefan's *Häutungen*

I   Gender and Genre: Theoretical Considerations

Contrasted with the treatment of historical context and autobiographical discourse in *Die Reise* and the *Erkundungen*, the relationship of recent women's autobiographies to the women's movement and to the problem of autobiography appears well documented. Karin Struck's *Klassenliebe* has come to occupy a central place within critical narratives about the rise of women's autobiography (as well as New Subjectivity) during the 1970s.[1] Verena Stefan's *Häutungen* is universally considered the central autobiographical text of the New Women's Movement.[2] Indeed, of the texts treated here, it is only Inga Buhmann's *Ich habe mir eine Geschichte geschrieben* that has received comparatively little critical scrutiny.[3] Our point of departure here is the disparity between the practice of women's autobiography and the elaboration of critical discourses about women's writing noted by Evelyne Keitel's 'Frauen, Texte, Theorie' in 1983.[4] Recent critical studies of women's writing in the Federal Republic have acknowledged a specific historical relationship between autobiographical writing and the New Women's Movement. Yet the poststructuralist feminist aesthetic informing, for example, Richter-Schröder's *Frauenliteratur und weibliche Identität* of 1986 and Renate Becker's *Inszenierungen des Weiblichen* of 1992 all but dissipates the historicity of texts like *Häutungen* or *Ich habe mir eine Geschichte geschrieben*. Contrasting Struck's *Klassenliebe* with Buhmann's and Stefan's autobiographies, our aim here is to offer an analysis of autobiographical texts by women that is sensitive to the context and the manner in which they take up the genre of autobiography. In order to provide a framework within which we can grasp the relationship between history and autobiography in our texts, a brief

---

1   Karin Struck, *Klassenliebe. Roman* (Frankfurt am Main, 1973). Subsequent references are provided in the main body of the text using the abbreviation *K*.

2   Verena Stefan, *Häutungen. Autobiografische Aufzeichnungen Gedichte Träume Analysen* (Munich, 1975). Subsequent references are provided in the main body of the text using the abbreviation *H*.

3   Inga Buhmann, *Ich habe mir eine Geschichte geschrieben* (Munich, 1977). Subsequent references are provided in the main body of the text using the abbreviation *G*.

4   Keitel, 'Frauen, Texte, Theorie', p. 830.

discussion of the history and theory of women's autobiography is a necessary preliminary in this first part of the chapter. The second part of the chapter then examines the relationship between history, life history and form in Struck's *Klassenliebe* and Buhmann's *Ich habe mir eine Geschichte geschrieben*. In contrast with the diary form of *Klassenliebe*, it argues, the synthetic and teleological narrative of Buhmann's autobiography provides a medium in which female subjectivity and historical discourse are brought into a dialogue through the collective agency of the New Women's Movement. The third and final part of the chapter focuses on Stefan's *Häutungen*. Taking on critiques of the text's essentialism in the light of recent debates about the 'identity politics' of oppositional movements, it argues that *Häutungen* provided the women's movement with a potent symbolic fiction in which a feminist politics is strikingly linked to a concept of autobiographical self-invention.

If theorists of women's autobiography are broadly agreed on a central point, it is that both classical autobiography and the generic definitions based upon it are predicated upon the exclusion of women. According to Marianne Vogt's 1981 *Autobiographik bürgerlicher Frauen*, autobiography developed from the eighteenth century on through the models provided by '"Selbstbiographien berühmter Männer"'; confined within bourgeois society to the domestic sphere women were barred from the 'Teilnahme am öffentlichen Diskurs' in which the genre was grounded.[5] The social status of women, as Kay Goodman puts it in 'Weibliche Autobiographien' (1985), was simply at odds with the key values of universality and representativeness as the generic paradigms of autobiography were established:

> [Die] geschichtliche und gesellschaftliche Rolle [der Frau] beschränkt sich meistens auf das Gebiet der Liebe und Familie – besonders um 1800. Dieser 'privaten' Rolle geht andererseits in aller Regel das 'öffentliche' Interesse ab. Es ist kein hinreichender Stoff für Autobiographien. Wie sollen Frauen, die sich nicht öffentlich zeigen dürfen, ihr Leben öffentlich erzählen?[6]

For women literate enough to write about themselves, their exclusion from autobiographical discourse had fundamental thematic and formal consequences. In her introduction to *Women's Autobiography: Essays in Criticism* (1980), Estelle C. Jelinek has argued that where male autobiographers sought public significance in their lives, the subject matter available to women was the domestic detail of their personal lives. In contrast

---

5   Marianne Vogt, *Autobiographik bürgerlicher Frauen*, pp. 15 and 25.
6   Kay Goodman, 'Weibliche Autobiographien', in *Frauen Literatur Geschichte. Schreibende Frauen vom Mittelalter bis zur Gegenwart*, ed. by Hiltrud Gnüg and Renate Möhrmann (Stuttgart, 1985), pp. 289-99 (p. 291).

with the coherent shape which a sense of public achievement could lend the autobiographies of men, Jelinek suggests, the episodic, serial and ultimately private forms of 'diaries, journals and notebooks' provided women with better vehicles for the repetitive and monotonous character of their experience than 'autobiograph[y] proper'.[7]

Theorists of women's autobiography have sought to rethink the premises of the genre from a perspective that takes into account the forms of self-expression historically available to women. With regard to the adoption of the synthetic and teleological forms of 'autobiography proper', however, they are divided. For Jutta Kolkenbrock-Netz and Marianne Schuller in 'Frau im Spiegel. Zum Verhältnis von autobiographischer Schreibweise und feministischer Praxis' (1982), for example, the genre's role in legitimating as universal a male concept of self militates against the appropriation of established autobiographical forms in order to articulate the personal and political concerns of women.[8] By contrast, Laura Marcus's *Auto/biographical discourses* of 1994 has claimed that notwithstanding the exclusive character of theorists' 'focus on the auto/biographies of historically significant individuals', autobiography always also upholds an inclusive emphasis 'on historicity as a medium shared by all'; a 'mode of understanding' that historicity, it is a discourse to which potentially 'every individual has access'.[9]

It is this emphasis on autobiography as a mode of understanding the medium of historicity that informs this discussion. For against the claim that autobiography is unsuited to articulating the political concerns of women, recent critical histories offer a suggestive account of the connection between women's relation to the genre on the one hand, and the social and historical choices open to them on the other.

Goodman suggests that at the time of the genre's emergence autobiography proper never excluded women in theory, though it clearly did so in practice.[10] If, as Cynthia S. Pomerlau notes in 'The Emergence of Women's Autobiography in England' (1980), autobiographical narratives are shaped and 'defined by the choices one makes' (or is able to make), then the synthetic and teleological narratives of autobiography proper surely become increasingly important for the self-definition of women with the hard fought increase in the

7   Estelle C. Jelinek, 'Introduction: Women's Autobiography and the Male Tradition', in *Women's Autobiography: Essays in Criticism*, ed. by Estelle C. Jelinek (Bloomington and London, 1980), pp. 1-20 (p. 19).
8   Jutta Kolkenbrock-Netz and Marianne Schuller, 'Frau im Spiegel. Zum Verhältnis von autobiographischer Schreibweise und feministischer Praxis', in *Entwürfe von Frauen in der Literatur des zwanzigsten Jahrhunderts*, ed. by Irmela von der Lühe (Berlin, 1982), pp. 154-74 (p. 155).
9   Marcus, pp. 135-36.
10 Goodman, 'Elisabeth to Meta', p. 310.

social and historical opportunities available to them.[11] This view is corroborated with respect to German autobiography by Goodman, who notes toward the end the nineteenth century a striking increase in the autobiographical productivity of women. As they entered the arenas of political discourse, moreover, Goodman argues that autobiography furnished individuals like the women's campaigner Helene Lange and the socialist Lily Braun with an ideal medium at the start of our own century with which to justify their public engagement.[12]

This dialectic of autobiography and historical choice provides a framework in which we can place Buhmann's and Stefan's autobiographies. The sociologist Anthony Giddens has suggested that the second wave feminist movements of the Western world embraced a 'life politics' or a 'politics *of* choice' intent upon mobilising and expanding the range of opportunities for self-actualisation collectively and individually available to women.[13] If this is so, then within the New Women's Movement, autobiography – conceived as Marcus's 'mode of understanding' – surely provided a crucial means of reflecting on such opportunities and on women's individual and collective relation to them. Let us pursue this point by turning to the texts by Struck and Buhmann.

II   From the Diary to Autobiographical Narration: *Klassenliebe* and *Ich habe mir eine Geschichte geschrieben*

Although it only appeared in February 1973, Karin Struck's *Klassenliebe* had sold 54,000 copies by the end of that year. A literary sensation, Struck's first work proved as controversial as it was popular. The controversy surrounding the text centred on its treatment not only of class relations, but also of sexual liaisons within the *Werkkreis Literatur der Arbeitswelt*. (This was an organisation of writers and workers, founded in 1968 and committed to producing a working-class literature, with which both Struck and *Klassenliebe*'s narrator, Karin, were marginally involved.)

The fascination of *Klassenliebe*'s treatment of class relations lay in the personal inflection that the text gave them. Critics focused on Karin's – the narrator's – 'Lage zwischen den Klassen' (*KL*, 51): alienated from her proletarian origins by her education, and yet uncomfortable amongst the

---

11 Cynthia S. Pomerlau, 'The Emergence of Women's Autobiography in England', in *Women's Autobiography: Essays in Criticism*, ed. by Estelle C. Jelinek (Bloomington and London, 1980), pp. 21-38 (p. 25).

12 Goodman, 'Weibliche Autobiographien', p. 297.

13 Anthony Giddens, *Modernity and Self-Identity: Self and Society in the Late Modern Age* (Cambridge, 1991), p. 214.

bourgeois intelligentsia on the one hand; and torn on the other between her proletarian husband H., a medical student and activist of the *Deutsche Kommunistische Partei* (DKP), and her lover Z., a bourgeois writer and radio editor. Franz Schonauer, in the *Deutsche Zeitung* (13 July 1973), considered it Struck's accomplishment '[daß sie den Klassen-] Konflikt nicht abstrakt reflektiert, sondern ihn als persönlichen Fall – darf man sagen als individuelles ["]Schicksal" – anschaulich macht'.[14] For other reviewers, however, the text's foregrounding of Karin's relationships with H. and Z. undermined the pertinence of its class observations. In *konkret* (May 1973), Rolv Heuer charged Struck with offering less a consideration of class issues than a 'Kolportageroman über Liebes- und Eheaffären unter Intellektuellen, die viel über Arbeiter reden'.[15] It was the critics' own preoccupation with these 'Liebes- und Eheaffären', however, that helped to surround the text with scandal.

Consistently questioning the genre designation of 'Roman' on *Klassenliebe*'s cover, critics submitted the text to an autobiographical reading that asserted the identity of its narrator and author. Their focus the affair of Karin and Z., moreover, they often approached the text as a roman-à-clef about sexual intrigues within the *Werkkreis Literatur der Arbeitswelt*. Many early reviewers speculated as to Z.'s identity.[16] But the scale of the conjecture surrounding the text is most forcefully illustrated by the fact that the writer Gerhard Zwerenz, widely presumed to be Z., felt obliged to deny ever meeting Karin Struck.[17] (In fact, Z. was the poet Arnfried Astel.)[18] At any rate, such widespread speculation certainly suggests that the person of Karin Struck, rather than the text's literary merits, dominated *Klassenliebe*'s reception.

A topic that has become increasingly important to the critical discussion of *Klassenliebe* is the text's treatment of gender and its relationship to the feminist politics of the 1970s. In 1973, only Alice Schwarzer took note of the issue of femininity in the text. In the satirical *pardon* (July 1973), she accused male reviewers of ignoring the problem of '[das] Frausein' in *Klassenliebe*. Beneath 'Karins eigenem Klassenraster', she argued, 'zeichnen sich von Seite zu Seite immer aufdringlicher die Konturen ihrer Betroffenheit als

14 Franz Schonauer, 'Schwierigkeiten beim Aufsteigen', *Deutsche Zeitung*, 13 July 1973, p. 12.
15 Rolv Heuer, 'Bon Jour, Proletariat', *konkret*, May 1973, pp. 44-45 (p. 45).
16 For example, Karl Krolow, 'Karin diskutiert sich ins Leben. Karin Strucks "Klassenliebe"', *Die Tat*, 19 May 1973, p. 25.
17 See 'Z. – oder die schrecklichen Folgen der Legende, Karin Strucks Liebhaber gewesen zu sein' in Gerhard Zwerenz, *Die schrecklichen Folgen der Legende, ein Liebhaber gewesen zu sein. Erotische Geschichten* (Munich, 1978), pp. 134-59 (p. 154).
18 Heinrich Peukermann, 'Der Weg vom Werkkreis in den Mediendschungel. Karin Struck – oder wie junge Autoren vermarktet werden', *Die Tat*, 22 July 1983, p. 9.

Zugehörige zum weiblichen Geschlecht ab'.[19] The text's relationship to the feminist politics of the 1970s has loomed ever larger, above all in scholarly accounts of the text. By and large, though, scholars have been circumspect in their assessment of *Klassenliebe*'s feminist credentials.[20] Struck's relationship to the New Women's Movement was to become progressively more controversial during the 1970s; but with much of that controversy surrounding her treatment of motherhood in the novel *Die Mutter* (1975) it is largely beyond our scope here. *Klassenliebe* itself has, however, come to occupy (in addition to its signal value for the rise of New Subjectivity) a crucial position in critical narratives about the women's writing of the 1970s. For Becker and Weigel, for example, the text, though ambivalent in its relation to a feminist politics, nonetheless marks a crucial step in the evolution of a first person feminist literature of 'Selbstfindung' that came to fruition in Stefan's *Häutungen*.[21] However if, as Becker and Weigel suggest, such a literature only came to fruition in this latter text, what renders the process of 'Selbstfindung' represented within *Klassenliebe* unsatisfactory? The text's diary form holds the key.

Speculating as to the identity of Karin's lover, Z., critics have proved adept at reading *Klassenliebe* autobiographically. However, where the issue of autobiographical writing is concerned, little attention has been paid to the diary form in which the text is written. Clearly, a satisfactory critical account of the text must consider how the narrator's subjectivity is constructed both in relation to class and gender, and in the form of diary. Let us begin our discussion of *Klassenliebe* by turning to a fundamental tension articulated within Karin's diary: a tension between a subjectivity that is perceived as deficient or fragmented on the one hand, and a desire for self-actualisation on the other.

In *Klassenliebe*, Karin's diary revolves around her perception that she lacks a coherent sense of identity – '*Ich* hatte nie ein Ich', she writes (*KL*, 180). This sense of lack is rooted in her doubly marginal position within the discourses of subjectivity: marginal first, on account of her class origins; and second, on account of her gender.

Related to her working-class origins is a crippling sense of speechlessness which Karin first experiences in the face of more privileged schoolmates.

19   Alice Schwarzer, 'Die mit dem Penis schreiben. Was die Männer der Literaturkritik an Karin Strucks "Klassenliebe" so erregt hat', *pardon*, July 1973, pp. 18-19 (p. 18).
20   See for example Leslie Adelson, 'The Question of a Feminist Aesthetic and Karin Struck's *Klassenliebe*', in *Beyond the Eternal Feminine: Critical Essays on Women and German Literature*, ed. by Susan L. Cocalis and Kay Goodman (Stuttgart, 1982), pp. 335-49.
21   Renate Becker, *Inszenierungen des Weiblichen*, pp. 74-77 (p. 74); Weigel, *Die Stimme der Medusa*, pp. 55-56.

Recalling her childhood, she writes: 'drinnen im Klassenzimmer wurde über mich Gericht gehalten, und ich weinte nur, ich konnte nichts anderes als weinen, ich konnte nicht reden, ich hatte keine Sprache, ich konnte mich nicht verteidigen' (*KL*, 105). Significantly, Karin's university education, which alienates her from her class origins but cannot simply erase them or integrate her into the bourgeoisie, exacerbates her speechlessness, trapping her, as noted above, 'zwischen den Klassen' (*KL*, 51):

> Welche Sprache kann ich sprechen? Ich spreche eine Niemandssprache in einem Niemandsland. In einem Zwischenreich. Weder Bayrisch noch Pommersch noch Westfälisch noch Platt noch Bürgerlich noch Proletarisch.
>
> (*KL*, 82)

Although *Klassenliebe* foregrounds Karin's position with respect to class, her gender too plays a crucial role in debarring her from the self-actualisation she craves. For her gender serves to bind Karin into relationships in which her subjectivity is always mediated to her by the men around her. Her husband's horrified reaction, for example, to her nakedness during a sauna reveals the extent to which, not least in her most intimate relationships, Karin is always already defined as the object or the potential object of male desire: '"ich habe dich gesehen, man konnte dich sehen", sagt H. zu mir [...]. Traurig war H., daß ein anderer Mann einen Zipfel meines nackten Körpers sehen konnte' (*KL*, 14). If it is rooted objectively in the discourses of class and gender, Karin's impoverished sense of identity finds powerful subjective expression in images of bodily fragmentation or mutilation – like her vision of lying 'auf einer Autobahn verstümmelt' (*KL*, 9; also 11).

Against this fragmented subjectivity, *Klassenliebe* projects the goal of self-actualisation. This goal is formulated right at the start of the text using, in altered form, a quotation from the text of the *Internationale*:[22] 'Ein Nichts zu sein, ertragts nicht länger, ein Ich zu werden, strömt zuhauf' (*KL*, 11). Here, Struck binds the anthem's commitment to class politics into the call for a politics that comes to rest with the needs of the human subject. Accordingly, *Klassenliebe* points to two converging strategies designed to promote the desired goal of self-actualisation. The first, social change, is located within the realm of politics; the second, the writing of a diary as an act of self-authorship, is perceived initially as the vehicle of a more subjective form of change.

Klassenliebe's politics recognisably draw on the discourses of the left (mixing an orthodox class politics with anti-authoritarian positions) and of the incipient New Women's Movement. Marcuse's critique of the 'functionalization of language' in *One-Dimensional Man*, for example, visibly

---

22   Renate Becker, *Inszenierungen des Weiblichen*, p. 74.

informs Karin's perception that the language of advertising serves the purpose of social control by assimilating concepts to the technological norms of the consumer society.[23] Remarking on the advertisement 'Ariel: für wirklich reine Wäsche', Karin observes how the attribute of 'Reinheit' is transformed into another concept, 'chemisch rein[...]', and thus robbed of its capacity to transcend the established universe of discourse (*KL*, 36). Yet *Klassenliebe* also outstrips Marcuse's position to expose how language encodes the norms of a male-dominated society: 'Ehebruch? Seiten-Sprung? Wörter aus einer anderen Welt. Gangsterwelt. Nicht meine' (*KL*, 14). In pointing to the male bias of the language of sexual relations here, *Klassenliebe* anticipates *Häutungen*'s more explicitly feminist critique of the imbrication of language and sexual domination.

Klassenliebe draws on the discourses of both the left and feminism, but it is most incisive where it brings them to bear on one another. Charging the left with a gender-blindness that recognises oppression only if it is organised around the industrial means of production, Karin adopts a feminist stance: 'Daß Kinder und Haushalt eine Arbeit ist, noch dazu, das begreifen [die Linken] nicht. Unbezahlte Arbeit' (*KL*, 104). Conversely, *Klassenliebe*'s narrator rejects on the grounds that it derives 'lediglich aus sozialen Privilegien bürgerlicher Bildung und Herkunft' (*KL*, 164) the radical feminist claim that oppression is gender- rather than class-based. Rather, *Klassenliebe* cuts through the ideological constraints of both the left and the New Women's Movement to advocate a revolution abolishing 'alle Verhältnisse [...], in denen der Mensch ein erniedrigtes Wesen ist: *alle*, da gibt es keine Prioritäten, nichts wird aufgeschoben' (*KL*, 23). Karin's desire for the abolition of injustice thus actively embraces the private sphere: to dismiss questions concerning human needs as '"unpolitisch"', she suggests, 'ist nur ein Schreckwort' (*KL*, 23).

If Karin's vision of social transformation embraces human beings' subjective needs, conversely her diary, perceived initially as the vehicle of a personal self-assertion, widens out to reveal aspirations of a very public character. Against her marginality within the discourses of class and gender, the diary for Karin holds out the promise of a kind of self-authorship: 'Ich muß mein Leben klar und durchsichtig machen. Schreiben als Beschwörung meiner Selbst', she writes (*KL*, 209). On an immediate level, the diary strives for self-assertion through appealing to the self-presence of the voice, which appears to offer Karin a means of transcending her profound sense of speechlessness. Sometimes, for example, writing her diary takes on for Karin the incantatory power of a 'Rosenkranzgebet' (*KL*, 12, 160). Yet above the self-presence of the voice, *Klassenliebe*'s narrator seeks to counteract her sense of speechlessness through literary aspirations of a public nature.

23   Marcuse, *One-Dimensional Man*, pp. 85-86.

Karin's desire for self-assertion through writing emerges most forcefully in *Klassenliebe* where she articulates '[den] Wunsch, Schriftsteller zu werden' (*KL*, 45). This wish, paradoxically, is both deferred and fulfilled in the text. It is deferred where Karin's diary projects her intent into the future, asking 'Wo kann ich in die Lehre gehen, schreiben zu lernen?' (*KL*, 270); and it is fulfilled where the declaration of intent is published as literature – as *Klassenliebe* itself. The desire on Karin's part to become a writer is surely central to the text's ambivalent autobiographical status, in which autobiographical claims of a 'Schreiben bei völliger Öffnung des Leibes und der Seele' (*KL*, 53) are offset by a process of fictionalisation signalled by the title designation of 'Roman'. And it illuminates one of *Klassenliebe*'s most striking features: its allusiveness. Alluding to a range of authors from Schiller and Novalis (*K*, 42, 258) to contemporary writers like Christa Wolf and Thomas Bernhard (*K*, 223, 276), Karin's diary conducts an assimilation or 'EINVERLEIBUNG DER BÜCHER' (*K*, 228) through which she seeks to transform her utterances into literature, to become literature herself. Moreover, through the public, literary aspirations that it expresses, her diary's initially private self-assertion is bound into a broader conception of writing as social practice. It is as such that Karin defends the political value of writing and its promise of self-actualisation against the dogmatism of the left. 'Was gehen uns die Parolen der linken Bürgersöhnchen an, Literatur sei Scheiße?', she asks, 'Gar nichts. [...] Ohne Phantasie ist der Sozialismus nichts' (*KL*, 118).

It is clearly erroneous to claim, as Heinrich Peukermann does, that *Klassenliebe* lacks a 'klar erkennbaren gesellschaftlichen Bezug'.[24] Setting the politics of class against gender and pointing to the possibility self-actualisation through social transformation and self-authorship, the text engages, on the contrary, with a wealth of political and literary issues. Whether Karin's politics or her diary in fact afford her the self-actualisation that she craves is another matter, however. Already some of *Klassenliebe*'s early critics have charged the text with displacing political conflicts into private ones. Indeed, anti-theoretical tendencies within *Klassenliebe* demonstrably combine with the diary form to displace not only political conflicts, but also their resolution into the private sphere.

Klassenliebe's anti-theoretical tendencies, first, stem from a mistrust of the dogmatism of the left following the student movement's proletarian turn after 1968. For Karin, the student left's growing penchant for theoretical abstraction excises from political discourse the needs of the human subject. As she puts it:

---

24 Peukermann, p. 9.

> Fragen wir D., was er in den letzten Semestern 'politischer Arbeit' an
> wirklichem Erfolg gehabt hat, kann er nicht antworten. 'Aufklärungsarbeit',
> 'die Gesellschaft', 'der Kapitalismus', 'weiterkommen', 'aufbauen', lauter
> Wörter, mit denen ich nichts anzufangen weiß.
>
> (KL, 77)

If it charges the left with a political or theoretical dogmatism that ignores the subjective needs of human beings, *Klassenliebe* falls victim to a reverse tendency. It privileges subjective experience over politics. *Klassenliebe* certainly embraces a concept of social transformation that encompasses subjective experience. Ultimately, though, Karin's critique of the left's dogmatism reinforces the perception on her part of an irreducible tension between the normative and homogenising formulations of political discourse on the one hand, and the heterogeneity and singularity of experience on the other. That Karin values the latter over the former is apparent right at the start of the text in her account of a 'Gewerkschaftsschulung' which she helps to lead:

> Am ersten Tag der Wochenendschulung wollten wir mit den jungen Arbeitern
> über die Geschichte der Arbeiterbewegung diskutieren. Ein Student referierte.
> Danach saßen alle steif und starr und schwiegen. Nach dem Mittagessen gingen
> die Kollegen nach draußen einen Feldweg entlang (wir wohnten auf dem Land).
> An einer Wiese blieben alle stehen: zwei Bauern oder Arbeiter in blauen Kitteln
> waren dabei, zwei Bullen einzufangen. Dieses Schauspiel verfolgten alle mit
> großer Lust bestimmt eine halbe Stunde lang: die Bullen waren ziemlich wild.
>
> (KL, 7)

Here, the monotony of political discourse, which leaves the seminar's participants (or rather non-participants) 'steif und starr', is set unfavourably against the visual pleasure afforded by the scene with the bulls, which the spectators watch 'mit großer Lust'.

Karin's preoccupation in *Klassenliebe* with the singularity of experience finds a formal counterpart in the diary. In a study of the diary as a literary form, Peter Boerner outlines the salient differences between the autobiography and the diary:

> der Tagebuchschreiber [steht] stets unter dem unmittelbaren Eindruck dessen
> [...], was er erfahren, gesehen oder gedacht hat, [während] der Autobiograph
> dagegen die Fakten seines Lebens schon in ihrer zeitlichen Entwicklung
> überschaut [...]. Das Tagebuch sieht die Dinge lediglich aus dem erlebnisnahen
> Moment der Niederschrift und bietet damit weithin ungeformte Gegenwart, die
> Autobiographie beruht auf der inzwischen gewonnenen Distanz und kann
> deshalb das Vergangene bereits gestalten.[25]

---

25   Peter Boerner, *Tagebuch* (Stuttgart, 1969), p. 13.

126

As a literary form, in other words, the diary promises an immediate relationship to the singularity of lived experience, from which the autobiographer is distanced through time and through the interpretative, shaping activity of autobiographical memory. In *Klassenliebe*, the diary certainly proves the ideal vehicle for what Weigel characterises as a shapeless, associative style through which Karin presents her personal experience 'ohne Distanz, ohne Begriffsanstrengung, ohne thematische und formale Konzeption'.[26] Yet as F.-Michael Kümmel's 'Eine (sich) erinnernde Literatur. Versuch einer literaturtheoretischen Schreibens der 70er Jahre' (1988) observes, the diary form's immediacy also entails risks for the diarist:

> Der Tagebuchschreiber sieht nur eine kurze Zeitspanne, kann die Ereignisse nicht direkt einordnen, da ihm das Wissen bezüglich ihrer Relevanz fehlt. Er notiert seine Gefühle und Regungen bezogen auf den Augenblick und geht dabei bewußt das Risiko des Irrtums ein. So wird das Tagebuch zu einer unmittelbaren subjektiven Form.[27]

In *Klassenliebe* the premium placed on the immediacy and singularity of human experience is related both to a hostility toward theoretical and political discourses, and to a suspicion of any kind of formal distance. For Karin's project of self-actualisation through social transformation, however, this is counterproductive. Surely no political programme can do without normative assumptions that are obtained by abstracting from and adjudicating between competing political claims from the perspective of a coherent ethical or theoretical position. Eschewing distance in favour of immediacy, in short, *Klassenliebe* dispenses with the politics in its plea for a politics encompassing subjective needs, leaving only subjectivism. *Klassenliebe*'s often perspicacious insights about class and gender are at best fragmentary, and rarely advance beyond a critique of the left or the feminist movement. All too often, however, the associative style of the diary displaces them before they can even unfold. Take, for instance, a reference that Karin makes to Marcuse, which is immediately swamped by her relationship with Z.: 'Marcuse: das spezifisch Weibliche in die Politik einbringen. Lieber Z., eine schöne Liebeserklärung [...]' (*KL*, 61). Consistently, Karin's political commitments are displaced by the stuff of the *journal intime*. On one occasion, Karin reports a meeting of the *Werkkreis Literatur der Arbeitswelt* only because of a rendez-vous with Z. 'weitab vom Gemurmel der diskutierenden schreibenden Arbeiter' (*KL*, 9). Though Karin's project of self-actualisation aims at calling into question

---

26   Weigel, *Die Stimme der Medusa*, p. 101.
27   F.-Michael Kümmel, 'Eine (sich) erinnernde Literatur. Versuch einer literaturtheoretischen Einordnung des autobiographischen Schreibens der 70er Jahre', *die horen*, 33, no. 4 (1988), 9-18 p. 12.

received distinctions between the private and the political, *Klassenliebe* ultimately tends to reproduce them by displacing political concerns with private ones. We can observe this mechanism of displacement at work in the process of autobiographical memory in the text too. Admittedly, Karin's diary does grasp aspects of her past experience – like the speechlessness that she experiences on account of her class origins – in political terms. More often, though, far from emphasising the more universal aspects of her socialisation, the memories that it records possess a private, talismanic quality. As much as the speechlessness experienced at school, it is the snow lying by the school bus stop, or the darkness enveloping her on the journey home from the house of a school friend that haunts the narrator of *Klassenliebe* (*KL*, 102-03, 143).

The tendency to displace political questions with private experience most poignantly undermines Karin's project of self-actualisation where she seeks the resolution of political conflicts in the private sphere. For it is increasingly in the imaginary plenitude of a union with her lover Z. that Karin seeks a sense of self-actualisation. 'Lieber Z.', she writes, '[...] Ich will mich dir ganz öffnen. Ich will, daß *du* dich mir ganz öffnest. [...] Ich will mit dir Hochzeit machen' (*KL*, 114). Addressing Z. here in the second person, Karin's diary sheds its more public aspirations to become the site of an imagined, but in reality unattainable, bond with Z.. Finally, it is in bearing Z. a child – Karin calls the child Elias (*KL*, 130) – that she invests a desire for integrity as a woman: 'Liebe, Liebe, Sanftheit, ein Kind. Eine Frau sein. Eine Mutter sein. Einmal richtig. Einmal ganz' (*KL*, 91).

Karin's hope for self-actualisation in the roles of lover and mother offer no solution to the powerful sense of fragmentation and lack at *Klassenliebe*'s heart. On the contrary, it puts her in a position where her subjectivity is defined in relation to and even by Z.. This is confirmed when Karin gives Z. access to her diary (*KL*, 191) and through a kind of censoring activity (granting or withholding his approval from her) he acquires the power to shape her tastes and needs. 'Wenn Z. etwas nicht wert findet,' Karin writes, 'so verliert es auch für mich an Wert. So weit bin ich' (*KL*, 188). This hardly amounts to an act of self-authorship on Karin's part.

The sense of lack around which Karin's diary circles is objectively grounded in the discourses of class and gender. But in the final analysis, her reluctance to abstract from her experience, a reluctance linked to her mistrust of political discourse and her preference for the immediacy of the diary, forces her into the search for private and imaginary solutions. Yet Karin's private solutions to political problems are no more than palliatives. Indeed, when Z. voices disquiet at the prospect of fathering a child by Karin (*KL*, 203-04), she is forced to invest ever greater hope for self-actualisation in giving birth to Elias (*KL*, 269, 281) and in her diary, conceived as a parallel form of gestation. As the diary proceeds, though, its promise of self-actualisation recedes. The endeavour to fix an elusive self-presence in

Klassenliebe – 'Ich bin Ich. Ich bin Karin', she writes (*K*, 48) – frequently reveals a more sombre reality: that she never transcends her deficient sense of self at all. As Karin puts it: 'Ich bin nicht mehr "Ich". War ich schon "Ich"? Angst vor der Leere' (*KL*, 181).

Compared to the sensation of *Klassenliebe*, the publication of Inga Buhmann's *Ich habe mir eine Geschichte geschrieben* by the left-wing Trikont press in 1977 proceeded quietly. Buhmann's autobiography certainly met with approval within the New Women's Movement. In the feminist literary journal *mamas pfirsiche* (1978), for example, Ilse Braatz praised Buhmann for emphasising 'in all ihren politischen Aktivitäten immer auch die persönlichen, scheinbar ganz privaten Konflikten'.[28] Where it did attract attention beyond the confines of the feminist counterculture, the critical response to *Ich habe mir eine Geschichte geschrieben* was more ambivalent. In the *Literaturmagazin* in 1979, Klaus Hartung's 'Die Repression wird zum Milieu' commended the 'Anspruch von Solidarität' invoked by Buhmann's account of her involvement in the student movement; at the same time, Hartung claimed also to discern in the text an underlying, private 'Syntax der Scham' that provided the true motive of autobiographical cognition.[29]

More recently, Buhmann's autobiography has acquired a higher profile within critical debates about the relationship between autobiographical discourse and feminist politics. Critics have identified the relationship between the text's central retrospective autobiographical narrative and the diary entries, letters and other documents mounted within that narrative as fundamental to the political and aesthetic claims of *Ich habe mir eine Geschichte geschrieben*. But despite sharing poststructuralist assumptions about the relationship between language, female subjectivity and feminist politics, scholars such as Weigel and Becker have adopted conflicting positions with regard to the text's juxtaposition of conventional autobiographical narration with the more disparate subjectivity of the diary entries and letters. In 'Der schielende Blick. Thesen zur Geschichte weiblicher Schreibpraxis' (1983), Weigel claims that Buhmann's diary entries and letters destabilise the text's autobiographical narrative:

> Die Jetzt-Schreibende versucht nun nicht, mithilfe rückblickender Erinnerungsarbeit aus dem vorhandenen Material die Geschichte einer kontinuierlich und episch beschreibbaren *Entwicklung* zu gestalten, aus der das heutige 'Ich' sich als (aus)gebildetes herleitete und erhellte. Das damalige 'Ich'

---

28   Ilse Braatz, 'Inga Buhmann: Ich habe mir eine Geschichte geschrieben. Rezension', *mamas pfirsiche*, 9/10 (1978), 195-96 (p. 195).

29   Klaus Hartung, 'Die Repression wird zum Milieu', pp. 73 and 71.

und das rückblickende 'Ich' werden nicht versöhnt. Häufig steht die Autorin ihren eigenen früheren Texten fremd gegenüber.[30]

By contrast, Becker identifies in Buhmann's autobiography a 'Logo-/Phallozentrismus' that destroys the heterogeneity of a 'weibliche Ökonomie' of language within the text. The text's retrospective autobiographical narrative, she claims, subjects the diary entries and letters mounted within it to a homogenising 'Hierarchisierungsprozeß' in which '*alle* Tagebuchaufzeichnungen in den Text hineingenommen und der nachträglichen Bewertung des sich erinnernden Ich unterworfen werden'.[31]

Weigel and Becker rightly place the relationship between autobiographical narration and diary at the heart of *Ich habe mir eine Geschichte geschrieben*. Arguably, their shared preference for the heterogeneity of the diary over the synthetic force of Buhmann's central autobiographical narrative (though they disagree over the extent to which the former is realised in the text) rests on mistaken assumptions about the political value of polysemic textual practices. We will suggest here that in *Ich habe mir eine Geschichte geschrieben* both the diary and the autobiographical narrative serve the goal of self-actualisation. However, where Buhmann's diary cannot transcend the private immediacy of her experience, the synthetic perspectives of the autobiography proper offer her a more powerful tool with which to grasp herself as subject and object of her own life history and, through the collective agency of the New Women's Movement, of the historical process.

At the heart of *Ich habe eine Geschichte geschrieben* stands, as in *Klassenliebe*, a tension between a sense of identity characterised by fragmentation or 'Zerrissenheit' (*G*, 23) on the one hand, and a desire for a more coherent subject position – a certain 'Verbindlichkeit' or 'Eindeutigkeit' (*G*, 41) – on the other. The opening of the text links Buhmann's sense of 'Zerrissenheit' to an inability to accede to the status of a self-determining subject. This inability is defined along two axes, the one historical, the other private. First, Buhmann is defined, even with respect to the act of her conception, as an object of the historical process. 'Mein Vater sagte mir immer mit Stolz, daß ich bewußt gezeugt worden bin. Es war Krieg – und man konnte ja nie wissen', she writes (*G*, 8). Second, she is socialised within a network of private relationships to conform to the gendered roles which her father and grandfather impose upon her as a young girl. 'Ebensowenig wird es ein Zufall sein,' she notes, 'daß mein Vater sowie mein Großvater mich häufig mit ihren verstorbenen Müttern verglichen' (*G*, 22). In contrast with her grandfather, whose letters

---

30   See Weigel's 'Der schielende Blick. Thesen zur Geschichte weiblicher Schreibpraxis' in Inge Stephan and Sigrid Weigel, *Die verborgene Frau. Sechs Beiträge zu einer feministischen Literaturwissenschaft* (Berlin, 1983), pp. 83-137 (p. 114).

31   Renate Becker, *Inszenierungen des Weiblichen*, pp. 131-32.

breathe the very spirit of the economic reconstruction of the 1950s (*G*, 15-17), Buhmann herself is thus subjected to a dual process of objectification that bars her from self-actualisation both with respect to her own life history and to the historical process.

It is the endeavour to transcend this object status that *Ich habe mir eine Geschichte geschrieben* chronicles. The 'Suche nach einer neuen Verbindlichkeit' (*G*, 41) that is a central motif in the text takes the form of various attempts on Buhmann's part to posit herself, against her enforced 'Objektstatus als Frau' (*G*, 126), as a subject. These attempts range from a project to master historical discourse – 'mir die gesamte Weltgeschichte autodidaktisch zu erarbeiten' (*G*, 34) – that Buhmann undertakes as a student in the mid-1960s, to her involvement in the student and the women's movements of the 1970s. They also include travel, through which Buhmann strives to constitute herself as subject by plotting her own itinerary (*G*, 29-32); and writing poetry, which affords her an unprecedented sense of certainty: 'Es war für mich völlig klar, wie man zu schreiben hatte, und was einfach nicht mehr ging – so zerrissen und unsicher sonst mein Leben damals war' (G, 54). Crucial too is the promise of self-actualisation offered by the diary and the autobiographical act.

The diary extracts included in *Ich habe mir eine Geschichte geschrieben* are the most substantial of a number of materials – including letters, pamphlets and speeches – mounted within the text's central autobiographical narrative. These materials share a documentary impetus which attests to the veracity of what is narrated (Buhmann's autobiography possesses nothing of *Klassenliebe*'s indeterminacy). Citing *Subversive Aktion*'s 'Juli-Manifest für die Phantasie', for example, testifies to Buhmann's marginal involvement with this group in the mid-1960s. It also presents the group's central tenets in unmediated form:

> 1. *Phantasie ist Veränderung*
> 2. *Verändert wird nicht nur Kunst, sondern auch Individuum, Gesellschaft und Lebensform*
> 3. *Der Künstler darf die Phantasie nicht gebrauchen, wie der Schüler die Leisten*
> [...]
>
> (*G*, 60)

Analogously the diary, which forms the bulk of the text's fourth to the ninth chapters, documents states of mind that might otherwise elude Buhmann's memory as autobiographer. Yet over and above its documentary value, the diary represents a form of self-assertion. Chronologically co-extensive with the events narrated within the text, it is necessarily set against the less immediate, but more interpretative, perspective of the text's central autobiographical narrative.

In *Ich habe mir eine Geschichte geschrieben*, Buhmann's diary offers her first of all a crucial means of resistance to her objectification within historical discourse and within the constrictive relationships of her family. When her attempts to press consciousness-widening drugs into the service of a radical subjective experience of self-actualisation fail, for example, Buhmann is branded by her father as a 'gefährliche Person' (*G*, 90) and briefly incarcerated in an asylum. Yet her diary offers a steady point of resistance to the pathologising medical discourses ranged against her:

> Das, was mir in der Klapsmühle die Stärke gab, mich doch noch als jemand zu fühlen, der Widerstand leistet, war mein Tagebuch − dort fand ich meine eigentlich[e] Identität, konnte mich aussprechen und Gedanken klären; dort durfte ich sagen, was ich dachte, ohne deshalb als abnorm angesehen zu werden [...]
>
> (*G*, 70)

Linked to the diary's role as a site of resistance is its powerful critical potential. Already with her growing involvement in the *Sozialistischer Deutscher Studentenbund*, the SDS, during the late 1960s, it provides Buhmann with a critical perspective from which to question student activists' ideas about female sexuality. A diary entry of 1 October 1966, for example, rejects the relevance for women of the '*Unterordnung der prägenitalen Ansprüche unter den genitalen Primat*' (*G*, 169) theorised by the Reichian psychoanalysis fashionable within the student movement.

Given its capacity for resistance and its critical potential, it is hardly surprising that Buhmann's diary should embrace, more forcefully than Struck's *Klassenliebe*, a conception of writing as a form of self-authorship or self-invention. A diary entry dating from a long stay in Paris during 1965 and early 1966 explicitly formulates this conception. Buhmann writes '*Du willst der Grund deiner selbst sein, dich selbst schaffen, erschaffen, durch alle Abhängigkeiten hindurch*' (*G*, 135). Like Karin's diary in *Klassenliebe*, however, Buhmann's diary succumbs to a subjectivism that strives to solve material problems with imaginary solutions. Focusing on personal relationships and the emotional states generated by them, it unfolds within the parameters of what she terms her 'Vorstellungen eines radikalen Individualismus' (*G*, 100). Yet at base, this radical individualism amounts to a solipsism − '*Da sind wir wieder: Ich bin meine Welt*' (*G*, 136), her diary intones − that ignores the material determinants of Buhmann's sense of 'Zerrissenheit' (*G*, 23). The excision of social mechanisms of cause and effect from her diary has perilous consequences for her project of self-invention. As a result, her attempt in Paris to play out to her own advantage the role of a French composer's 'Geliebte' (the very 'Verkörperung von Freiheit und Leidenschaft', she believes, *G*, 119) ends in the solitary trauma of a backstreet abortion after he withdraws emotional and financial support (*G*, 119-21). The unsatisfactory character of the diary as a means of self-invention is further evidenced by the narrator's persisting inability to posit herself as a subject using the first person 'Ich'. Instead, she uses the diary to conduct tortuous dialogues with herself in the second person singular. Berating herself for failing to fulfil the imperative of self-invention, Buhmann writes for example: '*Du wirst weder Verbrecherin sein noch Heilige, noch hundertprozentige Bürgerin, noch Bäuerin, noch Revolutionärin*' (*G*, 139).

Buhmann's diary might appear to justify Bernward Vesper's mistrust of self-invention as a concept which risks losing sight of material realities that cannot simply be conjured away. However, Buhmann's growing social and political commitment is related by the central autobiographical narrative of *Ich habe mir eine Geschichte geschrieben*. Though her involvement in *Subversive Aktion* before her 1965 trip to Paris is characterised by only '*ein distanziertes Engagement*' (*G*, 98), she is impelled upon her return to Germany to greater political commitment by reading Marcuse's *Eros and Civilization* and Simone de Beauvoir's *Le deuxième sexe* (1949). Indeed, she moves to Frankfurt 'um mich jetzt endlich mit der Frankfurter Schule gründlich auseinanderzusetzen und um eine "gute Sozialistin" zu werden' (*G*, 162). Despite joining the SDS and engaging herself practically whilst working as a 'Bürohilfskraft' (*G*, 162) in a mail-order company, Buhmann is driven by the penchant of Frankfurt's student left for 'intellektuelle[...] Analyse' (*G*, 178) on to Berlin, the centre of anti-authoritarianism. The political climate she finds in Berlin at the height of the student movement allows her to combine theoretical and practical interests more satisfactorily. She attends workshops on 'Wirtschaftsgeschichte und den Problemen der Dritten Welt' (*G*, 181) on the one hand, and participates in the demonstrations that followed the death of Benno Ohnesorg in June 1967 on the other (*G*, 183-87). Crucially, these demonstrations prove instrumental in granting Buhmann, as part of the student movement, a new sense of historical agency that is marked within her autobiographical narrative by a pronominal shift into the first person plural. Referring to the attempt on Dutschke's life in April 1968, for instance, Buhmann articulates the anti-authoritarian 'Manipulationsthese' as follows: 'Wir sahen in Springer den Bösewicht, den eigentlichen Täter, der die Massen verhetzt und verdummt[,] und hatten die Hoffnung, das würde sich ändern, wenn es uns gelänge, eine wirkungsvolle Aufklärungsarbeit in der Bevölkerung und vor allem unter den Arbeitern zu entfalten' (*G*, 199).

The autobiographical narrative of *Ich habe mir eine Geschichte geschrieben*, in short, provides Buhmann entry into social and historical discourse in a way that her diary cannot. But nor is it free from ruptures between the realms of subjectivity and history, between the private and the political. If her diary privileges subjective experience over social fact, Buhmann's autobiographical narrative for its part threatens to dissolve her subjective experience into the anonymity of historical discourse. The first person singular 'Ich' is all but obliterated from Buhmann's account of the turbulent events that followed the attempt on Dutschke's life (*G*, 194-201). Moreover, Buhmann reports that despite her greater involvement in the student movement, she continued to maintain a sceptical distance toward her political commitments, a distance that points to a persisting rupture between her subjective experience and the historical process:

> es wäre übertrieben zu sagen, daß ich nun alle Skrupel über Bord gepackt und mich voll den politischen Ereignissen und meinem Engagement hingegeben hätte. Eine gewisse Distanz ist bei mir nie verloren gegangen.
>
> (*G*, 185)

Bernd Neumann has argued that autobiographical discourse represents a medium in which autobiographers mediate their status as subjects and objects of their life history with their role as subjects and objects of the historical process.[32] For Buhmann, the central autobiographical narrative of *Ich habe mir eine Geschichte geschrieben* provides a tool with which subjectivity and history are brought into a dialogue. In essence, Buhmann's autobiography follows a dialectical movement. The diary extracts comprising the bulk of the text's fourth to ninth chapters issue into a pernicious solipsism (*G*, 58-177); and the initial entry into historical discourse as part of the student movement in Berlin in the tenth and eleventh chapters proceeds at the expense of the specificity of Buhmann's subjective experience (*G*, 178-203). The closing chapters, however, from twelve to twenty-one, are devoted to mediating Buhmann's subjective experience and her political involvement (*G*, 204-74). Moreover, they do so by elaborating her progressive commitment to a politics grounded in personal experience that anticipates, and leads to, the theory and practice of feminism. This process begins with a *Basisgruppe* consisting of young workers that Buhmann forms in Spandau in 1968 (*G*, 204-08). Though the formation of *Basis-* and *Stadtteilgruppen* is often seen as part of the student movement's turn from anti-authoritarian positions to more orthodox forms of class politics, it is her *Basisgruppe* that wins Buhmann over to an understanding of politics as a process that departs from and comes to rest with the needs of human beings. She writes: 'Nur wenn wir in der Lage wären, uns selbst zu verändern, neue Beziehungen zwischen uns herzustellen, würden wir auch die Kraft haben, für eine neue veränderte Gesellschaft zu kämpfen' (*G*, 210). Yet as her autobiographical narrative makes clear, the grasp of human needs fostered by her involvement in the *Basisgruppe* in 1968 was essentially blind to questions of gender:

> Später nahmen auch [die] Frauen [der Arbeiter] an den Sitzungen teil. Ich bekümmerte mich damals wenig um ihre Probleme, nahm auch nicht wahr, daß

---

32   Neumann, *Identität und Rollenzwang*, pp. 1 and 21.

sie oft nicht kommen konnten, weil sie bei ihren Kindern bleiben mußten. Zu einem sehr viel späteren Zeitpunkt erzählten sie mir, daß sie darunter gelitten hätten, wie ihnen ihre Männer die schönen emanzipierten Studentinnen der Basisgruppe als Beispiel und Idealbild vorgehalten hatten, um sie unter Druck zu setzen.

(*G*, 220)

As her work with the *Basisgruppe* progresses, Buhmann's initial blindness to gender-specific forms of oppression yields to a mounting concern for the problems of the proletarian women of Spandau. While the *Basisgruppe* succumbs under the pressure of the student movement's proletarian turn to a narrowing focus on agitation on the shop floor ('Betriebsarbeit', *G*, 222), Buhmann's political activities shift toward the working mothers of Spandau and the proletarian women attending a *Berufsschule* in Berlin-Wilmersdorf, with whom she produces a newsletter entitled *Hexenschuß* (*G*, 263-70). Buhmann's growing commitment at the end of the 1960s to women's problems radicalises from a gendered perspective the relationship between politics and human needs that she perceived already in her initial work with the *Basisgruppe*. Yet even here, the needs addressed are not her own; a disjunction between her social and political commitment and her subjective experience remains:

Tatsächlich begann ich damals immer mehr, mich mit Frauenproblemen auseinanderzusetzen. Doch durfte es erstmal nicht um mich selbst gehen, sondern um die unterdrücktesten, die ausgebeutetesten der Arbeiterklasse, die ungelernten Arbeiterinnen.

(*G*, 261)

Only the inception of the New Women's Movement's struggle against §218 brings about a reconciliation. Precisely as a form of identity politics – 'the tendency to base one's politics on a sense of personal identity'[33] – feminism enables Buhmann to balance her political commitment and her subjective experience. In the New Women's Movement as the organised political expression of her needs, Buhmann thus appears as a historical actor on her own behalf. It is no coincidence that with this reconciliation of subjective needs and political discourse, the autobiographical narrative of *Ich habe mir eine Geschichte geschrieben* comes to close, a close that marks a new beginning also:

Ich nahm jetzt [1971] mehr an den Frauenaktivitäten der Basisgruppe teil. Wir machten in Spandau eine §218-Kampagne mit einem Theaterstück, Unterschriftenlisten, Broschüren, Flugblättern und vielen Diskussionen. Wir

33   Diana Fuss, *Essentially Speaking: Feminism, Nature and Difference* (London and New York, 1989), p. 97.

zogen mit unseren Ständen auf alle belebten Plätze. [...] Es gab sehr heftige Diskussionen und auch Abwehr, doch wir konnten miteinander reden. Diese Erlebnisse waren sehr schön und machten wieder Mut. Ich wollte das fortsetzen.

(G, 275)

The precise complexion of Buhmann's feminism is not clearly articulated in her autobiography. At times, it appears indebted both to a socialist feminism that links the oppression of women to their position in relation to the industrial means of production; and to a radical feminism for which the determinants of women's oppression are irreducible to the structures of class society. Nonetheless, it is clearly a feminist politics that provides the autobiographical narrative of *Ich habe mir eine Geschichte geschrieben* with its *telos*. What, then, is the relationship between feminist politics and autobiographical discourse in the text?

On account of their historical role in legitimating as universal a male concept of self, some critics have rejected the synthetic forms and linear narratives of autobiography as unsuitable for articulating a feminist politics. Yet *Ich habe mir eine Geschichte geschrieben* reveals a more productive way of grasping the relationship between feminist politics and autobiographical discourse. For conceived in inclusive terms as a 'mode of understanding' to which potentially all individuals have access, autobiographical discourse provides women too with a medium in which life history and history can be mediated to one another. In Buhmann's autobiography, crucially, it is a feminist politics, itself a dialectic of the personal and the political, that serves to ground the text's central autobiographical narrative.

Approximately midway in the text, Buhmann offers a methodological reflection that expresses a profound ambivalence towards the autobiographical act. Reflecting on the diary entries that she mounts into her autobiographical narrative, she writes:

> Es ist äußerst schwierig für mich, nach alldem, was sich in den letzten Jahren an neuen Erkenntnissen und Lebensformen in der Frauenbewegung entwickelt hat, meine damaligen Erfahrungen und Interpretationen so wiederzugeben, wie ich sie im Tagebuch vorgefunden habe, aber jede Kürzung und Veränderung wäre eine Fälschung.

(G, 127)

At first sight, Buhmann's ambivalent conception of the autobiographical might appear to resemble that of Vesper in *Die Reise*. Does the shaping force of the autobiographical act amount to a legitimate interpretation of the autobiographer's past from the perspective of present 'Erkenntnissen und Lebensformen', or to an act of 'Fälschung'? Is the autobiographer's task, however futile, to uncover and present without 'Kürzung oder Veränderung' an autobiographical truth that pre-exists the autobiographical act?

136

As Buhmann's narrative progresses, it is precisely the interpretative aspect of the autobiographical act that is valorised. Feminist politics not only represents the *telos* of Buhmann's autobiography. It provides the ideological assumptions and perspectives from which, in the present of narration, the very impulse toward autobiographical cognition departs. *Ich habe mir eine Geschichte geschrieben* covers only the beginnings of the New Women's Movement, although the text indicates Buhmann's continuing commitment to it in analeptic utterances about 'neue[...] Erkenntnisse[...] und Lebensformen in der Frauenbewegung'(*G*, 127). Because the text is written from this perspective of a commitment to feminist politics, however, a feminist interpretation of gender provides a key to unlocking its meaning.

Like Karin's diary in *Klassenliebe*, the subjective immediacy of the diary in *Ich habe mir eine Geschichte geschrieben* is not well suited to grasping the social and historical dimensions of Buhmann's experience. By contrast, the feminist perspective underpinning the text's central autobiographical narrative allows her to evaluate from a gendered perspective the significant factors shaping her experience. Thus Buhmann is retrospectively able to highlight the sexism of the student groups to which she belonged, criticising, for example, the 'soziologische Elite' of the SDS in Frankfurt for using their 'frisch erlernten Jargon [...] als arrogantes Machtmittel vor allem gegen Frauen' (*G*, 162). Similarly, the interpretative force of autobiographical discourse foregrounds tendencies and revalues events which may have seemed trivial at the time, only to prove significant within the larger context of Buhmann's development. A good example here is the way that Buhmann's autobiographical narrative sets a letter of 18 November 1965 against the solipsism of her diary at this time in order to highlight a direction in her thinking that was only much later to come to fruition. 'Tatsächlich gab es auch andere Töne'(*G*, 147), Buhmann states, reviewing in retrospect the subjectivism of her diary – and then she cites the letter to her sister Ilsedore: '*Wir müssen es lernen, zugleich Frau und ganz zu sein [...]. Wir sollen [...] eine eigene Sprache finden, einen eigenen Ausdruck, das ist der Sinn der wirklichen Emanzipation der Frau. Frau, nicht Objekt*' (*G*, 148).

Renate Becker rightly asserts that the autobiographical narrative of *Ich habe mir eine Geschichte geschrieben* amounts to a process of hierarchisation that privileges the perspectives of the present of narration over the narrated past.[34] Yet far from embodying, as Becker claims, a pernicious phallocentrism, Buhmann's autobiography shows that such a process is really a political necessity. Rita Felski has observed that 'feminism as an oppositional ideology necessarily relies on the privileging of certain ethical and political values and normative assumptions'; and that predicated on the 'absence of fixed identities', the poststructuralist feminist aesthetic favoured by critics like

34   Renate Becker, *Inszenierungen des Weiblichen*, p. 131.

Becker is 'unable to provide any grounds for making such political choices or guidance in the adoption of certain political and cultural strategies rather than others'.[35] Indeed, Buhmann's *Ich habe mir eine Geschichte geschrieben* certainly shows Becker's mistrust of conventional synthetic and linear forms of autobiographical narrative to be misplaced. Bringing as it does subjectivity and history into a dialogue, Buhmann's autobiography formulates its author's entry, as part of the collective agency of the New Women's Movement, into historical discourse. It does so, crucially, through its capacity to privilege and clarify, from the coherent perspective of a feminist interpretation of gender in the present of narration, the political values and normative assumptions that are fundamental to feminism as an oppositional movement.

III   The Essential Fiction of West German Feminism: *Häutungen*

Renate Becker's *Inszenierungen des Weiblichen* theorises a 'dialektisches Verhältnis von Frauenbewegung und Frauentexten'.[36] By disputing the political value of a text like Inga Buhmann's autobiography, however, her study demonstrates insufficient sensitivity to that relationship. A dialectic of feminism and autobiography is certainly at work in this text, for it is a feminist politics that anchors the autobiographical narrative in which Buhmann formulates her entry, through the collective agency of the New Women's Movement, into the historical process. It is Stefan's *Häutungen* of 1975, though, which best illustrates the needs and functions which autobiographical discourse in turn fulfilled within the West German New Women's Movement. Taking on the controversial issue of the text's essentialism in the light of recent debates about the identity politics of oppositional movements, we will argue here that *Häutungen* not only functioned as a form of political discourse within the New Women's Movement, but also offered it a potent symbolic fiction of identity formation.

Born out of Verena Stefan's active involvement in feminist politics, *Häutungen* has become the key literary document of the New Women's Movement. It is perhaps surprising, given its subtitle of 'Autobiografische Aufzeichnungen', that the text should reveal so little about its author's engagement in feminist politics in Berlin during the early 1970s (Stefan had moved from Bern to Berlin in 1968). It barely mentions her participation in the radical feminist *Brot und Rosen* group during the §218 campaign, and refers only in passing to her co-authorship, as part of that group, of the important *Frauenhandbuch Nr. 1* (1972) on contraception and abortion (*H*, 15). Nonetheless, the text's

35   Felski, pp. 45-46.
36   Renate Becker, *Inszenierungen des Weiblichen*, p. 57.

138

resolutely political treatment of women's oppression and female sexuality ensured it a wide feminist readership; it sold over 200,000 copies by the start of the 1980s. Indeed, already *Häutungen*'s immediate popularity proved such that its publisher, the Frauenoffensive press in Munich, used the profits to secure financial independence from its parent company, Trikont. On a practical level alone, *Häutungen* thus contributed significantly toward the process of countercultural consolidation that characterised West German feminism during the second half of the 1970s.

What is striking about *Häutungen*'s popularity within the New Women's Movement is that it was achieved, as Riki Winter puts it in her 1981 contribution to the *Kritisches Lexikon zur deutschsprachigen Gegenwartsliteratur*, not through the 'marktüblichen Public-Relations-Strategien' but through 'Mundpropaganda'.[37] From the perspective of *Häutungen*'s critical reception this is significant because when the text received the attention of both the West German feuilletons and of explicitly feminist reviewers, it did so on account of the profile that it had already attained within the women's movement. When *Die Zeit* portrayed *Häutungen* to its readership as the 'Bibel der Frauenbewegung' (24 September 1976), for instance, it may have been to tarnish the text with the suggestion of fanaticism.[38] Yet for all the ambiguity of such a designation, it attests to the interest that *Häutungen* generated beyond the parameters of the New Women's Movement also. In contrast to the reception of *Klassenliebe*, moreover, where critical interest tended to focus on the text's author, critical debate about *Häutungen* centred squarely on its political claims.

In the feuilletons of the West German press, the critical response to *Häutungen* ranged from wholesale approval to scepticism. In a review appearing in the *Süddeutsche Zeitung* (7 April 1976) – and the *Frauenoffensive Journal* (1976) –, the novelist Christa Reinig lauded Stefan's assault on the patriarchal ideology inscribed in language. 'Dieser Autorin ist es gelungen,' Reinig wrote, 'die Sprache der Männer aufzubrechen und ihre Vokabeln den Frauen nutzbar zu machen'.[39] Although convinced of its significance, other critics were more circumspect in their evaluation of the text. In the *Frankfurter Allgemeine Zeitung* (16 March 1976), for example, Lothar Baier fought off a sense of voyeurism that confronted him as a male reader. However, despite welcoming the provocation which it represented 'gerade auch für Männer', Baier criticised *Häutungen* for resorting to a

37 Riki Winter, 'Verena Stefan' (1981), in *Kritisches Lexikon zur deutschsprachigen Gegenwartsliteratur*, ed. by Heinz Ludwig Arnold (Munich, 1978-), p. 2.

38 Renate Just, 'Schluss mit dem Klagen', *Die Zeit*, 24 September 1976, ('Zeitmagazin') pp. 16-18 and 50-55 (p. 17).

39 Christa Reinig, 'Das weibliche Ich', *Süddeutsche Zeitung*, 7 April 1976, ('Literatur') p. 3; also in *Frauenoffensive Journal*, 5 (1976), 50-51 (p. 50).

'naturlyrische[...] Kitsch' in order to represent homosexual experiences beyond heterosexual norms.[40]

In the publications of the New Women's Movement and in left-wing journals with feminist interests, the critical tone was generally more insistent. In discussions by Ann Anders in *Ästhetik und Kommunikation* (1976) and Ute Tempel in *mamas pfirsiche* (1976), affirmation was from the outset tempered with critique, with both critics suspicious of Stefan's use of nature imagery to evoke a femininity liberated from patriarchal prescriptions. Where Anders expressed misgivings about 'Naturmetaphern [...], weil wir durch sie traditionell entschärft und unseres eigenen Körpers entfremdet wurden', Tempel dismissed *Häutungen*'s appeal to nature simply as a 'Neuauflage banaler Klischees'.[41] Significantly, though, both Anders and Tempel emphasised the constructive spirit of 'Zustimmung und Kritik' in their approach to the text.[42]

For the feminist monthly *Courage* (September 1976), Brigitte Classen and Gabriele Goettle resolutely refused the imperative of solidarity. Their focus the equation of femininity and nature underpinning *Häutungen*'s vision of emancipation, Classen and Goettle emphasised the regressive implications of the natural metaphors within the text. Already the eponymous metaphor of 'Häutung' (the shedding of an old skin) for them undermined the notion of personal transformation that it sought to convey:

> Schon in "Brehms Tierleben" könnte [Stefan] erfahren, daß bei dem Prozeß der Häutung zwar eine neuere und bessere, doch bis ins Detail gleiche Haut nachwächst. Die Oberfläche mag in Verenas Fall neu sein [...], aber immer noch gilt die gleiche Biologie: die der Frau als Mädchen, Blondine, Mutter und Natur.[43]

The appeal to nature, in short, reproduced the very patriarchal construction of femininity which *Häutungen* purported to contest.

Throughout the 1980s and into the 1990s, academic studies of feminist literature in the Federal Republic have tended to amplify the initial critiques of *Häutungen*. The text's nature imagery has been a recurrent target of criticism, even in sympathetic treatments like Ricarda Schmidt's *Westdeutsche*

---

40 Lothar Baier, 'Nicht länger Teil eines Paares oder Abrechnung mit dem Patriarchat. "Häutungen" − die autobiographische Erzählung einer Feministin', *Frankfurter Allgemeine Zeitung*, 16 March 1976, p. 20.

41 Ann Anders, 'Fiktiver Brief an Verena Stefan', *Ästhetik und Kommunikation*, 25 (1976), 120-21 (p. 121); Ute Tempel, 'wie können frauen als "menschen" schreiben?', *mamas pfirsiche*, 4/5 (1976), 31-43 (p. 36).

42 Anders, p. 120; see also Tempel p. 35.

43 Brigitte Classen and Gabriele Goettle, '"Häutungen" − eine Verwechslung von Anemone und Amazone', *Courage*, September 1976, pp. 45-46 (p. 45).

Frauenliteratur der 70er Jahre (1982).[44] However, *Häutungen*'s political claims have been most forcefully contested by those critical studies of the West German women's writing of the 1970s informed by a poststructuralist feminist aesthetic. As well as attacking the text's nature imagery, Karin Richter-Schröder's *Frauenliteratur und weibliche Identität* of 1986 and Renate Becker's *Inszenierungen des Weiblichen* of 1992 have extended their critique to questions of language and of form. Where language is concerned, Becker's more generous approach applauds the text for exposing the male bias of a supposedly neutral everyday language that in reality legitimates serious 'Übergriffe auf den weiblichen Körper'.[45] For Richter-Schröder, however, *Häutungen*'s endeavours to highlight the relationship between language and sexual domination are unsophisticated. Stefan's linguistic experiments – splitting words or refusing to capitalise nouns – never extend, she asserts, beyond the 'Druckform'.[46] With regard to form, the position of the two critics is closer. Becker acknowledges Ricarda Schmidt's claim that the narrative of *Häutungen* is less chronological than circular; but for Becker, this claim is an evasion, for the text's powerful teleological drive undermines the heterogeneity and discontinuity that might qualify it as a form of *écriture féminine*.[47] Becker's understanding of *Häutungen*'s autobiographical form thus has more in common with that of Richter-Schröder, for whom 'die notwendig retrospektive Erzählstruktur autobiografischen Schreibens zu einer Darstellung der eigenen Entwicklung [führt], in der heterogene Momente stets einer übergeordneten Sinnstruktur subsumiert werden können'.[48]

The increasingly harsh critical treatment of Stefan's *Häutungen* returns us, albeit in the case of an individual text, to a point noted earlier in our discussion of the theoretical problem of women's autobiography. What is striking about the text's reception is a discrepancy between its popularity within the New Women's Movement, and the progressively more stringent critical response that it has elicited. *Häutungen*'s political claims – not least its equation of femininity with nature – certainly require thorough scrutiny. At the same time, it seems also churlish to dispute the text's radical potential when it provided significant practical impulses toward the establishment of a feminist counterculture during the mid-1970s, and clearly had a forceful impact on many of the women who read it. According to Barbara, one of five 'Oberschülerinnen' interviewed in a feminist edition of *Kursbuch* in 1977,

---

44 Ricarda Schmidt, *Westdeutsche Frauenliteratur in den 70er Jahren* (Frankfurt am Main, 1982), pp. 76-86 (p. 84).
45 Renate Becker, *Inszenierungen des Weiblichen*, pp. 82-83 (p. 82).
46 Richter-Schröder, p. 170.
47 Renate Becker, *Inszenierungen des Weiblichen*, pp. 87-88; Schmidt, p. 117.
48 Richter-Schröder, p. 155.

Häutungen offered a valuable demystifying critique of the role of women in a male-dominated society. 'Zumindest begann ich,' Barbara recounts of her politicisation, 'intensiver über meine Rolle als Frau nachzudenken, und habe Frauenbücher wie *Der kleine Unterschied*, die Frauen-Offensive-Journale und *Häutungen* nur so verschlungen'; all this, she observes, 'hat mir bestimmt sehr vieles klar gemacht'.[49] These remarks are significant because they indicate that *Häutungen* answered certain needs within the New Women's Movement, whatever criticisms may have followed. Clearly, we need an approach to the text that is sensitive to the historical context both of its composition and of its reception. Let us turn to Evelyne Keitel's 'Verständigungstexte – Form, Funktion, Wirkung' (1983), which offers us a useful model for understanding the discursive function of autobiography within the New Women's Movement.

The focus of Keitel's 'Verständigungstexte' is the way in which autobiographical texts serve the self-definition of oppositional movements. Keitel's model of the relationship between the texts and the movements has two related aspects. First, she argues, the texts must be examined in relation to 'bestimmte strukturelle Mängel innerhalb der gegenkulturellen Formationen, auf die sie sich beziehen'.[50] At issue here is a 'Theorielosigkeit, ja Theoriefeindlichkeit' within recent oppositional movements, in the face of which autobiographical 'Verständigungstexte' take on some of the functions of political and theoretical discourse. These functions are assumed through highlighting the universal character of the experience represented in the texts: '[es] werden jene subjektiven und individuellen Erfahrungen, auf denen ein Normensystem basiert, über die Person des Protagonisten exemplarisch dargestellt'. Here, one aspect of Keitel's model merges into the other. For Keitel suggests also that the autobiographical 'Verständigungstexte' of oppositional movements must be seen in terms of a specific construction of a 'lyrische[s] Ich' that allows them to address their readers effectively. Their protagonists, in short, are delineated broadly so as to stress the 'Allgemeingültigkeitsanspruch[...]' of their experience above the 'Idiosynkratische oder Individuelle'. This encourages readers to bring their own experience to bear on the text in the act of its 'Konkretisation im Rezeptionsprozeß'. The literary productions of oppositional groups thus have a dual function. First, they provide a means of clarifying and disseminating the normative assumptions on which an oppositional politics is based; second, they relate these assumptions to the experience of readers, whom they draw into the

---

49 Ulla/Birgit/Susan/Sabine/Barbara, '"Ich möchte lernen, ich selbst zu sein". Siebzehnjährige Oberschülerinnen schreiben über sich', *Kursbuch*, 47 (1977), 143-58 (p. 151).

50 Evelyne Keitel, 'Verständigungstexte–Form, Funktion, Wirkung', *The German Quarterly*, 56 (1983), 431-55 (p. 432). See pp. 437-49 for subsequent references to Keitel in the discussion above.

evaluation of these assumptions – a task to which autobiographical discourse, with its traditional claim to universality and singularity, is well suited. Taking Keitel's theory of the function of the autobiographical 'Verständigungstexte' of oppositional movements as a point of departure, let us turn to *Häutungen*. We will begin by examining in what sense the text functioned as a form of political discourse.

In a dialogue which Veruschka (who is named only once as the text's narrator and protagonist: *H*, 103) conducts with a less politicised comrade from the New Women's Movement (*H*, 82-89), *Häutungen* already claims a communicative function for itself. However, to understand precisely what it was that *Häutungen* sought to communicate, we must briefly set the text in relation to the ideological debates within West German feminism at the time of its publication.

1975, the year *Häutungen* was published, saw the end of the New Women's Movement's campaign to abolish §218, the abortion law of the Federal Republic. The campaign closed with only a partial success, ending with the institution in 1976 of a restrictive *Indikationslösung* allowing abortion only on compelling medical, criminological or social grounds; the desired *Fristenlösung* originally passed by the *Bundestag* in 1974, which had legalised all abortion within the first three months of pregnancy, had been revoked by the *Bundesverfassungsgericht*. A process of retrenchment and reorientation ushered in by the end of the fight against §218 was characterised above all by the eruption of ideological differences that had to a greater or lesser extent remained latent within the New Women's Movement under the fragile cohesion provided by the campaign to decriminalise abortion. After 1975, divisions between socialist feminism and radical feminism in particular came to a head.[51]

Set against this process of ideological diversification, it is no coincidence that *Häutungen* appeared almost simultaneously with (and is mentioned by the 'Oberschülerin' Barbara above in the same breath as) another key feminist text of 1975: Alice Schwarzer's *Der 'kleine Unterschied' und seine großen Folgen*. Some commentators have seen in *Häutungen* an expression of the politics of lesbian separatism.[52] But when contrasted with Schwarzer's radical feminist text, it becomes clear rather that *Häutungen* too articulates above all central tenets of radical feminism. For Stefan concurs with Schwarzer that the exploitation faced daily by women is a gender-specific form of oppression that is irreducible to the terms of class or race. Where Schwarzer argues in *Der 'kleine Unterschied'* that nothing, 'weder Rasse noch Klasse, bestimmt so sehr ein Menschenleben wie das Geschlecht',[53] *Häutungen* asserts that '*Sexismus*

51 Burns and van der Will, pp. 140-43.
52 Renate Becker, *Inszenierungen des Weiblichen*, p. 103.
53 Schwarzer, *Der 'kleine Unterschied'*, p. 178.

geht tiefer als rassismus als klassenkampf (*H*, 34). Whilst such a privileging of one type of difference over another is open to question, the similarity between Schwarzer's and Stefan's formulations surely suggests that both texts relate to what Keitel terms a 'einen genau definierbaren Diskussionsstand innerhalb der Frauenbewegung'.[54] Like the individual 'Protokoll' narratives that make up Schwarzer's text, *Häutungen* also grounds the point in female experience. This is evident, for example, in Veruschka's account of her relationships with her two male lovers: the student activist Samuel and the American 'Black Panther' Dave. Her relationship with Samuel teaches Veruschka that the economic reductionism of the political left is blind to the real needs of women:

> Samuel wühlte in seinen aktenordnern. das 'pillenproblem' schien ihm geläufig zu sein (er interessierte sich für die profite der pharmazeutischen industrie). wieso sprach er nicht mit mir, die ich die pille schluckte, darüber?

(*H*, 16)

Likewise, Veruschka's relationship with Dave shows that the racial discrimination he suffers as a black man does not predispose him toward sensitivity to her oppression as a woman. She notes: 'Dave bekämpfte die herr schaft der weissen über die schwarzen und stellte täglich die herr schaft der männer über die frauen neu her' (*H*, 35).

Der 'kleine Unterschied' and *Häutungen* also converge in their understanding of the site and the mechanisms of female oppression. In *Der 'kleine Unterschied'*, Schwarzer identified 'die Sexualität' as the 'Angelpunkt der Frauenfrage': here, she wrote, 'liegen Unterwerfung, Schuldbewußtsein und Männerfixierung von Frauen verankert. Hier steht das Fundament der männlichen Macht'.[55] Stefan's *Häutungen* too contains a critique of heterosexual relations that advances much the same propositions. More powerfully than the interview, commentary and analysis format of Schwarzer's text, however, autobiographical discourse allows in *Häutungen* a greater variety of ways in which such points can be made, providing a medium in which materials as diverse as accounts of experience, memories and dreams are brought together. In the text, above all the authenticity and authority of Veruschka's experience underwrites a critique of heterosexual intercourse as the mechanism through which female worth is defined – 'koitus [als] tribut für [...] gesellschaftliche anerkennung' (*H*, 35). This occurs notably in Veruschka's account of her attempt to be deflowered in the belief that 'mann würde mich als vollwertig behandeln' (*H*, 12). But other means too help to throw *Häutungen*'s critique into relief – like a poem whose symmetry

---

54   Keitel, 'Frauen, Texte, Theorie', p. 836.
55   Schwarzer, *Der 'kleine Unterschied'*, p. 7.

emphasises how the sexual act produces a pattern of domination and submission that amounts to the negation of the female partner's needs:

> Der eine küsste leidenschaftlich und wild, so dass ich
> zähne spürte, nichts als zähne –
> Und ich küsste leidenschaftlich und wild.
> Der andere küsste sanft und fand alles andere unreif und
> unerwachsen –
> Und ich küsste sanft und erwachsen.

(H, 42)

In addition, *Häutungen* also makes use of more traditional and impersonal forms of analytic or essayistic discourse in its critique of the ideology of heterosexual relations. Take the following remorseless demystification of the myth of romantic love (which parodies also the 'love is...' slogans popular at the time):

> liebe ist oft nichts anderes als eine schreckreaktion. eine reaktion auf den schreck, dass die wirklichkeit so brutal anders ist, als die vorstellung von ihr. durch liebe lässt sich brutalität eine weile vertuschen. liebe ist oft nur die beschichtung von abhängigkeiten aller art, von der abhängigkeit beispielsweise, die bestätigung durch einen mann zu brauchen. eine schicht liebe kann abhängigkeiten eine weile verbrämen. liebe ist eine tausendfache verwechslung von begehrt sein und vergewaltigt werden.

(H, 26)

In *Häutungen*, the interplay of experience-based, poetic and more essayistic discourses must be seen as part of a single communicative strategy. The relationship between them is essentially dialectical: on the one hand, essayistic passages draw their authority from the authenticity of Veruschka's experience; and on the other, the broader intersubjective significance of that experience is underlined by the more analytical passages. More insistently than the 'Protokoll' narratives of *Der 'kleine Unterschied'*, autobiographical discourse in *Häutungen* foregrounds also the debilitating subjective effect for Veruschka of the subjugation into which she is forced by established patterns of heterosexual relations. She describes her unfulfilling state of dependency as an addiction to 'die droge sexualität' (H, 72), an addiction which forces her to cling ever tighter to her male partners in order to compensate for the sense of self of which they deprive her. She writes: 'ich brauchte [Dave], weil ich mich nicht hatte' (H, 26).

However, notwithstanding the fact that, like *Der 'kleine Unterschied'*, *Häutungen* formulates central positions of radical feminism, we should not lose sight of striking differences between the two texts also. Schwarzer's more conventional analytical discourse, for instance, enables *Der 'kleine Unterschied'* to address the economic dependency of women, a topic never

145

taken up by *Häutungen*.[56] Conversely, where Schwarzer's text never advances beyond a critique of the established patriarchal order, *Häutungen*'s powerful narrative drive renders it more boldly utopian in its projection of an alternative to that order. This alternative, put briefly, takes the form of an exploration of the possibilities for self-actualisation afforded by non-hierarchical relationships between women, including sexual relationships based on a mutual '"[...] hingabe, die mit *zuwendung* zu tun hat, nicht mit unterwerfung [...]"' (*H*, 88). In projecting this alternative to the status quo, *Häutungen* admittedly seems to shift from radical feminist critique toward the lesbian separatist position noted by some critics. What is important, however, is arguably the manner in which such relationships between women are paradigmatic for a wider woman-based solidarity and autonomy. Veruschka certainly indicates as much in her discussion with her less politicised comrade (*H*, 82-89):

'[...] unter sich können [die frauen] die rollen loswerden, wenn sie es wirklich wollen−, wobei ich finde, dass es grundsätzlich darum geht, dass eine frau mit sich selber zurecht kommt, nicht darum, ob sie schon mal mit einer andern frau geschlafen hat− [...]'

(*H*, 84)

The wider symbolic significance so accorded to non-hierarchical relationships between women is central to *Häutungen*. For however self-absorbed her path of self-actualisation seems to become, Veruschka never ceases to affirm, even late in the text, the 'stellenwert, den die arbeit mit frauen in meinem leben einnimmt' (*H*, 102).

Verena Stefan's *Häutungen*, then, not only outlines, in an immediate and accessible form, the central principles of radical feminism. In addition to offering a radical feminist critique, it also points to possible alternatives to the established patriarchal order. Against the background of what some commentators have seen as the 'untheoretical' character of the New Women's Movement in the Federal Republic,[57] *Häutungen* thus claims for itself some of the functions of political discourse that Keitel associates with the 'Verständigungstexte' of oppositional movements. But Keitel also suggests that in such texts a specific construction of the 'lyrische[s] Ich' offers readers a surface for processes of identification and projection. Clearly, we have already begun to explore this issue with respect to *Häutungen*, because the premium that radical feminism places upon female experience makes it difficult (if not meaningless) to separate questions about the text's politics neatly from its

56   Schwarzer, *Der 'kleine Unterschied'*, pp. 220-28.
57   Edith Hoshino Altbach, 'The New German Women's Movement', in *German Feminism: Readings in Politics and Literature*, ed. by Edith Hoshino Altbach and others (Albany, N. Y., 1984), pp. 3-26 (p. 3).

construction of female subjectivity. However, a more detailed consideration of *Häutungen* as an autobiographical construction of the self will not only enhance our understanding of the text's appeal within the New Women's Movement; it can also provide us with a purchase on the most controversial issue associated with the text: its essentialism.

Häutungen uses a variety of textual strategies to address its reader. These include the range of experience-based, lyrical and analytical discourses outlined above. The text addresses questions to its reader, asking 'Wer schuf diese gesellschaft, die frauen hasst?' (*H*, 39). And in the figure of Veruschka's less politicised comrade from the New Women's Movement, it constructs a subject position for its reader, defusing her anticipated objections and dispelling her doubts. Nowhere, however, does *Häutungen* address that reader more forcefully than through the figure of Veruschka and her narrative of self-actualisation.

The figure of Veruschka is certainly sketched with the breadth which for Keitel encourages readers to bring their experience to the 'Verständigungstexte' of oppositional movements. Where *Klassenliebe*'s Karin asserts the singularity of her experience, *Häutungen* emphasises the broader gender-specific nature of Veruschka's experience. Describing how she was manhandled on the street by two immigrant workers, Veruschka appropriates from the rhetoric of anti-authoritarianism the topos of colonisation to assert that such treatment represents 'eine all tägliche behandlung einer kolonisierten in einer stadt der ersten welt' (*H*, 21). Another way in which *Häutungen* asserts the wider gender-specific character of Veruschka's experience is through stripping it of the specificity provided by references to time and space. *Häutungen* grounds the authority of its political statements in the authenticity guaranteed by its subtitle of 'Autobiografische Aufzeichnungen', yet references to time and place are minimal in the text, as if to elicit from the narrator's personal situation the contours of the oppression of women as a whole. To this end even the narrator herself remains largely nameless. She figures in the text above all in the intersubjectivity of first and second person pronouns – the 'ich' that she uses herself and the 'du' which others address to her. Just once she is named Veruschka by her female lover Fenna (*H*, 103).

At over twenty years remove from *Häutungen*'s publication it would be fanciful to suggest that we can reconstruct precisely how the text affected its empirical readers. Yet initial critical responses to the text suggest that it was frequently successful in fostering the processes of identification and projection outlined by Keitel. Kathrin Mosler certainly spoke for more than just herself when she affirmed in the *Frauenoffensive Journal* (1976) that she found in *Häutungen* 'Situationen wieder, die wir schon kennen'.[58] Significantly, though, it is the more hostile response of critics like Brigitte Classen and Gabriele

---

58   Kathrin Mosler, 'Hundert Blumen', *Frauenoffensive Journal*, 5 (1976), 6-8 (p. 7).

Goettle which suggests the extent to which women in the New Women's Movement felt able to identify with *Häutungen*. For them, precisely the text's appeal – 'vielleicht 30 000 Frauen, die alle meinen, "genau so wars bei mir"' – was what made their forceful critique so necessary.[59]

Renate Becker has dismissed approaches to women's writing based, like Keitel's, on a model of literary communication and the concomitant hypothesis of 'einer "idealen Leserin"' as utopian.[60] Whether the ideal of subversive textuality favoured by Becker herself is any less utopian is debatable. More significantly, however, Becker's refusal to countenance as politically fruitful the mechanisms of identification and projection posited by Keitel blinds her to *Häutungen*'s most powerful appeal to its readers: its narrative of self-actualisation.

According to Peter Brooks's *Reading for the Plot: Design and Intention in Narrative* (1984) narrative represents one of the most fundamental categories through which human beings organise and make sense of their experience. Predicated, moreover, upon 'the possibility of transmission' it has a dynamic and communicative aspect.[61] Thus narrative potentially constitutes a powerful force in the self-definition of feminism as an oppositional ideology. As Felski puts it with respect to the topos of 'self-transformation' in feminist fiction: insofar 'as narrative constitutes one of the most important ways in which ideologies are concretized in relation to life experience, the emergence of new plots for women which emphasize autonomy rather than dependence is to be welcomed'.[62] For its part, *Häutungen* unfolds a powerful emancipatory and hortative narrative that runs along the converging axes of the female body and the voice. Let us briefly consider this narrative before concluding our discussion.

The body stands at the heart of the representation of female subjectivity in *Häutungen*, and it is the 'Aufhebung der Entfremdung vom eigenen Körper' that drives its narrative.[63] The relationship that *Häutungen* posits between the female body and female subjectivity is primary, natural and unashamedly essentialist. Early in the text, Veruschka recalls a fleeting sensation of bodily integrity that she experienced as an adolescent:

> in einer dieser abendlichen stunden war es, dass das gefühl, tatsächlich lebendig
> zu sein, sich so heftig in mir ausbreitete, dass ich regungslos stehenblieb.
> sekundenlang spürte ich deutlich jede faser und jede pore der haut, die meinen

---

59 Classen and Goettle, p. 46.
60 Renate Becker, *Inszenierungen des Weiblichen*, p. 78.
61 Peter Brooks, *Reading for the Plot: Design and Intention in Narrative* (Cambridge, Mass. and London, 1984), pp. 3-7 and 27.
62 Felski, p. 152.
63 Schmidt, p. 86.

körper umschloss. blitzschnell flossen die prickelnden poren wieder zu einer
ganzheitlichen empfindung zusammen

(H, 9)

Yet within the symbolic order of patriarchy the narrator is alienated from her body as its surface is inscribed with male desires. *Häutungen* expresses this process of alienation using the metaphor of eviction: 'obwohl ich zeitweilig ein gefühl dafür bekam, dass ich mein körper rundum bewohnen konnte,' Veruschka notes, 'wurde ich stückweise daraus ausquartiert' (*H*, 10). Against the monolithic sexual ideology of patriarchy, the intrusion of nature into the urban monotony of Berlin (the 'grünfall der birken' at the start of the text, *H*, 5) and Veruschka's memory of her 'ganzheitlichen empfindung' trigger her quest to recover her 'verloren gegangene eigenkörperlichkeit' (*H*, 17). This quest is for Veruschka a difficult one. 'Entzugserscheinungen', *Hautungen*'s second chapter (*H*, 59-81), uses the metaphor of addiction to emphasise the painful struggle that marks her endeavour to overcome her experience of self-alienation. Only through a difficult separation from Samuel and a tentative process of 'ertasten betrachten besprechen' (*H*, 98) that Veruschka conducts together with her female lover Fenna can she perceive the contours of a less alienated relationship to her body.

The relationship to her body that Veruschka achieves is characterised above all by a pleasurable and positive experience of female bodily processes, such as menstruation (*H*, 107-08), whose rhythms are perceived as natural. It is here that *Häutungen* deploys the natural metaphors that have proved so contentious. The lips of the female genitals are described as 'blütenblätter' (*H*, 98), and the lining of the vagina as 'korallenwände[...]' (*H*, 107). From the wider perspective of autobiographical writing, the centrality the text accords to the body is certainly of interest, for it represents a significant departure from the imperious notion of 'Geist' or 'Bewußtsein' that critics of classical autobiography like Misch have regarded as the hallmark of autobiographical subjectivity.[64] Undeniably, though, it entangles the text in the problematic essentialism attacked by many critics, since Veruschka's discovery of her body amounts to the rediscovery of an originary harmony between the female body and external nature.

A further powerful impetus to *Häutungen*'s autobiographical narrative is provided by Veruschka's desire to find a voice. Alienated from her own body on the one hand, she is severed on the other from the linguistic resources necessary to articulate her needs. Veruschka outlines the profound sense of speechlessness that characterises her experience of her relationship with Dave thus: 'keine übung, keine tradition im reden, keine ansprüche. reden ein stummer wunsch' (*H*, 27). Against this overwhelming speechlessness,

---

64 Misch, I (Pt. 1), 11.

Veruschka's reappropriation of her own body and her burgeoning relationship with Fenna provide her with the desire to voice her needs: 'Jetzt will ich reden, um die anerkennung meiner neuen vorstellungen durchzusetzen, ich beginne erst, sie zu leben, ich kann noch nicht viel berichten' (*H*, 61), she writes. That her accession to language and to speech too is a faltering process, however, is illustrated by her attempt to explain her desire for a new life to Samuel:

> Ich beginne zu sprechen, während Samuel abwartend an seiner pfeife zieht. in meinem kopf ist der satz eingraviert − du sprichst ja so langsam, dass mann zum schluss schon vergessen hat, was du eingangs sagtest − [...] meine worte erreichen ihn nicht.
>
> (*H*, 62)

Here, it is not only her faltering speech but also Samuel's inability to understand her needs that thwarts Veruschka's endeavour to communicate those needs to him. But just as *Häutungen*'s essentialism has attracted criticism, so too the topos of the '"Überwindung der Sprachlosigkeit"' in fact widespread in feminist fiction has been attacked for its oversimplification of the 'konfliktreiche Beziehung zwischen Frauen, Weiblichkeit und Sprache'.[65]

In *Häutungen*, Veruschka's quest to recover her 'verloren gegangene eigenkörperlichkeit' (*H*, 17) goes hand in hand with her search for a voice. Indeed, they converge in her desire for an uncorrupted language with which to articulate her experience of her body. Critics have noted *Häutungen*'s critique of the imbrication of language and sexual domination, which asserts the impossibility of writing about the female body without interrogating the extent to which sexual domination is inscribed in language.[66] Veruschka takes this critique to a logical conclusion when she rejects existing anatomical designations for her body as oppressive:

> klitoris hat nichts zu tun mit der stelle an meinem körper, die klitoris genannt wird. um ein anderes wort dafür zu finden, muss ich noch länger anders leben als damals, da ich noch glaubte, mit klitoris etwas verbinden zu können.
>
> (*H*, 98)

Here, Veruschka acknowledges the impossibility of finding alternative terms outside patriarchal systems of representation. Yet the goal of an autonomous and uncorrupted language for female experience and the female body provides a powerful utopian horizon within the text as Veruschka affirms 'Ich führe ein anderes leben und spreche eine andere sprache' (*H*, 62) and insists 'Ich beginne, mich beim namen zu nennen' (*H*, 98). Indeed, *Häutungen*'s narrator

---

65   Weigel, *Die Stimme der Medusa*, p. 8.
66   See especially Schmidt, pp. 60-68.

150

certainly appears to acquire a perhaps symbolic power to name when, in the final section of the text ('Kürbisfrau', *H*, 119-24), her narrative shifts into the third person and she renames herself Cloe (after the Chloë in Virginia Woolf's *A Room of One's Own* of 1929, Schmidt and Becker surmise).[67]

Critics have acknowledged *Häutungen*'s status as the central literary document of the New Women's Movement in the Federal Republic. Yet they have also dismissed the text's political and aesthetic claims, rounding on its essentialism and contesting the naivety of its grasp of the relationships between language, female subjectivity and literary form. We have argued, by contrast, that the text's political and aesthetic claims must be seen precisely in the context of the needs and goals of the New Women's Movement, where *Häutungen* took on functions of political discourse and concretised radical feminist principles in a powerful narrative of self-actualisation. This is to situate *Häutungen* squarely within the practice of an identity politics in which the questions about experience and emancipation, about self-alienation and self-expression addressed by the text answer, as Felski puts it, a legitimate cultural need on the part of an oppositional movement that cannot just be dismissed from the perspective of more complex theoretical positions. For according to Felski:

> Literature does not simply constitute a self-referential and metalinguistic system, as some literary theorists appear to believe, but is also a medium which can profoundly influence individual and cultural self-understanding in the sphere of everyday life, charting the changing preoccupations of social groups through symbolic fictions by means of which they make sense of experience.[68]

Crucially, recent studies of women's writing to have taken up of the concept of identity politics, like Felski's *Beyond Feminist Aesthetics* and Diane Fuss's *Essentially Speaking: Feminism, Nature and Difference* (both of 1989), provide an interesting purchase on the question of essentialism that has dogged *Häutungen*.

Felski and Fuss argue for a flexible approach to questions of identity, authenticity and essence in women's writing which is able to consider them from a perspective that takes into account the broader oppositional needs of feminism. For Felski, a major task facing feminist criticism today is to develop an 'analysis of the subject which is not theoretically inadequate' but which can also account for the way in which precisely 'a supposedly conservative subject-based politics has been a powerful and effective force in mobilizing large numbers of women to assess critically and change aspects of their own lives'.[69] We must acknowledge, in short, that 'questions of

---

67 Schmidt, p. 104; Renate Becker, *Inszenierungen des Weiblichen*, p. 102.
68 Felski, p. 7.
69 Felski, p. 54.

subjectivity, truth, and identity may not be outmoded fictions but concepts which still possess an important strategic relevance'.[70] For her part, Fuss mounts a resolute defence of the political value of essentialism for oppositional movements. In the service of the dispossessed and the disenfranchised, she argues, the claim to possess an essence may constitute a 'rallying cry to stimulate personal awareness and political action':

> The point [...] of defining women from an essentialist standpoint is not to imprison women within their bodies but to rescue them from enculturating definitions by men. An essentialist definition of "woman" implies that there will always remain some part of "woman" which resists masculine imprinting and socialization [...]. To claim that "we are women from the start" has this advantage — a political advantage perhaps pre-eminently — that a woman will never be a woman solely in masculine terms, never be wholly and permanently annihilated in a masculine order.[71]

If this is so, is it not possible that *Häutungen*'s essentialism, however problematic, may also represent a call to 'personal awareness and political action'?

The claims of Felski and Fuss force us to reconsider the problem of essentialism in the text. Moreover, a strength of their respective arguments is that we are not enjoined to adopt an essentialist position in order to appreciate its radical potential. On the contrary, Fuss suggests the concept of essence itself represents a political tool that can in turn be deconstructed as a strategic fiction.[72] That this claim is not sophistry is demonstrated by the way it helps to pinpoint a paradox at the heart of *Häutungen*'s narrative of self-actualisation that has to date escaped critical scrutiny.

Häutungen's narrative of self-actualisation, we suggested, centres on Veruschka's related quests to recover her 'verloren gegangene eigenkörperlichkeit' (*H*, 17) and to find a voice. We can glimpse here what surely amounts to a tension in the text between the essentialism inherent in the idea of a return to an original bodily integrity and the constructive force of narrative. Fuss's perception that essentialism itself may represent a construct or a strategic fiction helps us to grasp this tension as a highly productive one. For on the one hand, *Häutungen* appeals to the notion of a female essence in order to mobilise and empower its (female) readers. Yet on the other, it combines this essentialist rallying cry with a clear imperative to construct an identity. *Häutungen*'s essentialism is generally acknowledged; but the fact that it combines this with the imperative of self-invention is less well understood. In the text, the notion of self-invention embraces the erotic practices through

70   Felski, p. 70.
71   Fuss, pp. 97 and 61.
72   Fuss, pp. 2-6.

which Veruschka and Fenna build their relationship. Veruschka writes: 'wir schaffen uns neu durch ertasten betrachten besprechen' (*H*, 98). It also encompasses Veruschka's autobiographical act, through which she seeks to right the patriarchal 'fälschung meiner eigenen geschichte' (*H*, 57). The first part of this chapter examined how some feminist critics of autobiography have linked women's relationship to the genre to the historical choices available to them; it contemplated also the possible connection between autobiography as a discourse of life and narrative choices on the one hand and feminism on the other as a politics of choice intent upon mobilising the range of opportunities historically open to women. This problematic of choice and opportunity features already in Buhmann's *Ich habe mir eine Geschichte geschrieben*. Grounding her autobiographical narrative in feminist politics allows Buhmann to expand and to realise, both in her social practice and her autobiographical act, what she describes as the '*Möglichkeiten meiner Selbst* ' (*G*, 95). Yet it is foregrounded in *Häutungen* too. Here, the marginal figure of the narrator's friend Nadjenka throws into relief the extent to which Veruschka's path of self-actualisation and self-invention is contingent upon mobilising the choices open to her (by joining a women's group or leaving Samuel, for example). Nadjenka thus functions in the text as a negative 'doppelgängerin[...]' (*H*, 106) to Veruschka, unable to make the decisions or take the steps that she, Veruschka, does make or take:

> [Nadjenkas] leben schnürt ihr die kehle zu. [...] Nie eine wahl gehabt. sekretärin gelernt, weil kein geld da war für etwas anderes, geheiratet, um von zuhause wegzukommen, um endlich zuhause zu sein, ein kind bekommen, nach vielen jahren schliesslich ein kind um —
>
> (*H*, 106)

Häutungen's significance for the New Women's Movement is in no small measure explained by the way it formulated and presumably helped to disseminate the positions of radical feminism. But over and above this, its appeal to women readers surely lay in it its powerful central narrative of self-actualisation. For that narrative provided the women's movement with a compelling symbolic fiction, in which the rallying cry of a call to essence was combined with a more complex grasp of the self as an open-ended nexus of possibilities, and of self-invention as a process dependent upon seizing those possibilities. If feminism is, as Giddens has suggested, a 'politics of choice', it is not hard to grasp how *Häutungen* could become West German feminism's essential fiction.

Conclusion

The aim of this study has been to offer an approach to autobiographical texts of the 1970s that grasps them both as historical documents and as contributions to the genre of autobiography. In the interpretative framework established in our introductory chapter and in close readings of individual texts, we have examined the rich and varied ways in which texts by Vesper, Brinkmann, Struck, Buhmann and Stefan engage both with the discursive contexts of their production and with the problematic of autobiographical writing. In addition to offering some reflections on our approach to our texts, we will close now by considering some of the literary and political issues raised by them.

Setting them in the context of shifts of political discourse within the Federal Republic, our first concern has been to illuminate how our chosen autobiographical texts engage with the discourses of the student and feminist movements of the 1960s and 1970s. Yet at the same time, we have never lost sight of the problem of autobiographical writing in them. Explicitly or implicitly, autobiography involves assumptions about the limitations and possibilities of the act of self-representation, and this perception too has informed our textual analyses.[1]

That questions about our texts' status as historical documents and as instances of autobiographical writing are ultimately inseparable is forcefully demonstrated above all by the women's autobiographies analysed above. Admittedly, some of the force of *Klassenliebe*'s reflections on the relationship of class and gender are undermined by a preference for the immediacy of the diary form. But in Buhmann's *Ich habe mir eine Geschichte geschrieben* and Stefan's *Häutungen* autobiography represents the very discursive medium of the identity politics of feminism. For in Buhmann's text it is a feminist politics that grounds an autobiographical narrative of self-actualisation through and in the collective agency of the New Women's Movement; and in *Häutungen*, it is an autobiographical narrative that concretises and dramatises in relation to female experience a feminist politics of the private and the political.

Combining the autobiographical with the political as effectively as they do, the women's autobiographies examined here throw into relief important questions about the relationship between text and context, and between the political and aesthetic value of autobiographical writing. The examination in this study of the relationship between our texts and the social and ideological contexts of their composition has comprised an exploration of the way these texts take up the discourses of anti-authoritarianism and of the New Women's Movement. This surely does not need repeating here. Yet in ways less

---

1   The 'theoretical dimension' of every autobiography is asserted in Sheringham, p. ix.

immediately apparent it has considered also the more complex manner in which the texts in turn grasp their own status and function within the oppositional politics of the student and women's movements, and their own value for the project of transformative social and political action.

With the exception perhaps of *Klassenliebe*, the horizon of social action is evident enough in the case of the women's autobiographies examined here. Although the diary form of *Klassenliebe* undermines the political perspectives and commitments of its protagonist Karin, the enormous success enjoyed by the text upon its publication at least fulfils one of her public aspirations – to become a writer. By contrast, the autobiographies of Buhmann and Stefan contribute more self-consciously to the oppositional politics of the New Women's Movement. Intended for reception within the movement (*Häutungen* after all constructs a subject position for its anticipated reader in the figure of Veruschka's less politicised comrade), *Ich habe mir eine Geschichte geschrieben* and *Häutungen* have a dual function. Bringing a feminist interpretation of gender to bear on the experience of their narrator-protagonists, they can be understood as forms of political discourse that disseminate and clarify the premises and positions of feminism within the women's movement. Yet they also represent emancipatory case studies, symbolic fictions of identity formation designed to empower readers to assess and to change critically aspects of their lives.[2]

By contrast, the way that Vesper's *Die Reise* and Brinkmann's *Erkundungen für die Präzisierung des Gefühls für einen Aufstand* set themselves in relation to the question of social and political transformation is more complex. In his letters to his publisher, März, Vesper's hope that his autobiography could provide the anti-authoritarian student movement with a revolutionary case history emerges clearly. But this movement lacked the vibrant culture of autobiographical self-expression later so central to the politics of the New Women's Movement. Perhaps in part because writing autobiography was so alien to the political culture of the student movement, the narrative of personal radicalisation inscribed within *Die Reise* is ultimately undermined by the perception that autobiographical and revolutionary practices are mutually exclusive. Moreover, the fact of his suicide and the delay in the publication of the text ensured that, in the fraught climate of the 'deutscher Herbst', *Die Reise* did in any case not meet with the interpretation that Vesper might have desired. An 'anti-authoritarian' readership willing or able to read the text as a revolutionary case history had ceased to exist.

For their part, the *Erkundungen* take up an anti-authoritarian discourse of the manipulation of human needs by the mass media. But on account of Brinkmann's hostility toward the left after the decline of the student movement, the possibility of transformative social and political action does not

2   Felski, p. 54.

figure within his autobiographical notes. For on the one hand the *Erkundungen* grasp the autobiographical act as the site of a retreat from a social and political reality dominated by the pervasive 'Bewußtseinsindustrie' that the mass media came to represent for Brinkmann. On the other, they formulate a radical concept of self-invention which, grounded in the metaphor of the random processing of information, proceeds as a textual performance that does not aspire to engage with a world beyond its parameters. The very subject capable of transforming the social and political institutions of the world has been dissolved into information.

Thus a final question raised by our texts is the relationship between their political and aesthetic value. Again, it is the women's autobiographies examined here that bring the issues involved most crisply into focus. It is clear that in our discussion of texts by Struck, Buhmann and Stefan we have been dealing with a single context: that of feminism. But by treating three women's texts in a single chapter we have necessarily implied that they are less complex than the texts by Vesper and Brinkmann, to which we have devoted a chapter each. As far as their engagement with the problematic of autobiographical writing is concerned this is arguably true. The complex connections drawn in Vesper's *Die Reise* and Brinkmann's *Erkundungen* between the discourses of anti-authoritarianism and the act of self-presentation surely make these the more fascinating literary texts. But as a case study of the way in which text and context are related and interact, our discussion of Struck's *Klassenliebe*, Buhmann's *Ich habe mir eine Geschichte geschrieben* and Stefan's *Häutungen* is in crucial respects more revealing. Less complex these texts may be, but the boldness with which the autobiographies of Buhmann and Stefan press autobiographical discourse into the service of the identity politics of feminism forces us to put the literary scholar's perhaps inevitable preference for subtlety and complexity into perspective. *Ich habe mir eine Geschichte geschrieben* and *Häutungen* remind us, in short, that we should not fall into the trap of confusing the aesthetic value of texts with their political value. These two texts force us confront the fact that the political value of literature is 'not merely constituted through stylistic differences', or through differing degrees of aesthetic sophistication and complexity.[3] Rather it is itself a complex function of the way in which texts interact with the contexts of their production and of their reception.

3   Felski, p. 157.

Bibliography

I: Principal Primary Texts

Brinkmann, Rolf Dieter, *Erkundungen für die Präzisierung des Gefühls für einen Aufstand: Reise Zeit Magazin. (Tagebuch)* (Reinbek, 1987)

Buhmann, Inga, *Ich habe mir eine Geschichte geschrieben* (Munich, 1977)

Stefan, Verena, *Häutungen. Autobiografische Aufzeichnungen Gedichte Träume Analysen* (Munich, 1975)

Struck, Karin, *Klassenliebe. Roman* (Frankfurt am Main, 1973)

Vesper, Bernward, *Die Reise. Romanessay*, ed. by Jörg Schröder (Jossa, 1977)

—, *Die Reise. Romanessay. Ausgabe letzter Hand*, ed. by Jörg Schröder and Klaus Behnken (Jossa, 1979)

—, *Die Reise. Romanessay. Ausgabe letzter Hand*, ed. by Jörg Schröder and Klaus Behnken (Berlin and Schlechtenwegen, 1981)

—, *Ergänzungen zu: Die Reise. Romanessay. Aus der Ausgabe letzter Hand*, ed. by Jörg Schröder and Klaus Behnken (Jossa, 1979)

—, *Die Reise. Romanessay. Ausgabe letzter Hand*, ed. by Jörg Schröder and Klaus Behnken (Reinbek, 1983)

II: Other Primary Materials (including further texts by Brinkmann, Struck and Stefan)

Baumann, Bommi, *Wie alles anfing. Mit einem Vorwort von Heinrich Böll und einem Nachwort von Michael Sontheimer* (Berlin, 1991)

Becker, Jürgen, *Felder* (Frankfurt am Main, 1964)

Böll, Heinrich, *Die verlorene Ehre der Katharina Blum oder Wie Gewalt entstehen und wohin sie führen Kann* (Cologne, 1974)

Brinkmann, Rolf Dieter, *Le Chant du Monde. Gedichte 1963-1964* (Olef, Eifel, 1964)

—, *Raupenbahn* (Cologne and Berlin, 1966)

—, 'Sex und Politik', *konkret*, June 1966, p. 8

—, 'Angriff aufs Monopol. Ich hasse alte Dichter', *Christ und Welt*, 15 November 1968, pp. 14-15

—, *Godzilla* (Cologne, 1968)

—, *Keiner weiß mehr. Roman* (Cologne and Berlin, 1968)

—, *Die Piloten. Neue Gedichte* (Cologne, 1968)

—, 'Der Film in Worten', in *ACID. Neue amerikanische Szene*, ed. by Rolf Dieter Brinkmann and Ralf-Rainer Rygulla (Berlin and Schlechtenwegen, 1969), pp. 381-99

—, ed., *Silverscreen. Neue amerikanische Lyrik* (Cologne, 1969)

—, 'Notizen 1969 zu amerikanischen Gedichten und zu dieser Anthologie', in *Silverscreen. Neue amerikanische Lyrik*, ed. by Rolf Dieter Brinkmann (Cologne, 1969), pp. 7-32

—, *Gras. Gedichte* (Cologne, 1970)

—, 'Wie ich lebe und warum (1970)', in *Trivialmythen*, ed. by Renate Matthaei (Frankfurt am Main, 1970), pp. 67-73

—, *Westwärts 1 & 2. Gedichte* (Reinbek, 1975)

—, *Rom, Blicke* (Reinbek, 1979)

—, *Der Film in Worten. Prosa. Erzählungen. Essays. Hörspiele. Fotos. Collage. 1965-1974* (Reinbek, 1982)

—, and Rygulla, Ralf-Rainer, eds., *ACID. Neue amerikanische Szene* (Berlin and Schlechtenwegen, 1969)

Brock, Bazon, *Bazon Brock, was machen sie jetzt so? Die 'Blaue Illustrierte' — eine Autobiographie* (Darmstadt, 1968)

Chotjewitz, Peter, *Vom Leben und Lernen. Stereotexte* (Darmstadt, 1969)

Dittberner, Hugo, *Das Internat. Papiere vom Kaffeetisch* (Darmstadt und Neuwied, 1976)

Döblin, Alfred, *Berlin Alexanderplatz. Die Geschichte vom Franz Biberkopf* (Olten and Freiburg, 1961)

Goethe, Johann Wolfgang von, *Sämtliche Werke nach Epochen seines Schaffens. Münchner Ausgabe* , ed. by Karl Richter and others, 21 vols (Munich, 1985-), XVI: *Aus meinem Leben. Dichtung und Wahrheit*, ed. by Peter Sprengel (1985)

Härtling, Peter, *Nachgetragene Liebe* (Darmstadt and Neuwied, 1980)

Hoffmann, Freia, *Ledige Mütter. Protokolle, Analysen, Juristische Informationen, Selbstorganisation* (Frankfurt am Main, 1975)

Kerouac, Jack, *On the Road* (New York, 1957)

Lang, Roland, *Ein Hai in der Suppe oder Das Glück des Philipp Ronge. Roman* (Munich, 1975)

März Texte 1 (Darmstadt, 1969)

Matthaei, Renate, ed., *Trivialmythen* (Frankfurt am Main, 1970)

Meckel, Christoph, *Suchbild. Über meinen Vater* (Düsseldorf, 1980)

Frank O'Hara, *Lunch Poems und andere Gedichte*, trans. and ed. by Rolf Dieter Brinkmann (Cologne, 1969)

Runge, Erika, *Bottroper Protokolle* (Frankfurt am Main, 1968)

—, *Frauen. Versuche zur Emanzipation* (Frankfurt am Main, 1969)

Salzinger, Helmut, 'Das lange Gedicht', in *Super Garde. Prosa der Beat- und Pop-Generation*, ed. by Vagelis Tsakiridis (Düsseldorf, 1969), pp. 167-91

Schneider, Peter, *Lenz. Eine Erzählung* (Berlin, 1973)

Schwarzer, Alice, *Frauenarbeit — Frauenbefreiung* (Frankfurt am Main, 1973)

—, *Der 'kleine Unterschied' und seine großen Folgen. Frauen über sich — Beginn einer Befreiung* (Frankfurt am Main, 1975)

Struck, Karin, *Die Mutter. Roman* (Frankfurt am Main, 1975)

Timm, Uwe, *Heißer Sommer* (Munich, 1974)

Tsakiridis, Vagelis, ed., *Super Garde. Prosa der Beat- und Pop-Generation* (Düsseldorf, 1969)

Wellershoff, Dieter, *Die Schattengrenze. Roman* (Cologne, 1969)

Weiss, Peter, *Notizbücher 1971-1980*, 2 vols (Frankfurt am Main, 1981)

Zwerenz, Gerhard, *Die schrecklichen Folgen der Legende, ein Liebhaber gewesen zu sein. Erotische Geschichten* (Munich, 1978)

III: Secondary Literature on Brinkmann, Buhmann, Stefan, Struck and Vesper

BRINKMANN

Adam, Wolfgang, '*Arkadien* als *Vorhölle*. Die Destruktion des traditionellen Italien-Bildes in Rolf Dieter Brinkmanns *Rom, Blicke*', *Euphorion*, 83 (1989), 226-45

Braun, Michael, 'Finsterer Alptraum Gegenwart. Aus dem Nachlaß von Rolf Dieter Brinkmann', *Badische Zeitung*, 12/13 December 1987, ('Magazin'), p. 4

Groß, Thomas, '"...jetzt, jetzt, jetzt ad infinitum!" Zum neuen Materialband aus dem Nachlaß von Rolf Dieter Brinkmann', *taz*, 10 July 1987, pp. 15-16

Hartung, Harald, 'Pop als "postmoderne" Literatur. Die deutsche Szene: Brinkmann und andere', *Neue Rundschau*, 82 (1971), 723-42

Heise, Hans-Jürgen, 'Einer nennt es Sprache. Der überschätzte Rolf Dieter Brinkmann. Pop-Poesie mit Klischees aus zweiter Hand', *Rheinischer Merkur*, 5 December 1980, p. 37

Karsunke, Yaak, 'Ins Gras gebissen. Rolf Dieter Brinkmanns Gedichtband', *Frankfurter Allgemeine Zeitung*, 27 June 1970, p. 21

Lampe, Gerhard, *Ohne Subjektivität. Interpretationen zur Lyrik Rolf Dieter Brinkmanns vor dem Hintergrund der Studentenbewegung* (Tübingen, 1983)

Philippi, Klaus-Peter, 'Ohne Sinn wird die Kultur zur Müllkippe. Ein nachgelassenes Tagebuch von Rolf D. Brinkmann', *Rheinischer Merkur*, 28 August 1987, p. 18

Pickerodt, Gerd, '"Der Film in Worten." Rolf Dieter Brinkmanns Provokation der Literatur', *Weimarer Beiträge*, 37 (1991), 1028-42

Piwitt, Hermann Peter, 'Rauschhafte Augenblicke. Hermann Peter Piwitt über Rolf Dieter Brinkmann: "Rom, Blicke"', *Der Spiegel*, 17 September 1979, pp. 252-57

—, '"Die ganze Häßlichkeit der Welt bin Ich." Hermann Peter Piwitt über Rolf Dieter Brinkmanns Nachlaßband "Erkundungen"', *Der Spiegel*, 3 August 1987, pp. 143-45

Schlösser, Hermann, *Reiseformen des Geschriebenen. Selbsterfahrung und Weltdarstellung in Reisebüchern Wolfgang Koeppens, Rolf Dieter Brinkmanns und Hubert Fichtes* (Vienna, Cologne and Graz, 1987)

Schulz, Genia, 'Kein Zugeständnis. Rolf Dieter Brinkmanns "Erkundungen"', *Merkur*, 41 (1987), 916-21

Späth, Sybille, *Rolf Dieter Brinkmann* (Stuttgart, 1989)

—, 'Gehirnströme und Medientext. Zu Rolf Dieter Brinkmanns späten Tagebüchern', *Literaturmagazin*, 30 (1992), 106-17

Willson, A. Leslie, 'Der schöne, einzigartige Brinkmann', *Literaturmagazin*, 36 (1995), 38-40

Zeller, Michael, 'In den Haß emigriert. Ein Einsamer auf dem "Idiotenschlachtfeld": Rolf Dieter Brinkmanns Tagebuch ist das Protokoll einer Selbstzerstörung', *Die Zeit*, 28 August 1987, p. 39

BUHMANN

Braatz, Ilse, 'Inga Buhmann: Ich habe mir eine Geschichte geschrieben. Rezension', *mamas pfirsiche*, 9/10 (1978), 195-96

STEFAN

Anders, Ann, 'Fiktiver Brief an Verena Stefan', *Ästhetik und Kommunikation*, 25 (1976), 120-21

Baier, Lothar, 'Nicht länger Teil eines Paares oder Abrechnung mit dem Patriarchat. "Häutungen" — die autobiographische Erzählung einer Feministin', *Frankfurter Allgemeine Zeitung*, 16 March 1976, p. 20

Classen, Brigitte, and Goettle, Gabriele, '"Häutungen" — eine Verwechslung von Anemone und Amazone', *Courage*, September 1976, pp. 45-46

Just, Renate, 'Schluss mit dem Klagen', *Die Zeit*, 24 September 1976, ('Zeitmagazin') pp. 16-18 and 50-55

Mosler, Kathrin, 'Hundert Blumen', *Frauenoffensive Journal*, 5 (1976), 6-8

Reinig, Christa, 'Das weibliche Ich', *Frauenoffensive Journal*, 5 (1976), 50-51

—, 'Das weibliche Ich', *Süddeutsche Zeitung*, 7 April 1976, ('Literatur') p. 3

Tempel, Ute, 'wie können frauen als "menschen" schreiben?', *mamas pfirsiche*, 4/5 (1976), 31-43

Winter, Riki, 'Verena Stefan' (1981), in *Kritisches Lexikon der deutschen Gegenwartsliteratur*, ed. by Heinz Ludwig Arnold (Munich, 1978-)

STRUCK

Adelson, Leslie, 'The Question of a Feminist Aesthetic and Karin Struck's *Klassenliebe*', in *Beyond the Eternal Feminine: Critical Essays on Women and German Literature*, ed. by Susan J. Cocalis and Kay Goodman (Stuttgart, 1982), pp. 335-49

Heuer, Rolv, 'Bon Jour, Proletariat', *konkret*, May 1973, pp. 44-45

Krolow, Karl, 'Karin diskutiert sich ins Leben. Karin Strucks "Klassenliebe"', *Die Tat*, 19 May 1973, p. 25

Peukermann, Heinrich, 'Der Weg vom Werkkreis in den Mediendschungel. Karin Struck — oder wir junge Autoren vermarktet werden', *Die Tat*, 22 July 1983, p. 9

Schonauer, Franz, 'Schwierigkeiten beim Aufsteigen', *Deutsche Zeitung*, 13 July 1973, p. 12

Schwarzer, Alice, 'Die mit dem Penis schreiben. Was die Männer der Literaturkritik an Karin Strucks "Klassenliebe" so erregt hat', *pardon*, July 1973, pp. 18-19

VESPER

Abosch, Heinz, 'Kein Weg ins Freie. Zu Bernward Vespers Buch "Die Reise"', *Neue Rundschau*, 89 (1978), 310-13

Becker, Peter von, 'Totgeboren ins deutsche Vater-Land. Bernward Vespers nachgelassener Roman-Essay "Die Reise"', *Die Zeit*, 11 November 1977, ('Literatur') pp. 11-12

Bhatti, Anil, 'Wozu schreiben? Bemerkungen anläßlich der Lektüre von Bernward Vespers "Die Reise"', in *Erzählung und Erzählforschung im 20. Jahrhundert. Tagungsbeiträge eines Symposiums der Alexander von Humboldt-Stiftung Bonn-Bad Godesberg, veranstaltet vom 9. bis 14. September 1980 in Ludwigsburg*, ed. by Rolf Kloepfer and Gisela Janetzke-Dillner (Stuttgart, 1981), pp. 309-17

Grütter, Emil, 'Faschistoide Sozialisation und Gesellschaftskritik in Bernward Vespers Autobiographie *Die Reise*', *Freiburger literaturpsychologische Gespräche*, 1 (1981), 63-77

Guntermann, Georg, 'Tagebuch einer Reise in das Innere des Autors. Versuch zu Vespers "Romanessay" *Die Reise*', *Zeitschrift für deutsche Philologie*, 100 (1981), 232-53

Lubich, Frederick Alfred, 'Bernward Vespers *Die Reise* — der Untergang des modernen Pikaro', in *Der moderne deutsche Schelmenroman — Interpretationen*, ed. by Gerhart Hoffmeister (Amsterdam, 1986), pp. 219-37

—, 'Bernward Vespers "Die Reise": Von der Hitler-Jugend zur RAF. Identitätssuche unter dem Fluch des Faschismus', *German Studies Review*, 11 (1988), 69-94

Mosler, Peter, 'Bericht über ein verlorene Generation oder Reise ohne Ankunft. Bernward Vespers Roman', *Frankfurter Allgemeine Zeitung*, ('Literatur') p. 5

Neumann, Bernd, 'Die Wiedergeburt des Erzählens aus dem Geist der Autobiographie? Einige Anmerkungen zum neuen autobiographischen Roman am Beispiel von Hermann Kinders "Der Schleiftrog" und Bernward Vespers "Die Reise"', *Basis*, 9 (1979), 91-121

Rathjen, Friedhelm, 'Das andere Ende der Kerze: Bernward Vesper', *Bargfelder Bote*, 185/186 (1994), 22-33

Schirnding, Albert von, 'Patre Absente. Eine Generation schreibt sich frei', *Merkur*, 34 (1980), 489-97

Schultz-Gerstein, Christian, 'Deutscher Sumpf', *Der Spiegel*, 11 July 1977, pp. 146-148

Schweikert, Uwe, 'Logbuch eines Verzweifelnden. Bernward Vespers "Die Reise"', *Frankfurter Rundschau*, 29 October 1977, p. 23

Vogt, Jochen, 'Schwierigkeiten mit der Selbstentblößung. Versuch über die "Die Reise" von Bernward Vesper', *Diskussion Deutsch*, 17 (1986), 289-99

IV: The Literary Context (including New Subjectivity, the Autobiography of the 1960s and 1970s and discussions of more than one author in I. above)

Anz, Thomas, 'Neue Subjektivität', in *Moderne Literatur in Grundbegriffen*, ed. by Dieter Borchmeyer and Viktor Zmegac (Frankfurt am Main, 1987), pp. 283-86

Becker, Renate, *Inszenierungen des Weiblichen. Die literarische Darstellung weiblicher Subjektivität in der westdeutschen Frauenliteratur der siebziger und achtziger Jahre* (Frankfurt am Main, Bern, New York and Paris, 1992)

Briegleb, Klaus, *1968. Literatur in der antiautoritären Bewegung* (Frankfurt am Main, 1993)

Dittberner, Hugo, 'Die autobiographische Tendenz', *Literarische Hefte*, 52 (1976). 69-71

Enzensberger, Hans Magnus, 'Gemeinplätze, die Neueste Literatur betreffend', *Kursbuch*, 15 (1968), 187-97

Frieden, Sandra, *Autobiography: Self into Form. German-Language Autobiographical Writings of the 1970s* (Frankfurt am Main, Bern and New York, 1983)

Hartung, Klaus, 'Die Repression wird zum Milieu. Die Beredsamkeit linker Literatur (Peter Schneider, Peter O. Chotjewitz, Inga Buhmann und Bernward Vesper)', *Literaturmagazin*, 11 (1979), 52-79

Helm, Ingo, 'Literatur und Massenmedien', in *Gegenwartsliteratur seit 1968*, ed. by Klaus Briegleb and Sigrid Weigel (Munich, 1992), pp. 536-56

Hinton Thomas, R., and Bullivant, Keith, *Literature in Upheaval: West German Writers and the Challenge of the 1960s* (Manchester, 1974)

Kosta, Barbara, *Recasting Autobiography: Women's Counterfictions in Contemporary German Literature and Film* (Ithaca and London, 1994)

Kümmel, F.-Michael, 'Eine (sich) erinnernde Literatur. Versuch einer literaturtheoretischen Einordnung des autobiographischen Schreibens der 70er Jahre', *die horen*, 33, no. 4 (1988), 9-18

McGowan, Moray, '"Neue Subjektivität"', in *After the 'Death of Literature': West German Writing of the 1970s*, ed. by Keith Bullivant (Oxford, New York and Munich, 1989), pp. 53-68

Mattenklott, Gundel, 'Literatur von unten – die andere Literatur', in *Gegenwartsliteratur seit 1968*, ed. by Klaus Briegleb and Sigrid Weigel (Munich, 1992), pp. 153-81

Reinhardt, Stephan, '"Nach innen führt der geheimnisvolle Weg, aber er führt auch wieder heraus." Unvollständige Bermerkungen zum neuen Irrationalismus in der Literatur', in *Nach dem Protest. Literatur im Umbruch*, ed. by W. Martin Lüdke (Frankfurt am Main, 1979), pp. 158-84

Richter-Schröder, Karin, *Frauenliteratur und weibliche Identität. Theoretische Ansätze zu einer weiblichen Ästhetik und zur Entwicklung der neuen deutschen Frauenliteratur* (Frankfurt am Main, 1986)

Roberts, David, 'Tendenzwenden. Die sechziger und siebziger Jahre in literaturhistorischer Perspektive', *Deutsche Vierteljahresschrift für Literaturwissenschaft und Geistesgeschichte*, 56 (1982), 290-313

Ruoff Kramer, Karin, *The Politics of Discourse: Third Thoughts on "New Subjectivity"* (Bern, New York, Frankfurt am Main and Paris, 1993)

Saunders, Barbara, *Contemporary German Autobiography: Literary Approaches to the Problem of Identity* (London, 1986)

Schmidt, Ricarda, *Westdeutsche Frauenliteratur in den 70er Jahren* (Frankfurt am Main, 1982)

Schnell, Ralf, *Die Literatur der Bundesrepublik. Autoren, Geschichte, Literaturbetrieb* (Stuttgart, 1986)

Türkis, Wolfgang, *Beschädigtes Leben. Autobiographische Texte der Gegenwart* (Stuttgart, 1990)

Walser, Martin, 'Über die Neueste Stimmung im Westen', *Kursbuch*, 20 (1970), 19-41

Weigel, Sigrid, *Die Stimme der Medusa. Schreibweisen in der Gegenwartsliteratur von Frauen* (Dülmen-Hiddingsel, 1987)

V: The History and Theory of Autobiography

Boerner, Peter, *Tagebuch* (Stuttgart, 1969)

Brodzki, Bella, and Schenk, Celeste, eds., 'Introduction', in *Life/Lines: Theorizing Women's Autobiography*, ed. by Bella Brodzki and Celeste Schenk (Ithaca and London, 1988), pp. 1-15

Bruss, Elisabeth, *Autobiographical Acts: The Changing Situation of a Literary Genre* (Baltimore and London, 1976)

Eakin, John Paul, *Fictions in Autobiography: Studies in the Art of Self-Invention* (Princeton, 1985)

Felski, Rita, *Beyond Feminist Aesthetics: Feminist Literature and Social Change* (London, 1989)

Goodman, Kay, 'Weibliche Autobiographien', in *Frauen Literatur Geschichte. Schreibende Frauen vom Mittelalter bis zur Gegenwart*, ed. by Hiltrud Gnüg and Renate Möhrmann (Stuttgart, 1985), pp. 289-99

—, *Dis/Closures: Women's Autobiography in Germany between 1790 and 1914* (New York, Bern and Frankfurt am Main, 1986)

—, 'Elisabeth to Meta: Epistolary Autobiography and the Postulation of the Self', in *Life/Lines: Theorizing Women's Autobiography*, ed. by Bella Brodzki and Celeste Schenk (Ithaca and London, 1988), pp. 306-19

Jelinek, Estelle C., ed., 'Introduction: Women's Autobiography and the Male Tradition', in *Women's Autobiography: Essays in Criticism*, ed. by Estelle C. Jelinek (Bloomington and London, 1980), pp. 1-20

Keitel, Evelyne, 'Frauen, Texte, Theorie. Aspekte eines problematischen Verhältnisses', *Das Argument*, 25 (1983), 830-41

—, 'Verständigungstexte—Form, Funktion, Wirkung', *The German Quarterly*, 56 (1983), 431-55

Kolkenbrock-Netz, Jutta, and Schuller, Marianne, 'Frau im Spiegel. Zum Verhältnis von autobiographischer Schreibweise und feministischer Praxis', in *Entwürfe von Frauen in der Literatur des zwanzigsten Jahrhunderts*, ed. by Irmela von der Lühe (Berlin, 1982), pp. 154-72

Marcus, Laura, *Auto/biographical discourses: criticism, theory, practice* (Manchester and New York, 1994)

Man, Paul de, 'Autobiography as De-facement', *MLN*, 94 (1979), 919-30

Mazlish, Bruce, 'Autobiography and Psycho-analysis: Between Truth and Self-Deception', *Encounter*, 35 (1970), 28-37

Misch, Georg, *Geschichte der Autobiographie*, 4 vols (Frankfurt am Main, 1949-69)

Neumann, Bernd, *Identität und Rollenzwang. Zur Theorie der Autobiographie* (Frankfurt am Main, 1970)

Pascal, Roy, *Design and Truth in Autobiography* (London, 1960)

Pomerlau, Cynthia S., 'The Emergence of Women's Autobiography in England', in *Women's Autobiography: Essays in Criticism*, ed. by Estelle C. Jelinek (Bloomington and London, 1980), pp. 21-38

Renza, Louis A., 'The Veto of the Imagination: A Theory of Autobiography', *NLH*, 9 (1977), 1-26

Schneider, Manfred, *Die erkaltete Herzensschrift. Der autobiographische Text im 20. Jahrhundert* (Munich, 1986)

Sheringham, Michael, *French Autobiography: Devices and Desires. Rousseau to Perec* (Oxford, 1993)

Spengemann, William, *The Forms of Autobiography: Episodes in the History of a Literary Genre* (New Haven and London, 1980)

Sprinker, Michael, 'Fictions of the Self: The End of Autobiography', in *Autobiography: Essays Theoretical and Critical*, ed. by James Olney (Princeton, 1980), pp. 321-42

Starobinski, Jean, 'The Style of Autobiography', in *Literary Style: A Symposium*, ed. by Seymour Chatman (London and New York, 1971), pp. 285-96

Vogt, Marianne, *Autobiographik bürgerlicher Frauen. Zur Geschichte weiblicher Selbstbewußtwerdung* (Würzburg, 1981)

VI: Other Works Consulted

Adorno, Theodor W., *Ästhetische Theorie*, ed. by Gretel Adorno and Rolf Tiedemann (Frankfurt am Main, 1970)

Altbach, Edith Hoshino, 'The New German Women's Movement', in *German Feminism: Readings in Politics and Literature*, ed. by Edith Hoshino Altbach and others (Albany, N. Y., 1984), pp. 3-26

Barthes, Roland, *Image, Music, Text*, trans. and ed. by Stephen Heath (London, 1977)

Bebel, August, *Die Frau und der Sozialismus*, 63rd edn (Berlin, 1974)

Becker, Jillian, *Hitler's Children: The Story of the Baader-Meinhof Terrorist Gang* (London, 1977)

Bedingungen und Organisation des Widerstands. Der Kongreß in Hannover. Protokolle Flugblätter Resolutionen, ed. by Bernward Vesper, *Voltaire Flugschrift*, 12 (1967)

Benjamin, Walter, *Das Kunstwerk im Zeitalter seiner Reproduzierbarkeit. Drei Studien zur Kunstsoziologie* (Frankfurt am Main, 1963)

Bergmann, Uwe, Dutschke, Rudi, Lefèvre, Henri, and Rabehl, Bernd, *Rebellion der Studenten oder Die neue Opposition* (Reinbek, 1968)

Bieling, Rainer, *Die Tränen der Revolution. Die 68er zwanzig Jahre danach* (Berlin, 1988)

Black Power. Ursachen des Guerilla-Kampfes in den Vereinigten Staaten. Zwei Analysen, ed. by Bernward Vesper, *Voltaire Flugschrift*, 14 (1967)

Bock, Hans Manfred, *Geschichte des 'Linken Radikalismus' in Deutschland. Ein Versuch* (Frankfurt am Main, 1976)

Böckelmann, Frank, and Nagel, Herbert, eds., *Subversive Aktion. Der Sinn der Aktion ist ihr Scheitern* (Frankfurt am Main, 1976)

Bopp, Jörg, 'Geliebt und doch gehaßt. Über den Umgang der Studentenbewegung mit Theorie', *Kursbuch*, 78 (1984), 121-42

Brooks, Peter, *Reading for the Plot: Design and Intention in Narrative* (Cambridge, Mass. and London, 1984)

Burke, Seán, *The Death and Return of the Author: Criticism and Subjectivity in Barthes, Foucault and Derrida* (Edinburgh, 1992)

Burns, Rob and van der Will, Wilfried, *Protest and Democracy in West Germany: Extra-Parliamentary Opposition and the Democratic Agenda* (Basingstoke and London, 1988)

Buselmeier, Michael, and Schehl, Günter, 'Die Kinder von Coca-Cola', *kürbiskern. Literatur und Kritik*, 1 (1970), 74-89

DER SPIEGEL oder Die Nachricht als Ware. Nachwort von Bernward Vesper, ed. by Bernward Vesper, *Voltaire Flugschrift*, 18 (1968)

Dutschke, Rudi, untitled contribution, in *Bedingungen und Organisation des Widerstands. Der Kongreß in Hannover. Protokolle Flugblätter Resolutionen*, ed. by Bernward Vesper, *Voltaire Flugschrift*, 12 (1967), 78-82

—, *Geschichte ist machbar. Texte über das herrschende Falsche und die Radikalität des Friedens*, ed. by Jürgen Miermeister (Berlin, 1980)

Engels, Friedrich, *Der Ursprung der Familie, des Privateigenthums und des Staates*, 6th edn (Stuttgart, 1894)

Enzensberger, Hans Magnus, *Einzelheiten* (Frankfurt am Main, 1962)

—, 'Baukasten zu einer Theorie der Medien', *Kursbuch*, 20 (1970), 159-86

Fichter, Tilman, and Lönnendonker, Siegward, *Kleine Geschichte des SDS. Der Sozialistische Deutsche Studentenbund von 1946 bis zur Selbstauflösung* (Berlin, 1977)

Fiedler, Leslie A., *The Collected Essays of Leslie Fiedler*, 2 vols (New York, 1971)

Firestone, Shulamith, *The Dialectic of Sex: The Case for Feminist Revolution* (New York, 1970)

—, *Frauenbefreiung und sexuelle Revolution* (Frankfurt am Main, 1975)

Frankfurter Frauen, eds., *Frauenjahrbuch '75* (Frankfurt am Main, 1975)

Frevert, Ute, *Frauen-Geschichte. Zwischen bürgerlicher Verbesserung und neuer Weiblichkeit* (Frankfurt am Main, 1986)

Fuss, Diana, *Essentially Speaking: Feminism, Nature and Difference* (London and New York, 1989)

Giddens, Anthony, *Modernity and Self-Identity: Self and Society in the Late Modern Age* (Cambridge, 1991)

Greer, Germaine, *The Female Eunuch* (London, 1970)

—, *Der weibliche Eunuch. Aufruf zur Befreiung der Frau* (Frankfurt am Main, 1974)

Habermas, Jürgen, untitled contribution, in *Bedingungen und Organisation des Widerstands. Der Kongreß in Hannover. Protokolle Flugblätter Resolutionen*, ed. by Bernward Vesper, *Voltaire Flugschrift*, 12 (1967), 42-48

—, *Protestbewegung und Hochschulreform* (Frankfurt am Main, 1969)

Holzer, Horst, 'Massenmedien oder Monopolmedien?', *kürbiskern*, 4 (1970), 622-37

Huyssen, Andreas, *After the Great Divide: Modernism, Mass Culture, Postmodernism* (Basingstoke and London, 1988)

Jameson, Fredric, *Postmodernism; or, The Cultural Logic of Late Capitalism* (London and New York, 1992)

Jay, Martin, *Marxism and Totality: The Adventures of a Concept from Lukács to Habermas* (Cambridge, 1984)

Kittler, Friedrich, *Aufschreibesysteme. 1800-1900* (Munich, 1985)

Kommune 2, *Versuch der Revolutionierung des bürgerlichen Individuums: Kollektives Leben mit politischer Arbeit verbinden!* (Berlin, 1969)

Krahl, Hans-Jürgen, *Konstitution und Klassenkampf. Schriften und Reden 1966-1970* (Frankfurt am Main, 1971)

Langguth, Gerd, *Protestbewegung. Entwicklung – Niedergang – Renaissance. Die Neue Linke seit 1968* (Cologne, 1983)

Leary, Timothy, *The Politics of Ecstasy* (New York, 1968)

Leary, Timothy, *Die Politik der Ekstase* (Hamburg, 1970)

McLuhan, Marshall, *Understanding Media: The Extensions of Man* (New York, 1964)

—, *Die magischen Kanäle* (Düsseldorf and Vienna, 1968)

Marcuse, Herbert, *Eros and Civilization: A Philosophical Enquiry into Freud* (Boston, 1955)

—, *One-Dimensional Man: Studies in the Ideology of Advanced Industrial Society* (Boston, 1964)

—, *Kultur und Gesellschaft*, 2 vols (Frankfurt am Main, 1965)

—, *Triebstruktur und Gesellschaft. Ein philosophischer Beitrag zu Sigmund Freud* (Frankfurt am Main, 1965)

—, *Der eindimensionale Mensch. Studien zur Ideologie der fortgeschrittenen Industriegesellschaft* (Berlin and Neuwied, 1967)

—, *An Essay on Liberation* (Boston, 1969)

—, *Versuch über die Befreiung* (Frankfurt am Main, 1969)

—, *Five Lectures: Psychoanalysis, Politics and Utopia* (Boston, 1970)

—, *Das Ende der Utopie. Vorträge und Diskussionen in Berlin 1967* (Frankfurt am Main, 1980)

Markovits, Andrei S., and Gorski, Philip S., *The German Left: Red, Green and Beyond* (Cambridge, 1993)

Miermeister, Jürgen, and Staadt, Jochen, eds., *Provokationen. Die Studenten- und Jugendrevolte in ihren Flugblättern 1965-1971* (Darmstadt and Neuwied, 1980)

Millett, Kate, *Sexual Politics* (New York, 1969)

—, *Sexus und Herrschaft. Die Tyrannei des Mannes in unserer Gesellschaft* (Munich, 1974)

Rabehl, Bernd, *Am Ende der Utopie. Die politische Geschichte der Freien Universität Berlin* (Berlin, 1988)

Reich, Wilhelm, *Die sexuelle Revolution* (Frankfurt am Main, 1966)

—, *Die Funktion des Orgasmus. Sexualökonomische Grundprobleme der biologischen Energie* (Cologne, 1969)

—, *Die Massenpsychologie des Faschismus* (Cologne, 1971)

Reiche, Reimut, 'Verteidigung der "neuen Sensibilität"', in *Die Linke antwortet Jürgen Habermas*, ed. by Wolfgang Abendroth and others (Frankfurt am Main, 1968), pp. 90-103

Rutschky, Michael, *Erfahrungshunger. Ein Essay über die siebziger Jahre* (Cologne, 1980)

Said, Edward, *The World, the Text, and the Critic* (London, 1984)

Sander, Helke, 'Rede des "Aktionsrates zur Befreiung der Frauen"', in *Autonome Frauen. Schlüsseltexte der Neuen Frauenbewegung seit 1968*, ed. by Ann Anders (Frankfurt am Main, 1988), pp. 10-38

Schenk, Herrad, *Die feministische Herausforderung. 150 Jahre Frauenbewegung in Deutschland* (Munich, 1980)

Schneemann, Anke, 'Autobiographie AG', *Schreiben 1. Frauenliteraturzeitung*, 3/4 June 1978, pp. 42-43

Schneider, Michael, untitled contribution, in *DER SPIEGEL oder Die Nachricht als Ware*. *Nachwort von Bernward Vesper*, ed. by Bernward Vesper, *Voltaire Flugschrift*, 18 (1968), 5-18

Schneider, Michael, *Den Kopf verkehrt aufgesetzt oder Die melancholische Linke. Aspekte des Kulturzerfalls in den siebziger Jahren* (Darmstadt and Neuwied, 1981)

Schrader-Klebert, Karin, 'Die kulturelle Revolution der Frau', *Kursbuch*, 17 (1969), 1-46

Stephan, Inge and Weigel, Sigrid, *Die verborgene Frau. Sechs Beiträge zu einer feministischen Literaturwissenschaft* (Berlin, 1983)

Ulla/Birgit/Susan/Sabine/Barbara, '"Ich möchte lernen, ich selbst zu sein". Siebzehnjährige Oberschülerinnen schreiben über sich', *Kursbuch*, 47 (1977), 143-58

'Vom SDS zum Frauenzentrum', no author, in *Frauenjahrbuch '75*, ed. by Frankfurter Frauen (Frankfurt am Main, 1975), pp. 9-48

Wimmer, Michael, 'Verstimmte Ohren und unerhörte Stimmen', in *Das Schwinden der Sinne*, ed. by Dietmar Kamper and Christoph Wulf (Frankfurt am Main, 1984), pp. 115-39

Wimsatt, Jr., W. K., and Beardsley, M. C., 'The Intentional Fallacy', *Sewanee Review*, 54 (1946), 468-80

Wulf, Christoph, 'Das gefährdete Auge. Ein Kaleidoskop der Geschichte des Sehens', in *Das Schwinden der Sinne*, ed. by Dietmar Kamper and Christoph Wulf (Frankfurt am Main, 1984), pp. 21-45

Britische und Irische Studien zur deutschen Sprache und Literatur